Of Swansea West

THE MUMBLES: Past and Present

Swansea 1880. Illustration from "The Cambrian" *By permission, South Wales Evening Post*

Of Swansea West

THE MUMBLES: PAST AND PRESENT

Norman Lewis Thomas

Gomer Press
1978

First Impression - 1978

ISBN 0 906199 026

Previous Books:

The Story of Swansea's District & Villages:
Volume One.

The Story Of Swansea's Districts & Villages:
Volume One. Enlarged & Revised.

The Story Of Swansea's Markets.

The Story Of Swansea's Markets & Additional
Historical Data.

The Story Of Swansea's Districts & Villages:
Volume Two & Abridged Volume One.

A Hundred Years In School: St Helen's 1874-1974.

Swansea: Old & New. (Co-authorship with D. G. Bowden).

Printed at
Gomer Press
Llandysul, Dyfed

To: The Public Library Staffs of the Principality
And especially to:

OYSTERMOUTH BRANCH LIBRARY

Iris Williams
Victoria Blewett
Susan Jenkins (Mrs.)
Ruth Vincent
Muriel Owen (Mrs.)
Megan Bell (Mrs.)
Angela France (Mrs.)

CONTENTS

PREFACE

"History is the chart and
compass for national endeavour."

A. Helps: "Friends In Council." Bk.i, Ch. 11.

It has been written that "No man is an island," (J. Donne: Devotions No. 17), and this is often the case when compiling a work of local history. Authors are indebted to past and present writers; precise acknowledgment is made, therefore, to those consulted in the process of my research within the relevant chapters of this book. Consequently, the use of asterisks, numbers and foot-notes is omitted on this occasion.

Herein, the Mumbles story is traced to modern times and embraces historical events, the rise and decline of former industries, marine affairs as well as aspects of the changing social and environmental scene. However, the account is not treated in isolation to the rest of the Gower Peninsula and Swansea. For centuries, Oystermouth Manor formed part of the Lordship of Gower; then grew as a village community placed within the Gower Union; and afterwards became an Urban District Council for a period in the nineteenth and twentieth centuries. Its absorption into the Swansea County Borough's extension programme occurred in 1918, and the Mumbles Ward, as such, has remained in existence, to date, for six decades. Therefore, these circumstances serve as a justification for some of the topics to be preceded by the addition of appropriate background information intended to create more interest in particular themes as a whole. The details concerned may also bring to light, in war or peace, facets of the important part played and valuable contribution rendered by the City of Swansea area to the over-all history of the United Kingdom.

Furthermore, it is considered, that no apology is due for the number of quotations recorded in the book; most of them are descriptive while others refer to actual localities or sites as they once were years ago. Detailed as numerous accounts are, no work can ever be complete, and this one is no exception to the rule.

I wish to record my warmest thanks and appreciation to the many people who have so kindly assisted me in the various stages of my research, whether by personal interviews or correspondence. In the first instance, grateful acknowledgments are herewith tendered to the following publishers for their permission to include short quotations in this book: Jonathan Cape Ltd., for a "Kilvert's Diary" entry, 18th April, 1872, Vol.

2, edited by William Plomer, pp. 187-88, re the Estate of Mr. F. R. Fletcher, Editor; J. D. Lewis & Sons Ltd., for "The Men Of The Mumbles Head" by Carl Smith, Chap. 1, p. 15, Chap. 2, p. 23 & Chap. 3, p. 68; Macmillan, London and Basingstoke, for "Walter Savage Landor" by Malcolm Elwin, a paragraph re Swansea Bay and Oystermouth Tramroad; and the Oakwood Press (Dorset) for "The Swansea & Mumbles Railway" by Charles E. Lee, Chap. 3, p. 20, Chap. 4, pp. 26-27, and Chap. 5, p. 30 and pp. 36-37.

The use of additional, brief extracts from other editions was granted and, in this respect, my many thanks are due to Mr. K. Bailey, Headmaster, and Staff Members, "Oystermouth School Centenary" 1878-1978 historical booklet; Mr. P. J. Harmer, General Manager, The South Wales Transport Co. Ltd. (National), Swansea, "The Chain Of Progress" 1960; Mr. R. Lawson, The Mumbles Railway Co. Ltd., Cheltenham, "A New Role For The Mumbles Railway" and a copy of the Company badge; Mr. E. I. E. Phillips, "Guide To All Saints, The Parish Church Of Oystermouth" and "Fifty Years At All Saints"; Dr. P. E. King and A. Osborn, "Oyster Dredging" and for artistic impressions of the Mumbles Railway by Mr. R. M. May, F.R.S.A., together with those photographs itemised and reproduced by kind permission of Swansea City Council, Dr. J. R. Alban, City Archivist, Archives Department; Mr. I. J. Lewis, Editor, South Wales Evening Post; and Messrs. Roger David Studios, Newton Road, Mumbles. Apologies are sincerely offered for any inadvertent omissions in acknowledgment to data supplied by personnel or sources consulted in the compilation of this work.

I am also indebted to the following individuals and bodies for relevant information or material so readily presented to me and whose kindness is herewith remembered: Mr. David Bennett, Director, Norton Limeworks Ltd., Mumbles, (now Associated Asphalt), Mr. E. L. Reynolds, retired technical adviser and Mr. A. Williams, retired foreman; Mr. D. N. W. Earp, Divisional Manager, Glamorgan Water Division, Welsh National Water Development Authority (now Wales Water), Mr. B. G. Harker and Mrs. M. I. Hinds (former Cllr. and Committee Member of the West Glamorgan Water Board); Mr. A. Cottle, Secretary, The Mumbles Railway Society and Mr. J. Llewellyn, Committee Member; Mr. A. C. Foy, Proprietor, Libby's Agency, Mumbles, and former Secretary, Mrs. E. M. Beynon; Capt. J. Rhydderch, Clerk & Chief Fishery Officer, South Wales Sea Fisheries Committee; Inspector R. Richards, Regional Controller, H.M. Coastguard Rescue H.Q., Mumbles, District Officer P. W. Cross and retired Inspector, Mr. E. Williams, M.B.E., Mumbles; Coxswain L. Derek Scott, B.E.M., Mumbles Life-Boat, Mr. E. Beynon, Mumbles Life-Boat's Hon. Secretary and R.N.L.I. H.Q., Poole, Dorset; the staffs of the Swansea Public Library Service; the Royal Institution Of South Wales; and the Uplands Bookshop Ltd., Swansea.

Among others who rendered help at all times were: Mr. Robert Barnes, Miss Victoria Blewett, Mr. Derek G. Bowden, Mr. Rowley Davies, Mr. Cyril Evans, Mr. Thomas H. Evans, Mr. Geoffrey Morgan, Miss Betty Nelmes, Dr. Michael O'Kane, Mr. Hywel Williams and Miss Iris Williams.

Floreat Swansea Norman L. Thomas

CHAPTER ONE

ANCIENT AND MODERN

"History is a pageant, not a philosophy."
Augustine Birreli: Obiter Dicta: The Muse of History.

"The Parish Registers date from 1719 . . .
"In 1849 several deaths were recorded from the visitation of cholera, and of varying ages. There are between 1783 and 1794 receipts in various pages of the registers from the Government stamp collector for the duty of three-pence upon each entry of baptism, marriage and burial, in accordance with a silly and mischievous Act passed in the reign of George III. There was a penalty of £5 for non-compliance. The person collecting got 2s. in the £, and, of course, the poor parson got the credit of charging for his own benefit. This Act was repealed in the latter year . . .
"The tithes have descended to various people from time to time until both tithes and advowson became the property of Mr. A. D. Berrington. The former were purchased at a sale by auction in February, 1885, by Mr. Jenkins, land agent, Swansea, for £2,250, and the latter subsequently by the late vicar, the Rev. Dd. Secretan Jones, for £200, the present possessor."

Alfred Hall: "History Of Oystermouth." 1899.

"Nature has done everything for Oystermouth; Art has as yet done nothing."

The Cambrian: 5th May, 1882.

The painstaking work of archaeologists over the years, past and present, has revealed evidence of Prehistoric man's activities in and around the Mumbles and Gower Peninsula. Stone implements, sometimes even wooden tools, as well as skeletal remains, have been assiduously unearthed, dated, assembled and exhibited in local and national museums. The Royal Institution of South Wales, Victoria Road, Swansea, for example, displays many such discoveries.

Among some Neolithic stone items found within the Mumbles area may be listed: a rhyolitic, polished axe discovered in a Newton field, circa

1882; a similar find, diorite, located somewhere in Oystermouth, circa 1909; and another cherty example, but with the butt end missing, was dug up in an allotment on Mumbles Hill, 1938. The Mumbles Hill fissure or cleft has revealed Prehistoric human remains, bones and teeth, which cannot be dated precisely.

Pleistocene fauna were found in the Inner Sound Cave, Oystermouth; Rothers Tor Cave, Oystermouth; and in Caswell Bay Bone-Cave, Bishopston. A chance find of the Early Iron Age was an upper stone of a beehive quern, i.e. a stone handmill for grinding grain, from nearby Clyne Common. These are but a few of an extensive number of sites discovered and listed by J. G. Rutter in his 1948 publication entitled "Prehistoric Gower: The Early Archaeology Of West Glamorgan."

At a later stage in history, Swansea, unlike Neath or Nidum which possessed an established Roman auxiliary fort, did not become a settlement during the Roman occupation of Britain. However, in 1860 when All Saints Parish Church, Oystermouth, was enlarged by the addition of a north aisle, fragments of a Roman mosaic pavement came to light during draining operations on its south side. Under heaps of removed soil, embedded in concrete, the tesselated floor was unearthed by workmen who, unfortunately, cracked the section into pieces before its true designation was recognised. Fortunately, some of the pieces were retrieved by the noted 19th century antiquarian and a mayor of Swansea, George Grant Francis, who then set them into a tablet arrangement and attached it to the west wall of the old church near the tower arch.

Other fragments of this Roman mosaic pavement were found on the north side of the churchyard together with several pieces of Roman pottery and fragments of black and red vases. Both Dillwyn and Morgan refer to the discovery of three Roman coins 196-235 A.D. unearthed during the digging of a foundation in the village, 1882; and another one, 98-117 A.D., came from an old well in 1837.

Consequently, there is a strong possibility that the site of this Norman Church was once a Roman "villa" or courtyard house, one of a few which were scattered along the coastal areas of South Wales. A number of these small marble or earthenware pieces much favoured by the Romans for the paving of their mosaic floors are in the possession of the R.I.S.W., and G.G. Francis' tablet can be viewed in the church.

In addition to the possible existence of a Roman villa here, it may well be that a Christian church was founded in Oystermouth at a very early date in time. In this respect, E. I. E. Phillips in his "Guide To All Saints, The Parish Church Of Oystermouth" writes:

> "If it be accepted that Christianity was established in Gower about the end of the Roman occupation of Britain, and that there was an early settlement

near Oystermouth, however small it may have been, the question arises whether a church was founded there at any time during the years between the end of the Roman occupation and 1141, the date of the documented gift of de Londres. It is quite possible, it is even most likely, and the supposition that that there was an early foundation is supported by a body of evidence that cannot be lightly set aside or disregarded. Legends, traditions and annals handed down for the most part in stories told by Nennius, writing in the ninth century, support it; so do the Iolo MSS; and so does the Liber Landavensis, which records gifts of lands and endowments to the Church of Llandaff, and is considered to contain rather more of history than of legend and tradition. These ancient writings record that St. Illtyd, the head of a great college of saints at Llan-Illtyd (Llantwit Major), retired in his old age to lead the life of a hermit in a cave at Loyngarth (Oystermouth) in the fifth century, and there built a church, which Nennius says was still standing in his day. In the early sixth century Urien Rheged ruled over the district of Gower after driving out Irish invaders, who for some years had occupied the land. Learning of the fame of Loyngarth, he instituted in it, and in his principal court of Llwchwr, a chair for the teaching of poetry and the arts. Of the first preceptor, Talhaiarn, the Iolo MSS tells that 'he presided in the chair of Urien Rheged at Caer-Gwyrosydd' (Loyngarth) and again that 'the chair was established at Caer-Gwyrosydd, or Ystumllwynarth, where Urien Rheged was accustomed to hold his national and royal court.'

". . . One of Taliesin's (c. 530-600) pupils, Rhun, is designated in the Welsh Calendar as 'a saint of Ystumllwynarth.' The chair at Caer-Gwyrosydd (the fortress of the armed men of Gower) was in all probability within the fortress, the llan, which may well have enclosed the ancient British church of Loyngarth.'"

The late William Henry Jones, a noted local historian and onetime archivist to Swansea Corporation, drew attention to the possibility that the church was built upon the site of a Roman building. In his "History of Swansea & The Lordship of Gower" he states:

"We have spoken of the discovery at Oystermouth of Roman tesserae, and pointed to the circumstance as proof of Roman occupation. Whether the pavement belonged to a domestic or ecclesiastical building the meagreness of the remains will not allow us to determine, but it requires no violent exercise of the imagination to recognise something in the fact that the discovery was made close to the ancient Norman parish church that would indicate the building to have been ecclesiastical. Were it so, there is much probability that any church which Nennius found at Loyngarth would have stood upon this anciently-selected site, and in this manner the mind quickly links up the occupation of Oystermouth in continuous succession from probably the earliest years of the Christian era until today."

There were numerous churches in and around Gower long before the arrival of the Normans according to ancient accounts; several of these within the Lordship of Gower were reputed traditionally to date as far back as the Roman occupation. Old Welsh place names with "Llan" preceding a particular Welsh Saint's name, such as Dewi, Illtyd, Cyfelach, etc., indicate the former existence of Early Christian cells or Celtic Church colonies. The word "Llan" refers to a fortified enclosure or a monastic village community.

The division of Wales into parishes, it should be recalled, was not a Welsh system, but an adoption of the parochial scheme introduced earlier into England by King Alfred. It suited the Normans to embrace this system for their own convenience or control. Whenever possible, they established their own churches on good pasture or defence sites, outside a settled district, or nearby, sometimes to the detriment of established Welsh churches. Local conditions, however, frequently determined the success or failure of such manoeuvres.

Norman Churches were, of course, generally dedicated to Latin Saints and made subject to the Latin Church system of control and purpose. In 1583 there were 23 parishes, each with its own parish church, located within the Lordship of Gower, of which, Oystermouth was one. With but two exceptions , the largest of these possessed Welsh names and were occupied by the Welsh. By contrast, some of the English parishes were very small; Nicholaston, for example, consisted of only 540 acres.

The majority of the old churches in the English parishes of Gower were built in the 12th and 13th centuries. The earliest documentary reference to the origin of the old parish church of Oystermouth is contained in the deed of 1141, whereby Maurice de Londres, the son of William de Londres, presented to the Abbey of St. Peter's, Gloucester, for the endowment of Ewenny Priory, six churches with their respective acres of land, as a perpetual tenure by free gift of charity. Oystermouth was one of the churches listed in the deed which was the foundation charter of Ewenny Priory.

A great deal of the Church's history is contained in the publication entitled, "Guide To All Saints, The Parish Church Of Oystermouth," written by E. I. E. Phillips. A recent additional booklet by the same author, "Golden Jubilee: 50 Years At All Saints," refers to the history of the parish during the first half century of its existence under the new Diocese of Swansea & Brecon.

The oldest sections of the present church date back to the 13th century, the history of which was investigated by the historian, E. A. Freeman during the last century. Its tower, south wall, and the east wall of the Lady Chapel, represent those parts identified with the Early English style of architecture. The embattled tower's exterior walls measure approximately 8 metres by 7 metres. Many of the Gower churches were fortified by the addition of square-like towers since they served as places of refuge in bygone times when the peninsula frequently sustained invasions by land and sea.

During the incumbency of the Rev. Samuel Davies, 1821-64, the church was enlarged by the addition of a north aisle in 1860. It was during the digging activities for the foundations of this aisle that pieces of Roman mosaic work, or tesserae, were discovered. Some superstitious villagers would never pick up these tesserae for fear of being tormented by fairies, a fact related to Alfred Hall by one of the Church Sextons, Thomas Harris. The addition of an organ chamber as well as a new vestry featured among subsequent alterations which took place in 1873.

A further substantial enlargement was effected in 1915 during Archdeacon Harold Williams' incumbency, 1898-1938. The north aisle was demolished and a splendid new building was constructed which today embraces the main church. The arcade, built in 1860, on the site of the old north wall to connect the north aisle to the nave of the old church, was retained to join the nave of the new church extension to that of the old. Although a great deal of the construction was executed during 1915 the complete plan was not finished until 1937. At present, the church consists of a chancel, nave, porch, tower, Lady Chapel and vestry.

As may be expected, there are numerous ecclesiastical and historical features of antiquity located within the church. Of particular interest is the pillar piscina in the Lady Chapel near the site of the old sedilia. An ancient square-shaped font, with scalloped base, records the date "R.T. 1251" scratched inside it. A very old stoup is present in the porch, while outside may be seen some intriguing corbels. On the west wall, inside the church, a slate tablet displays several pieces of the tessellated paving discovered in 1860. Their preservation together with others housed within the Royal Institution of South Wales is due to the supervisory care of George Grant Francis at the time of discovery. If in fact the site of the church was once a Roman villa, these tesserae represent the furthest known western example of a decorated mosaic pavement of the era in Britain.

The bells of All Saints are Spanish in origin, being cast originally for the Jesuit Church of La Campania, Santiago, in Chile. In early December, 1863, a fire broke out in the church during a festival service when the resulting conflagration caused the deaths of two thousand persons. Later, several of the bells were acquired by the late Aubrey Vivian, Esq., whose family had trading links with South America. Three of these bells were afterwards presented to the Church in circa 1865 by him. The largest one, E flat, was cast in 1753; the smallest, F sharp, in 1818; and the third one, F natural, is undated.

Among the communion vessels may be numbered a silver Elizabethan communion cup and paten cover, a Georgian almsplate and pewter ware. The handsome tower clock was the gift of a Mr. Francis Tippings, of Le Mayals, and was put up in May, 1875.

In addition to their intrinsic beauty, stained glass memorial windows sometimes reveal notable aspects of a parish's historical background and frequently commemorate the lives of citizens who have lived, worked, served and worshipped within the church community. Such is the case in respect of All Saints as E. I. E. Phillips so vividly recounts:

". . . Beginning with the Lady Chapel we may proceed around the church giving a brief description of each. The triple lancet windows behind the altar at the east end of the Lady Chapel are in memory of the Rev. Samuel Davies, who enlarged the church in 1860. The window over the ancient site of the sedilia commemorates Richard, Lewis, and Catherine Richards, the first of whom died in 1895 and the others in 1918. The small single-light window between the chancel arch and the door in the Lady Chapel is in memory of Edith Mary Catherine Richards, who died in 1923. The largest window on the south wall of the Lady Chapel was, at one time, a small window of two lights near the staircase leading to the rood loft. During the second half of the last century, the staircase was removed, the doorway bricked up and the window enlarged to one of three lights in the perpendicular style. The stained glass is in memory of Dame Catherine Prudence, wife of Sir John J. Jenkins, of the Grange, who later became Lord Glantawe. Dame Catherine died in 1900. The very large stained glass window in the north wall of the nave is a memorial to Lord Glantawe, who died in 1915. The theme is 'The Army of the Christian soldier,' represented by St. Michael, the warrior saint of heaven . . .

"The small window to the west of the side door near the pulpit is in memory of four men of the lifeboat 'Wolverhampton,' John Jenkins, William Rogers, William Jenkins and William Macnamara, who lost their lives on the 27th January, 1883, near the Lighthouse Rock, Mumbles, whilst trying to rescue the crew of the wrecked ship 'Admiral Prinz Adalbert.' On the east of the side door near the pulpit is a small window memorial to Violet Alice Lewis, given by Miss E. M. C. Richards in 1951. Behind the organ on the north wall of the chancel, is a window of three lights, which can only be seen from outside the church. It is in memory of Isabel Crawshay who died on the 8th November, 1863, aged 17. The beautiful window at the east end of the chancel, above the triptych over the altar, commemorates the late Col. David Lewis, who for twenty six years until his death in 1928 was a churchwarden. Rich colours have been used in this window with as little white glass as possible. The church is dedicated to 'All Saints' and it was therefore very appropriate that this theme should have been taken for the subject of the composition for the window in this position. In the centre is Christ in Glory; the Virgin and John the Baptist are on either side, and the angel and the three kings at the tomb below; the branches of the vine spread over the side lights, uniting the figures to Christ 'The True Vine'; the figures represent the patron saints of the six Welsh dioceses with the diocesan arms below: (1) Llandaff, St. Peter & St. Paul; (2) Swansea & Brecon, St. John; (3) Bangor, St. Deiniol; (4) Monmouth, St. Woolos; (5) St. David; (6) St. Asaph.

> "This window was removed and stored in the cellar under the church during the last war to safeguard it against damage from air raids. In the porch is a window 'in memory of a deeply regretted parent, deceased, 27th October, 1879.'"

Numerous other ornamental memorials are in evidence. Those killed in the two World Wars are remembered thus:

> "The exquisitely carved rood screen was erected as a memorial to ninety-eight men from the parish who lost their lives in the first world war, 1914-18; their names are inscribed on the panels. No other screen in Wales exceeds this one in beauty and in the fine carving of its craftsmen; *it is one of the loveliest things in the church.*
>
> "The men who died in the second world war, 1939-45, are remembered by a cross of Celtic Portland stone erected in the churchyard. Their names have been beautifully engraved on a roll of honour dedicated 'proudly and affectionately' to one of their number, a former choirboy, Flight Sergeant Gordon Pusey of the Royal Air Force, by four of his friends. At the time when the cross was erected a faculty was obtained for the removal of all tomb stones, headstones, crosses and kerbs. Because of the shortage of labour permission was obtained to enlist the assistance of 'displaced persons' from the camp at Scurlage, Gower, for this work."

On the 6th May, 1977, another large, striking stained glass window placed in the north wall of the Church was unveiled and consecrated by the Vicar, the Rev. Canon J. E. C. Hughes. This memorial window commemorates the heroism of the crew of the Mumbles Lifeboat, "Edward , Prince of Wales," who perished in tempestuous seas off treacherous Sker Point on the 23rd April, 1947, when attempting for the second time to rescue those aboard the doomed 7,000 ton Liberty vessel, S.S. "Samtampa." In all, 47 men were killed in the disaster, 8 of them being the crew of the Mumbles Lifeboat who were: Coxswain William J. Gammon, Gold Medallist, R.N.L.I., Thistleboon; Second Coxswain, William Noel, George Hotel; Bowman, William R. S. Thomas, Bracelet Bay; Motor Mechanic, William G. Davies, Lifeboat Cottage; Asst. Motor Mechanic, Ernest Griffin, Norton; Lifeboatman, William L. Howell, Clifton Terrace; Lifeboatman, William R. Thomas, George Bank; and Lifeboatman, Richard Smith, Hallbank.

The Mumbles Lighthouse, overturned lifeboat and the stricken "Samtampa" are all depicted in a most graphic portrayal, whilst the eight lifeboat crew members outlined at the top of the scene heighten still further the dramatic effect produced by the arrangement as a whole. During 1976-77, the "1947 Mumbles Lifeboat Disaster Memorial Window Appeal" raised three thousand pounds needed to pay for and install the window in the Parish Church. Lifeboat crew lives lost nationally during the years 1947-1972, numbered 51 crewmen; apart from the Mumbles Lifeboat, only two other lifeboat stations lost their entire crews of eight men within that 25 year period, the Broughty Lifeboat in 1959, and the Longhope Lifeboat, 1969. A well-illustrated and detailed history of the Mumbles Lifeboat service, from 1832 onwards, has recently been written by a serving member of the present Mumbles Lifeboat, Carl Smith. Published in 1977 by the Gomer Press, Llandysul, "The Men Of The Mumbles Head" will remain a valuable work of reference in this particular field of local history.

As E. I. E. Phillips reminds us in his "50 Years At All Saints," the Parish of Oystermouth has made a number of important contributions to the history of the first half century of the Diocese of Swansea and Brecon which came into existence on the 24th June, 1923. The Priory Church of St. John, Brecon, was selected as its Cathedral. In the first instance, two archdeacons have been appointed from its own vicars: the first Archdeacon of Gower, the late Rev. Harold Stepney Williams (1864-1954), and the fourth Archdeacon of Brecon, the Rev. William David George Wilkinson, who retired in 1969. Next, a parochial division was formed out of the western part of Oystermouth Parish which permitted the creation of the new parish of St. Peter's, Newton, while the building of "The Church Of The Holy Cross," Fairwood Road, West Cross, amidst an expanding housing estate in 1955, marked another tangible achievement.

With great determination, the Rev. H. Williams carried through an expansive building programme during his first twenty years as Vicar of Oystermouth and among the projects completed were: St. Peter's Church, Newton; a vicarage house; a day-school; Norton Mission Church; men's clubs; two church halls; and the enlargement of the Parish Church in 1915. The latter work was finally concluded in 1937. The new Parish of St. Peter's, Newton, came into being on the 4th February, 1933, when the Rev. W. J. Hickin was instituted to the living on that date.

An interesting account was recorded by the Rev. H. Williams about the baptism of two gypsy babies in 1907. The first child was baptised at St. Peter's Church, Newton, when two ladies of the congregation were godmothers. Under kind encouragement, the mother overcame her nervous reluctance, and accompanied by friends, she soon became at home in her unusual environment. The second baby was baptised in a gypsy van on Blackpill Common:

> "The Vicar happened to be passing that way one day and saw a woman vigorously waving her hand to him from a gypsy van. Going up to the van he found that there was another gypsy mother who wanted her baby baptised. As the child was not well and the gypsies were leaving next day, the mother was anxious to have the child baptised there and then. So, all kneeling down on the van floor, prayer was offered up and their little one was made a

member of Christ's flock, in the name of the Father, the Son and the Holy Ghost. Never was there a more reverent congregation."

The Rev. W. D. G. Wilkinson was Vicar of Oystermouth between 1939 and 1954, and eventually became Archdeacon of Brecon from 1955 to 1969. Of his duties at Oystermouth it has been written:

> "As Vicar of the Parish, Archdeacon Wilkinson worked assiduously for the good of his people in difficult and trying times. He gave encouragement to those in distress, comfort to those bereaved in battle of their sons, husbands or fathers, and succour to those made homeless by the operations of enemy aircraft over Swansea and its environs. For many of those in need he found temporary accommodation in the homes of the people in his parish and set a fine example by taking some into his own home. Indeed, with Mrs. Wilkinson, he cared for one homeless lady in the vicarage from the war years until he left Swansea to take up his appointment as Vicar of St. David with Llanilltyd, Brecon, in 1954. At all times he gave spiritual aid to his people and never spared himself in health or in illness."

The present Vicar, the Rev. James E. C. Hughes, was instituted and inducted to the living at Oystermouth on the 25th November, 1954. It was under the Rev. J. Hughes' guidance that "The Church Of The Holy Cross" came to be built in Fairwood Road, the site offered by Swansea Corporation, rather than the original location proposed at the Bellevue House grounds. The Bishop favoured the project together with the placing of the Curate's house close by on the same land. The Rev. Geoffrey Davies, a minor Canon at Brecon Cathedral, commenced duties at West Cross in July, 1956, and the new Church was dedicated by the Bishop on the 29th October, 1956, at an evening service attended by more than 400 people.

Several legible 18th century headstones remain in the present churchyard dedicated to the Mochresses, Robinses, Maddockses, as well as the Burts. A particularly well-preserved headstone, attached to the tower wall facing Church Park Place, refers to the Mochresses and Burts thus:

> "Here lyeth the body of John Mochress of this parish, Mariner who departed this life the fifteenth day of Decem'r, 1739. Aged 59 Years.
>
> ". . . also lieth . . . John Mochress, son to the above, . . . sixth day of May, 1759. Aged 42 Years.
>
> "lieth . . . of Mary Relict of ye above Jn. Mochress and late wife of Rd. Burt, who Died the 30th of August, 1788.
>
> "Above 60 Years I lived here
> Before my glass was past
> Then left this life in hope ye Christ
> Will rise me at the last.
>
> ". . . lieth the body of ye above Rich'd Burt . . . sixteenth day of April, 1805. Aged 79 Years."

Another early 18th century headstone, spelling as recorded, reads: "Here lyeth ye body of Susan the wife of Elieas Nicklas who died the 9th of March, 1729. Aged 33 Years." The names of the old Mumbles families, the Robinses and Maddockses, also reveal themselves, punctuation as originally set out: "Hear lyeth the body of john robin and his wife who died 1736"; "Here lieth the Body of Wm. Robins who Died this life, May ye 14th 1771"; Joan Maddocks in 1758; David Maddocks of the Dunns, 1760; and Ann Bydder, wife of Robert Byddor, 1797.

In the churchyard are interred the remains of Rear-Admiral Daniel Lawrence who died in 1854; and Major George Aikin, Bengal Artillery and onetime Captain in His Majesty's 37th Regiment of Foot, the grandson of James Aikin, Aide de Camp to the Duke of Marlborough, whose death was on the 21st August, 1807, aged 52 years. Lady Frances Morgan, daughter of Bennet, third Earl of Harborough, and wife of Major-General George Morgan, who died in 1841, was buried in the nave, near the chancel.

A much visited grave is that of Dr. Thomas Bowdler, 1754-1825, who expurgated or "bowdlerised" the works of William Shakespeare and Gibbon. It is situated on the right-hand side area of the main church doors. He died at the Rhyddings, aged 70, on the 24th February, 1825; donated twenty-five pounds to the poor of Box in Wiltshire, his birthplace, St. Boniface, Bonchurch, Isle of Wight, Oystermouth and Swansea; and left five shillings per annum for the repair of his grave. The author of "Letters from Holland," he also had two literary sisters, Jane and Hannah.

Together with the Church in Wales' four places of worship, All Saints, St. Peter's, Holy Cross and Clyne Chapel of Ease, within the Mumbles Council of Churches, are Bethany Baptist Church, West Cross; Baptist Church, Newton Road, 1908; Tabernacle Congregational Church, Newton Road, 1870; the third Mumbles Methodist Chapel on the present site, enlarged 1877; Paraclete Congregational Church, Newton, 1880; the Roman Catholic Church of "Our Lady Star Of The Sea," 1919; and the Christadelphian Meeting Room, Mt. Zion, 1850, The Dunns. In spite of past 19th century rivalries or restricted periods of co-operation, noticeable at times of economic crises and religious revivals, each denomination has made its singular contribution to the religious and social history of the Mumbles area. As elsewhere today, there is a far closer bond of co-operation between the different churches as borne out by the events of two World Wars and the active participation in local celebrations such as Ostreme.

The small, pleasant-looking building of Bethany Baptist Church, Norton, is situated at the end of a narrow, winding lane, off the busy Mumbles Road. According to the trust deeds, the Church was founded at West Cross in 1855, and as such is one of the oldest places of worship in the

Mumbles. It is also the third oldest English Baptist Church within the City of Swansea; the other two being, Mount Pleasant, 1825; and York Place, formerly Congregational, 1830. The late Cllr. Harry Libby's grandfather, on his mother's side of the family, was one of the founders of the Church.

Bethany was the meeting place for Baptists not only from the Mumbles, but also attracted worshippers from the English area of South Gower. Even today, it draws its congregation from a wide area which embraces Brynmill and Derwen Fawr in the east; Newton , Bishopston and Kittle westwards; as well as from the immediate vicinity of Norton and West Cross.

In the early days, the little Church, built in a field, was placed in a truly rural setting, with only a narrow lane and footpath leading to it. Either on horseback or in horse-drawn carts, the farmers and their families would converge here for the Sunday services and other special occasions.

Mr. Robert Barnes, Lay-Reader, writes of its architecture:

> "The Church itself was built to a characteristically English style. It possesses a fairly large porch and single aisle with raised pews sloping gradually towards the front of the church. This feature is unusual on the ground floor of Swansea churches, and not only enables all the congregation to see the speaker, but the speaker to see all the congregation! In keeping with the English tradition, there is no 'sedd fawr' or 'big seat'; instead there is a small railed off section which contains the Communion table.
>
> "Behind the Communion table is the pulpit, a very large rectangular raised space, under which is sited the Baptistry. Some wits have commented that Bethany is the only church in Mumbles which could hold small meetings in the pulpit, as it is so large!
>
> "To the Church's rear, and turning at right angles to it, is the Schoolroom. This building is considerably older than the Church itself, and is reputed to have been used as a place of worship before the construction of the present Church. *An interesting feature for all visitors to the Schoolroom is the seats. These are made up of seats removed from the old Mumbles Electric train trams after its closure, and are very useful and comfortable."*

Bethany has experienced variable fortunes over the years but has always been regarded as a centre of Evangelical witness in the Mumbles area. It has never been wealthy, nor probably ever will be, but through the generous, faithful giving of its members has survived; and moreover, it has seldom been without a pastor. Many Mumbles people will remember with affection the late Pastor, the Rev. Luther Morgan, whose tragic and sudden death in the pulpit of Bethany, in 1955, was a great loss to the Church.

The present Pastor is the Rev. F. S. Copleston, who was for some years a lecturer in Divinity and Greek at Barry Bible College. He has provided the church with a strong and vigorous leadership since 1958, and consequently its membership has grown. Progress has been made in other spheres under his pastorate: among other improvements may be numbered the much-needed surfacing of the approach lane, structural improvements to the Schoolroom as well as particular maintenance of the building as a whole.

It was, as a result of the initiative and drive of the deacons of Bethany, that the daughter church in Newton Road was founded in 1908 to serve the needs of an expanding area.

As Mr. R. Barnes recalls in his history of the Baptist Cause in the Mumbles district, "Centenary Of The Building Of The Church: 1867-1967," the original church, i.e. the present schoolroom was superseded by the 1867 building. From time to time, during the 1850's and 1860's, open-air tea parties and meetings attended by hundreds of people at a time testified to the growing numbers and brought in additional funds. Since the induction of the first minister, the Rev. J. Pugh, 1851-1862, eleven others to date have served Bethany.

An anonymous, authoritative author of "Catholic Life" in Swansea of the 19th and early 20th century, recalls the origins of "Our Lady Star Of The Sea" by Devon Place:

> "Services had been held at the Mumbles on and off for many years before a Mass Centre had been established. Father Gwydir (Rector Basil Gwydir, O.S.B., 1904-1914) had rented a small, disused chapel in 1910, but no serious attempt to establish a mission there was made before Father Egerton's time (Assistant Priest, St. David's, 1908-1911). Then, he began in 1915 to say Mass week by week at 8 a.m. on Tuesday, Thursday and Saturday, after which he acquired the Pavilion—known as Tom Owen's Pavilion—and converted it into a church. The new church was opened in July, 1919, when Abbot Hurley said the Mass and the Abbot of Caldy (island) preached. The first Rector was Abbot Hurley, who took up residence in 1921."

A "Dilston Cottage" in Mumbles used to be a place of refuge for all priests during the 1820's. The cottage was once owned by a Dr. Nicholl who shared the dwelling with his sisters. They had been educated at the Ursuline Convent, St. Omer, in France. This abode was also known to a Father James Fleetwood when he was Rector of Nelson Street Chapel, Swansea, during the years 1824-29.

Prior to the use of the pavilion, the Roman Catholics used a building on the Mumbles Road which was later rebuilt as the Central Hall. Tom Owen, a well-known comedian in his day, used to entertain audiences in a temporary building placed in the centre of what is today the Parade Gardens. Afterwards, he built his own pavilion on the site now occupied by the Roman Catholic Church.

It was at Newton that the authoress, poetess and hymnographer, Frances Ridley Havergal, (1836-1879), spent the closing days of her relatively short life; "Our Welsh retreat," as her sister, M. V. G. Havergal called it. The daughter of a writer of sacred music, she came to live with her sister, Maria, at Caswell Bay Road, in 1878.

Of an intellectual disposition, Miss Frances R. Havergal had a delicate constitution. Whenever possible, she would happily walk along the cliffs or down to Caswell Bay below. A visit to the top of the Mumbles Lighthouse was another pleasure, as well as watching the sailing vessels in Swansea Bay, many of which would have been the famous Swansea copper-ore barques.

Writing of her sister's brief time at the Mumbles, in a book published in 1880, by James Nisbet, Maria Havergal recounts:

> "She was so very tired that even the sea air and perfect rest failed to refresh her for some time. Afterwards, she thoroughly enjoyed the walks and scrambles on the cliffs; at low tide springing lightly over boulders to beds of sea-weeds, and rocky pools bright with sea anemones and then calling to me to watch the white-crested waves, 'the wind dashing them back like confirmation veils.' Or watching the vessels with all sails up entering the harbour, she would speak of the abundant entrance into the everlasting kingdom. Delighting in all knowledge she studied the Nautical Almanac and at the top of Mumbles Lighthouse learnt all the keeper could tell her . . .
>
> "We made her study cosy with home comforts and she called it her workshop. She arranged the pictures; by the door was her motto 'For Jesus' sake only' and her temperance pledge card.
>
> "In the South window, its sea view stretching over to Ilfracombe, stood her little table, flowers and easy chair. Her sofa faced the West window with the view of Caswell Bay and its rocks and there the sunsets came which we so often watched together."

With the aid of her American typewriter, Frances Havergal continued to write letters, articles and hymns, and receive her many friends. She could never really give up Teetotal work and once wrote:

> "I haven't taken up teetotal work, but teetotal work has taken me up!! Morgan and Scott made me accept a big, handsome, pledge book in February, and somehow the thing has fairly caught fire here. One led to another, and yesterday boys were coming all day to sign! I had 25 recruits yesterday alone, and a whole squad more are coming this evening! and we are going in for getting every boy in the whole village! And now, 'Please, Miss, mayn't the girls sign?' So I've got to open a girls' branch as well! So work grows!

She was loved by the village boys and girls, and to please them adopted the title of "The Newton Temperance Regiment." In the summer season especially, many of the youngsters worked as donkey-boys; for a few coppers, day-trippers were taken for short-rides or conveyed through Newton Village and down the hill to Caswell. Prospective customers were sought after as they alighted from the Mumbles Train at Oystermouth. "The cottagers around us soon won my sister's interest and regard," wrote Maria, "and she invited them to a Bible reading in our house . . . My dear sister Frances had promised to meet some men and boys on the village bank on May 21st. Though the day was very damp she went, taking her Bible and her temperance book with her. As she passed thro' the village of Newton, quite a procession gathered round her, her regiment of boys eagerly listening."

This true servant of God died at Newton on the 3rd June, 1879, and was buried in her father's tomb at Astley Churchyard. On the 9th June, at 6 a.m., many villagers and neighbours, assembled on the house lawn to pay their last respects as her flower-crowned coffin passed on its final journey.

Quite apart from countless articles, Frances R. Havergal had about twelve works published, mainly, of course, of a religious theme. Such titles as "Swiss Letters And Alpine Poems," "Bruey, A Little Worker For Christ," "Ministry Of Song," "Under The Surface," and "Life Echoes" represent a short cross-section of her books. All together, this much-travelled Christian wrote seven hymns for "Hymns Ancient And Modern," these being numbers 186, 203, 212, 259, 307, 356 and 485. A plaque commemorating the fact that she resided at Newton is set in the wall of her former home in Caswell Bay Road which stands today as a Victorian residence of character and elegance.

In 1977, the present Methodist Chapel building celebrated its centenary but the growth of Methodism in and around Mumbles spans a period of some 200 years. Members and joint authors of a detailed work of reference entitled, "Two Centuries Of Mumbles Methodism," Mr. Robert O. Roberts and Mrs. Megan Roberts record the rise of the Cause from the mid-18th century onwards.

Between 1764 and 1771, John Wesley visited the Society's followers or classes at Oxwich, a small but strong focal point of Gower membership, on five occasions. The famous preacher, abiding by his claim that the whole world was his parish travelled extensively; he refers in his diary to a visit made to Newton on the 28th August, 1958, where he preached in a barn, probably the old tithe barn:

> "I scarce ever saw such rain in Europe as we had for a considerable part of this morning. In one of the main streets the water ran with a stream capable of turning a mill. However, having appointed to preach at Newton, about six miles from Swansea, I was determined not to break my word though I supposed but few would attend. But I was mistaken; such a num-

ber of people came together as no house in the town would contain. A barn was soon prepared, and it pleased God to send a gracious rain upon their hearts."

The two previous Methodist Chapels erected on the same site were put up in 1814 and 1861. At one time in the mid-19th century, Mumbles possessed no fewer than three Methodist places of worship, Primitive, Reformed and Wesleyan; and four, if the Bible Christian Chapel of 1856 at Glen Road was included.

* * * *

Although today encompassed within the City of Swansea District boundary, the story of the Mumbles is inevitably bound up with the history of the Gower Peninsula as a result of the former's geographical location. Evidence of man's invasions and settlements in and around the peninsula spans many periods of time, and embraces the Palaeolithic, Mesolithic and Neolithic stages, the Bronze and Iron ages, the Roman occupation and the subsequent period referred to generally as the Dark Ages.

Norman infiltration of Gower commenced within thirty years after the Battle of Hastings and Swansea's first castle, circa 1099-1101 was erected by Henry de Newburgh and his knight-adventurers. This was most likely a mound surrounded by wooden palisades, a simple motte and bailey type of construction, followed by similar strongholds put up in Gower. These strategic, temporary strongpoints were later replaced by more durable stone-work fortifications which guarded the eastern entrance to the Lordship of Gower. The mouth of the river Tawe site, "Caer Wyr," fortress of Gower, provided protection not only against sea borne attacks but also from those landward approaches on either side of Kilvey Hill.

With the construction of Oystermouth Castle, and its subsequent rebuilt versions, emerged the manor of the same name alongside those somewhat larger Mediaeval demesnes of Gower created by the Norman conquest. Therefore, it is due to the latter's military occupation of the peninsula that a small but permanent settlement of people at Oystermouth was established, albeit, for some time afterwards, as victors and vanquished. As a stronghold, Oystermouth remained second only to Swansea in importance, and, for a brief interval, took over the role as the premier castle of Gower.

Throughout their existence, the castles at Swansea and Oystermouth were frequently damaged or razed to the ground by invasions of Welsh princes in revolt against their feudal overlords. However, the Norman defenders clung tenaciously to their immediate possessions, repaired or rebuilt their fortresses here and in other parts of the peninsula and managed to dominate the Lordship of Gower as a whole.

As was the usual pattern of habitation, the Normans occupied the more favourable, fertile limestone areas of land located in the south and west of the peninsula which became recognised as the Englishry or Gower Anglicana. The Welshry, Gower Wallicana, applied to the north and east uplands of Gower and supported scattered hamlets or individual farm holdings maintained by Welsh speaking inhabitants who held their lands under feudal tenure.

In essence, the Lordship of Gower was a minor Marcher Lordship, in contrast to those more powerful domains associated with the border counties, but, nevertheless, it was an important one and recognised warily as such by the Mediaeval Kings of England. The de Braoses were renowned for their skill, bravery and ferocious fighting qualities in the service of their sovereign over-lord. Such valuable military support for the crown helped to maintain the de Braoses' independent role as Marcher Lords. However, by the commencement of the 14th century, Edward I could no longer ignore the consequences of their oppresive misrule in Gower which had so alienated the English tenants of the Lordship.

Between the early 14th century and the close of the 18th century, it is very unlikely that the population of old Oystermouth ever passed the seven hundred mark. In the first Census return for 1801, a figure of 715 is recorded for the Parish of Oystermouth; and in 1811, 761 inhabitants are listed together with 200 dwelling-places. Within these centuries, from being one of Gower's twelve manorial estates of the Middle Ages, Oystermouth evolved into a small parish community of village proportions and became noted for its fine beds of oysters.

As in the case of Swansea, there are numerous impressions and topographical descriptions about Oystermouth and the Mumbles recorded by visitors, historians and authors of guide books throughout the centuries. John Leland, Henry VIII's antiquary, in the 16th century wrote:

> "A iii miles from Swineseye communely cawillid in englisch, Swansey, at the rode mowth of Tawe was a castel cawllid Est Wilthlunarde, otherwise *Ostermuth,* and of sum *Mummess.* Swansey is a market town and chief place of Gowerland."

J. H. Skrine, who completed two successive tours of late 18th century Wales, stated in his 1798 publication:

> "The remains of Swansea Castle consist chiefly of a massy tower with a curious light parapet upon Gallic arches; this castle and that of Oystermouth were built by Henry Beaumont, earl of Warwick, in the reign of Henry I. Oystermouth is a very fine ruin on the coast, at a distance of about four miles from Swansea, near the promontory of the Mumbles Head, which terminating in high hills, and stretching far out into the bay, affords a safe anchorage to ships passing up and down the channel."

Among quite a number of early 19th century travellers to South Wales was J. T. Barber. He undertook a rather stormy passage by sea in a hoy, i.e. a large one-decked vessel, commonly rigged as a sloop, from Bristol to Swansea, and his subsequent recollections of this short voyage produced a particularly amusing account when read in its entirety. In his, "A Tour throughout South Wales and Monmouthshire," 1803, Mumbles is described from the sloop thus:

> ". . . The two old French-horn players were lying at the door, soaking in the rain, but also asleep. From such a scene we gladly withdrew, and in a few hours found ourselves at the entrance of Swansea Bay, finely encircled with high varied hills; on our left were two isolated rocks called the Mumbles, at a small distance from the mainland, where the whitened town of Oystermouth appeared issuing from the water, beneath a lofty dark hill. At the bottom of the bay, the superior extent of Swansea lined the shore backed by an atmosphere of cloudy vapours produced from the numerous furnaces in its neighbourhood. At length I trod on Cambrian ground, and paid my half crown, with a willing engagement to forfeit a hundred times the sum if ever I should be again on board a Swansea Hoy."

In economic terms, the history of Oystermouth, and its later, wider appellation, the Mumbles, is the story of farming, limestone quarrying, fishing, oyster dredging, some iron mining and a watering place for visitors which developed into a popular holiday resort. These activities were, of course, a reflection of similar occupational trends elsewhere in Gower when limestone quarrying, oyster fishing (Port Eynon), coal mining (Penclawdd) and the quarrying of red ochre, all took place within the peninsula. As in the past, agriculture is the dominant pursuit in Gower while two large limestone quarries today have replaced the numerous smaller ones of yesteryear.

At Oystermouth and the Mumbles, the oyster fishing trade reached its peak by 1871 before its eventual sad decline. A little more than a century ago, upwards of thirty families were engaged in farming activities; flocks of sheep negotiating the narrow cliff laneways under supervision were a common sight to behold towards the end of the 19th century. Nowadays private housing developments have encroached upon much of what was formerly acres of farming land and the disappearance of the Woollacott Farm, Thistleboon, in the second half of the present decade is but a recent example. The limestone industry remained active throughout the 19th century and continued in operation for approximately 60 years of the present century, the principal site being established by the Norton Limeworks business.

(Among other aspects, separate, detailed chapters within record the histories of the Mumbles' limestone industry, the Mumbles Railway,

Mumbles Lighthouse, Oystermouth Castle and the oyster fishery of former renown).

The place names, Oystermouth and Mumbles, *as used today,* require, perhaps, some appropriate definitions when referred to in an historical context. "Mumbles" appertains to the village while "Oystermouth" is a parish which inclues Mumbles, Newton, Norton, West Cross, Lilliput and Brynau or Blackpill.

The name Mumbles was probably first applied to the two protuberant, rocky islets close to the headland situated at the far end of Swansea Bay by Viking navigators. There is a somewhat similar name, "Mumby" on the Lincolnshire coast. Several other versions may merit consideration in respect of their interpretations. The Danish word "Mumme" means "to mask," and this the two rocks off the mainland may be said to do to the up-channel voyager. Another Danish word "Marmles" together with the Latin "Mammac," both denote "breasts," as well the two tiny islands might appear to be when viewed within Swansea Bay. A Welsh derivation also suggests itself from "Mammoel," meaning "bare place or spot." In the 16th century, it is referred to as Mommulls and Mombles; and in the following century as Monmoul(e)s and Mumble Clifft. Abraham Rees in his "The Cyclopaedia," of 1819, records the location as "Mumble Point, a rock in the Bristol Channel, at the entrance into Swansea Bay. N. lat. 51° 37′. W. Long. 4° 3′." Apparently, there is no clear interpretation available in respect of the name Mumbles.

Ancient writings refer to Oystermouth in a number of instances. Taliesin, a noted bard of the 6th century writes of it as Caer-Gwyrosydd, "Fortress of the Gower horsemen" or armed men of Gower. There is also the story of Saint Illtyd, head of a great college of saints at Llan-Illtyd, i.e. Llantwit Major, who retired in his old age to lead the life of a hermit in a cave at Loyngarth (Oystermouth) in the 5th century, and there established a church, which Nennius, who wrote in the 9th century, stated was still standing in his day.

There are also the Welsh versions of the name. One of Taliesin's pupils, Rhun, is designated in the Welsh Calendar as "a Saint of Ystumllwynar-th." In another form, Ystumarth is seen as "a curved wooded ridge."

Among Mediaeval references is one in the Chartulary or Register of the Abbey of Gloucester which states: "Maurice de Londres, son of William de Londres, gave the Church of *Ostremuwe* in Goer" to the Abbey of St. Peter there, in the year 1141. From that date until 1367, the church was held by the Benedictine Monastery, Gloucester Abbey and its tithes and glebe (land) possessed by the Prior of Ewenny. Towards the close of the 13th century, the "Ecclesia de Oystremuthe" is mentioned, within the lists of Advowsons, i.e. the right of patronage or presentation to a church benefice, belonging to the Abbey. In 1319, a curious deed among the

Penrice Charters lists lands and tenements at "Constable's town in the fee of Oscroume."

It was, perhaps, inevitable that a popular derivation of the place name Oystermouth would be linked to the locality's long association with the breeding of oysters. George Grant Francis (1814-1882), was among those who held the opinion that the name had long been generally connected with the local staple in oysters.

For part of the 19th century and up until 1918, local and civic matters relating to Oystermouth Parish were looked after by its own council administration, the Oystermouth Urban District Council. Its offices were located in Dunns Lane on the site occupied today by the Public Library. A shed here also once housed the Fire Brigade Station. However, the Oystermouth U.D.C. was disbanded when Mumbles, together with other outlying districts such as Fforestfach and Sketty, elected to become part of the Swansea County Borough. A continuous, daily supply of water for domestic consumption via Cray reservoir rather than the two hours per day schedule then in existence and the all-round introduction of electricity from Swansea were among the significant factors which influenced a majority vote acceptance for inclusion within an expanded borough boundary.

* * * * * *

For the most part, the peninsula of Gower with the Mumbles is composed of a plateau which is between some 200 and 350 feet above sea level. The lower south-west zone consists of carboniferous limestone while the higher north-east area contains millstone grit and lower coal measures. Boulder clay, to a large extent, blankets the latter two measures.

Since time immemorial, the relentless, erosive action of the sea upon this plateau has produced or carved into being one of the most admired coastlines in the United Kingdom. The uniqueness of its small, sandy bays and tiny coves, together with a picturesque variety of scenic inland and coastal views, won for Gowerland the distinction of being selected as the very first of the nation's outstanding areas of natural beauty.

Vacillations or fluctuations in respect of relative land and sea levels associated with the Bristol Channel, as well as elsewhere, have taken place since the Pleistocene or "Ice Age" period. J. G. Rutter in his "Prehistoric Gower" states that "Pleistocene shore-lines on or near the present coast but above the present sea-level are clearly displayed by the so-called "Raised beaches," which in Gower form a prominent feature of the coastline. These consist of beach-platforms 20 to 30 feet above the present platform, frequently covered with beach deposits and sometimes bounded by "fossil" cliffs.

At a very much later period in history, the severe storms, savage gales, awesome tidal waves and destructive floods which occurred in the Bristol Channel during pre and post-Mediaeval times continued to affect and disturb those former lowlands which once abutted on to the foreshore of Swansea Bay. Eventually, the periodic but persistent inroads of the sea encroached and finally overwhelmed the forests, groves and meadows belonging to these low lying acres.

A document from the Harleian Miscellany makes reference to a mighty tidal wave which struck the South Wales coastal region in the early 17th century. Bristol, Newport, Cardiff, Aberavon and Swansea were among some of the places affected by its onslaught whereby upwards of five hundred persons perished. This event took place about 9 o'clock on the morning of the 20th January, 1607, when the maddened seas engulfed the flat, marshy lands and plains in its path.

Corporation records reveal that Swansea rendered some financial assistance to hard-hit Aberafon. "Aputt Swanzey XVI day of February, in the yeare of our Lorde, 1607 . . .

> Therefore, John David Edwards, Portreff of the towne of Swanzey, together with the Aldermen and Burgesses of the same, hath thought good in charity to bestowe the some of xxs. as theyer ffree gyft and benevolence to the forsed dystressed inhabitance of Avon towards the repayring of their forsed sea walles, and have delivered the same XXs. into the hands of Hopkin Griffith, one of the Burgesses of the said towne of Avon, the day and yeare above written."

The Mumbles foreshore and adjacent coastal waters suffered from the effects of this great tidal wall of sea and acres of flat, marshy lands and plains, together with farmsteads on Grove Island, referred to later as the Green Grounds, were wiped out of existence. In addition to this particular story, the Mumbles is mentioned in other accounts, albeit a mixture of facts, personal reminiscences or legends.

During the Mediaeval period, it would appear that the edge of the Swansea seashore curved some distance outside the Green Grounds from the Mumbles Head to Margam Woods. Within the perimeter of sand-dunes or "burrows" forests covered the slimy soil in which grew such trees as the silver birch, beech, holly, oak and yew. One legend makes reference to a bridle path, i.e. a path or way for horsemen, used by the Lords of Gower, and by the Mansels, Mowbrays and the Talbots in succession. The bridle path was supposed to extend from Penrice Castle to Margam Abbey, and for generations was used by the Abbots of the Abbey and other travellers to Gower. The path hugged the seacoast, passed some distance beyond the Mumbles Head and continued in the direction of Margam Woods. In all probability, the events of 1607 caused its final disappearance.

Old Gower traditions used to refer to a Silver Wood and the submerged forest or Crows' Wood in Swansea Bay.

E. E. Rowse, in his book, "In And Around Swansea," testifies to the encroachment of the sea along Swansea Bay in past centuries as well as throughout the 19th century by recording the reminiscences of an old Mumbles sailor. The latter considered that sea erosion in the bay had claimed approximately 100 yards of ground in the last century.

Under the title, "The Story Of The Miss Angels And Their Farm," he records the following account:

> "It was in the autumn of 1890 that I found myself one glorious afternoon, accompanied by two congenial companions, parading the Mumbles Beach . . . A large number of trawlers were still afloat, and the numerous skiffs and pleasure boats which skimmed across the bay in graceful attitude, made up a sight never to be forgotten. Calling for a boat, an old sea salt, on the look-out, struck a bargain with us, and after a few minutes' rowing we found ourselves far out in the bay, just under the Mumbles Head. We soon found the old sailor very agreeable and full of traditional stories, which he related to us quite freely. . . 'I remember the Mumbles for the last 70 years: (i.e. as far back as 1820); I am in my 79th year (born circa 1811). I consider that the sea has encroached nearly 100 yards since I was a boy, as the stumps and the roots of the trees along the shore testify. I know all about the Miss Angels. There were two sisters, one of whom was blind for a long time. They lived in yonder house close to the shore (the first house after leaving Norton for Swansea), and during the winter, when the waves rolled over the protecting wall, and threatened its destruction, they would move down to the 'Ship Hotel,' and remain there until the winter was over. One of the sisters lived in Angel Street, Swansea, in the house now known as the York Hotel, and died there. This was 30 years ago (circa 1860). It used to be told among the fishermen that the Angel family would become extinct. There used to live in the parish three families—the Robins, the Madocks, and the Angels. Each of these families opposed the laying down of a tesselated pavement in the church, and as the other parishioners were desirous that this should be done, they heaped curses upon the heads of those who opposed the scheme, and swore that they were accursed, and that their posterity would become extinct. And this has actually happened, as we have no Angels, nor Robins, nor Madocks left.
>
> "I have seen the maps and ancient pictures, which prove that a large extent of land, now submerged in the bay, and extending as far as the Green Grounds, formerly belonged to the Angel family. When Sir John Morris' father wished to work a quarry in the Mumbles hill, the Miss Angels insisted that he should pay them so much for 'way leave,' but this old Sir John stoutly refused to do. The Miss Angels determined, however, to defend their rights, and the case was tried at Carmarthen Assizes. After long contention, the judge expressed his dissatisfaction with the proofs of ownership, and the Miss Angels were mulcted in costs.
>
> "However, they were not to be turned aside from their purpose, so they

employed a barrister, and had the case tried at Hereford, and here again the case seemed to be going against the maiden ladies. It happened that the counsel for the defendants had been detained on the high road, and that, consequently, their case proceeded without him. Fortunately, however, he arrived before its conclusion, and, after apologising to the judge, he was allowed to cross-question the ladies. This elucidated many facts which had been withheld, and as the old documents were produced in court, which proved that all the lands in the neighbourhood of the church, as far out as the Green Grounds, belonged to the Angels, the jury were convinced, and the judge gave them a verdict which ultimately ruined Sir John Morris, and caused him to leave the country.

"The plan of this ancient property showed distinctly a farm house, where the sea now covers the Green Grounds, as well as a large meadow, which was crossed by a country stile; but all this has long ago disappeared, and the very memory of its existence only lingers in the minds of the very aged.

"It appears that the public records of the reign of Edward IV speak of the great floods which devastated Glamorganshire, and that this tremendous storm continued for several days. But the most extraordinary flood recorded took place in the early part of the reign of James I, when an Atlantic tidal wave swept up the Channel, scouring both coasts, and doing fearful damage. It overwhelmed Grove Island, and the farm and meadow lands on it, effacing for ever almost all traces of its exact whereabouts; although it is well known by means of an old map, that it was not far from the Mumbles rocks, and that it occupied the site now known as the Green Grounds. I am getting an old man now, but I can remember my grandfather speaking of the tradition which his ancestors had handed down, about the ancient wood, known as 'The Silver Wood,' and how it gradually disappeared, and what I heard has often been confirmed during my lifetime. I remember some of our men fishing up the horns of the antelope, the ox and the stag, and recovering tusks of the wild boar. I have oftentimes heard also of the tale of the last boar that was killed in Norton; how it was forcing its passage down one of the long lanes leading to the shore, but was speared by a spit, which killed it on the spot, and this is why the natives call the lane Boar-spit lane to this day."

Nine years later, another but shorter appraisal of the Green Grounds' tradition appeared when Col. W. Ll. Morgan in his "Antiquarian Survey Of East Gower," 1899, wrote:

"A slab of Forest stone was dragged up on the Green Grounds, 1885, bearing marks of a chisel and cement. It is supposed to have come from the old house of the Angels said to have existed on these lands. This idea mainly rests upon tradition, though there are said to be in existence deeds with plans of farms, where at present there is deep water, only no one has ever succeeded in finding these plans. However, it is certain that within 100 years the representatives of the Angel family did claim rights on the foreshore as part of the property swallowed up by the sea."

Even today, there are still some Mumbles residents who can recall to memory the local saying, "You can hear them out on the Green Grounds."

A late 17th century map housed in the R.I.S.W. records the name of the Maddocks family. The 1663 map drawn by Griffith Griffiths shows the land owned by them complete with a manor known as Dunns or Maddocks' Mews. A parish road once led to the village from this location. Within its grounds stood a leaping stock used by people to mount their horses; a house and stable yard; a large garden with trees and seats; a kitchen garden; a kitchen outlet and a large barn near the front courtyard. The courtyard or mount possessed five cannon which faced out over the sea. Since those days and the present time, the Dunns' area has witnessed numerous topographical changes.

Further references to submerged farmlands and the Angel and Robins families are made by Alfred Hall in his "History of Oystermouth," pages 6-7, published in 1899:

> "I have also heard that an innkeeper at the Mumbles had a picture of a farm at 'Grove Island,' but that it was destroyed by a servant. *The farm was connected by a path near the Inner Sound, and a stile leading to it was represented . . .*
>
> ". . . it has reached me that deeds belonging to property in the shape of farms belonging to the 'Angel' family in the bay, were a few years ago in the possession of a Gower Minister named Ford, of Pilewell, Pitton."

After the Rev. Ford's death in Swansea the elusive deeds in question were reputed to have been sent to Carmarthen. A William Robins and the Muckrosses are mentioned on page 19, their particular headstones, both of the mid-1730's, being amongst the oldest ones located in the parish graveyard.

Late Mediaeval records record the presence of coal deposits within the Lordship of Gower which, among others, included those at Clyne Forest and the Grange located in the Parish of Oystermouth. An Inquisition of 1319 investigated a number of alienations accomplished by William de Braose and his ancestors and one of those persons affected was John de Horton of Knelston whose lands contained "mines of sea coal near le Clun," i.e. Clyne. The latter area is again referred to by the Cromwellian Survey of 1650 in connection with the Manor of Oystermouth, namely:

> "There was also produced a grant under the hand of Walter Thomas dated 20th July, 1642, made to Richard Seys for digging of coales in Clyne Fforest and part of the other lands mentioned."

In bygone days, the coal worked in Clyne Forest was shipped from the beach at Blackpill but at a lower line of water than exists today.

Throughout intermittent periods of successive centuries coal continued to be exploited here until 1916.

In addition, arsenic was once manufactured in Clyne Woods, on the east side of Clyne Castle. Other small furnaces were also engaged in extracting naptha from timber but this process was abandoned early in 1841.

Although by no means inexhaustible, the following significant dates in respect of the 19th century history of Oystermouth and Mumbles may be noted: the Oystermouth Railway or Tramroad Company formed in 1804; a passenger service inaugurated on the Oystermouth Railway, 1807; turnpike road constructed between Swansea and Mumbles, 1826; iron-ore deposits mined on Mumbles Hill, 1845; some deaths from cholera sustained in 1849, but not comparable with Swansea's severe losses in the same year; Coastguard Look-out placed on Mumbles Hill, "Somerset House" area, 1850; new road section, opposite Oystermouth Castle, in the direction of Langland Bay, completed in 1856; Parish Church of All Saints enlarged and horse-drawn passenger service re-introduced, in two stages, between the Royal Institution of South Wales, Swansea, and Oystermouth, 1860; first Mumbles' R.N.L.I. lifeboat put into service, 1866; the National Schools opened in 1867; approximately sixteen million oysters landed and sold for nearly £50,000, 1871, a peak year; on the same site, third Methodist Chapel enlarged, and steam traction introduced on the Oystermouth Railway line, 1877; Board Schools opened in 1878, i.e., today's Oystermouth Infants' School and the Oystermouth Junior Comprehensive School; Oystermouth Waterworks Co. Ltd. commenced operations, 1882; the first Mumbles Lifeboat disaster recorded, 1883; Mumbles visited by P.M. Gladstone and party, 1887; and the new railway line from Oystermouth to Mumbles Head together with the opening of the Mumbles Pier completed in 1898.

Iron ore was formerly worked from a mine situated on Mumbles Hill, slightly beyond and overlooking the present Yacht Club. Although much of the workings were afterwards filled in, the cutting or rift at this point is clearly visible on inspection. Mining activities in this particular field continued, on and off, for a period between 1845 and 1899; small quantities of ore were also obtained from Langland at one time. The late Cllr. Harry Libby's grandfather was a manager of the mine in the 1850's.

After blasting operations, the pieces of rock-ore would be broken down to more containable sizes; some were rolled, dragged on sledges or transported in barrows to the beach. A little off shore, the waiting beached vessels were loaded up with iron ore which was then shipped across to Swansea and Briton Ferry. The loading procedure adopted was similar to that used by other sailing craft engaged in the transport of limestone from Mumbles.

Among the lodes or veins which intersected the Mumbles Hill, a few pockets of haematite iron ore were successfully exploited and at Newton. In spite of the limited quantities involved, this was a valuable source of iron with its high peroxide of iron content, known also as limonite. The silica of the millstone grit was once extensively worked by an adit or opening driven into Newton Hill.

Small two masted vessels were used to convey cattle and sheep across the Bristol Channel from Somerset and Devon to Mumbles throughout the 19th century. At appropriate times, the local farmers would meet the boats berthed on the beach to receive their live cargoes. Each animal was lowered down separately to sand level by means of a block and tackle suspended from the after jib. Such a procedure is clearly portrayed by the noted artist, Alfred Parkman, in his delightful, detailed painting entitled, "Mumbles 1881."

The noticeable growth of Mumbles' population in the 19th century is revealed by the following census figures: 1821, 1008; 1831, 1164; 1841, 313 houses & 1482; 1851, 430 houses & 1938; 1861, 547 houses & 2460; 1871, 742 houses & 3574; 1881, 3915; and 1891, 4132.

In 1849, Swansea suffered its second and more widely spread outbreak of cholera, when upwards of 200 people perished in the epidemic. Between the end of July and mid-September, 423 cases were reported and the total number of deaths had reached 148. The causes were basically the same as for the 1832 visitation: defective and inadequate water supplies, an almost complete absence of drainage facilities, and wretched, over-crowded conditions within the poorer sections of the town.

Several deaths from this deadly disease were also recorded in the Mumbles during the same year at a time when the containment of numerous infectious diseases presented an urgent problem for small or large public bodies in Wales. The over-crowded workers' tenements of the old borough were not Oystermouth's problem; her population was approximately one-fifteenth of Swansea's in 1849, the year when Merthyr lost some fourteen hundred people in the cholera outbreak there. (Swansea's inhabitants numbered 31,461 in 1851; Oystermouth's, 1,938). Primitive sanitary arrangements, a non-existent drainage scheme and insufficient water supplies obtained from wells and springs were, however, all too-evident in the Mumbles of the mid-19th century, and for some time afterwards.

In a scathing medical report produced in September, 1849, two Local Board of Health medical inspectors, George G. Bird, M.D., and Thomas A. Essery, found "Newton Village defective in a remarkable degree." Among other comments, they stated:

> "The site is particularly salubrious, but house ventilation is very defective; few persons open their windows, and many of these are so constructed

as not to admit of being opened. A large number of pigs are kept in this village, and they are permitted to wander over the roads and thoroughfares . . . In that part of Newton, called Nottage, there are several stagnant pools, the emanations from which are dangerous, and have no doubt tended greatly to produce epidemic cholera. It is in this part that the disease and choleric diarrhoea have most prevailed."

The government of the day, the talented administration of Sir Robert Peel (1788-1850) was aware of the basic causes behind such outbreaks. In the very early Spring of 1845, it had declared its intention to propose a bill for the general regulation of drainage and ventilation in all towns. The creation of adequate water supplies for public consumption, the construction of sewers, branch sewers and house drains etc., were to be entrusted to local administrative bodies.

In the first annual report of the Medical Officer of the Borough of Swansea, 1855, Dr. W. H. Michael, wrote that in considering "the sanitary condition of Swansea, there are two things of great and grave importance demanding attention, viz., Drainage and efficient Water Supply, the absence of both being a fruitful source of mortality." The horror of the town's 1849 outbreak heightened the need for urgent reforms. As a result, Swansca's first water undertaking was formed in 1851, as a Company, to supply water to the smelting industries and port. It built one reservoir, now the lake in Brynmill Park, and laid approximately two miles of mains to the harbour area at the mouth of the River Tawe. More than three decades were to pass after the 1849 epidemic, however, before the first supplies of piped water from the western corner of Caswell Bay were relayed to certain parts of the Mumbles. This was achieved by the placing of a steam pump at Caswell, installed by a private firm, the Oystermouth Waterworks Co. Ltd., early in 1882. (See separate chapter).

The ending of the wretched, mismanaged Crimean War, 1854-56, highlighted by the forthright dispatches of "The Times" was an occasion for much rejoicing at all levels of Victorian society. Following the Treaty of Paris, 30th March, 1856, numerous peace celebrations took place in Swansea throughout the following month as well as elsewhere in Great Britain. "The Cambrian" dated 30th May, 1856, duly noted that, "the Mumbles and Caswell attracted a fair share of visitors" in this respect. Bathing in Langland and Caswell Bays increased in popularity, while marine walks, visits to Oystermouth Castle and Church, remained permanent attractions for visitors.

Day trippers in particular were to increase noticeably in later decades as a result of improved transport and road facilities. In the latter respect, 1856 was also the year when the then Duke of Beaufort made a creditable contribution to the betterment of the Mumbles roadways' routes. On the 27th June for that year, "The Cambrian" reported:

"Our town readers will be glad to hear that the *new road* (branching off opposite Oystermouth Castle to Langland Bay) is at length completed. It was thrown open to the public last week, and we need hardly state it is a most desirable improvement, . . . we understand mainly indebted to the *liberality of His Grace the Duke of Beaufort.* Few places in the kingdom present more attractions for excursionists and picnics than the delightful neighbourhood of Langland and Caswell, which is as famed for its pellucid streams and splendid shells as for the beauty of its coast scenes. A good road therefore to such a locality is of great importance to Swansea, and we doubt not, with this improved mode of access, it will soon become a place of fashionable resort."

During the second half of the 19th century, a notable feature of village life was the holding of an annual summer regatta which used to attract large crowds from Swansea. Races were originally organised for the cutter design of rigged skiffs, those small vessels possessing one mast, a mainsail, a forestaysail, and a jib to bowsprit-end; upwards of thirty or more craft would participate. Other events took place nearer inshore such as diving and swimming contests, punt races and the inevitable greasy pole competitions. Sometimes a small fair would be in attendance, or a visiting band, while trades people plied their wares along suitable stretches of the shore line.

Even though, sadly, the number of sailing skiffs declined sharply towards the close of the Victorian era, the regatta continued to function at a time when competitive yachting headed the list of principal events. However, some of the remaining skiffs presented formidable opposition to smaller yachts taking part in the same class competitions. Wisely, headmasters of local Board Schools granted their pupils half-day holidays on regatta days and thereby avoided the occurrence of depleted attendances prompted by such important occasions.

During the first week of June, 1887, the famous British statesman, William Ewart Gladstone, with his wife and son, Rector Stephen Gladstone, paid a visit to Swansea as the welcomed guests of Sir H. H. Vivian, M.P. The public reception accorded the Prime Minister was an enthusiastic one locally; at his Singleton Estate, which the town's M.P. had opened to the people, an enormous procession took nearly two hours to file past Mr. Gladstone. In the same week, the Free Library, i.e. the Central Public Library, Alexandra Road, was formally declared opened by the Prime Minister who then delivered his famous speech on the Irish Question.

Sir Hussey and Lady Vivian also managed to arrange a short sightseeing tour of the Mumbles for their guests. A horse-drawn carriage was used for the journey and the Vivians, together with Lord Aberdare and others, accompanied the Gladstones on the visit. At the Mumbles, the carriage was left for a while in the village and the party proceeded on foot to inspect the bays. Meanwhile, arrangements had been made for the visitors, on their return, to call in at the noted oyster and temperance tavern of Harry Lockband and his wife, Ann. Their business was located near to the Mermaid Inn, in Beaufort Buildings, which is now the Ashleigh Hotel.

By the time the first of her distinguished visitors had arrived, who happened to be Prime Minister Gladstone, Mrs. Lockband had prepared a quantity of fresh oysters for consumption together with plates of brown bread and butter laid out neatly on the large parlour table. Mr. Gladstone remarked to the proprietor's wife that he did not care much for oysters personally but his wife and son were very fond of them. Therefore, he indicated his desire to wait awhile until the remainder of the party came in.

On their arrival, the visitors were served hot cups of tea with their meals and the entire fare received high commendation from all concerned. Mrs. Gladstone was later surprised to learn that the oysters were sold at the relatively cheap rate of one shilling per dozen. Sir Hussey added that prices were even cheaper in his younger days, a fact substantiated by Mrs. Lockband who recalled her mother having sold old Squire Vivian at Singleton ten dozen oysters for one shilling. Such amounts were then carried on their heads by some of the Mumbles womenfolk to places such as Blackpill, Singleton and the outskirts of Swansea. This was traditionally known as a "long hundred."

Afterwards, the Lockbands received a letter of thanks from the Gladstones which earned their establishment the title of being known as the Gladstone Restaurant or the Gladstone Oyster & Refreshment Bar. Before her death in 1908, at the age of 78, Mrs. Lockband remarried as Mrs. J. H. Humphries and remained in business for 32 years.

At first, Oystermouth was part of the Swansea Union, formed in 1836, but later it came within the Gower Union, Swansea County Court District, diocese of St. David's, archdeaconry of Carmarthen, and the deanery of East and West Gower. By the end of the Victorian era, the Urban District of Oystermouth closely resembled a boot in profile: its upper border abutted on to the Parish of Brynau, from which it was separated by the West Cross brook; and its back border was divided from the Parish of Bishopston by the Clyne Common waters which disappeared below ground to emerge afterwards near the Caswell Pumping Station. The heel, arch and sole were formed by the seaskirt rocks which extended from Whiteshell Point to the Mumbles Head; and its receding front composed by the shallows of Swansea Bay, from the Sounds to West Cross Railway Station. This irregular shape was about one mile in width at its upper part and nearly three miles in length at its base. As constituted by the Local Government Act of 1894, an urban district, such as Oystermouth's, was broadly defined as an area which did not yet have a population large enough to enable it to obtain a charter and thereby become a municipal corporation. (Afterwards, when part of the Swansea County Borough, the Mumbles Ward boundary continued to resemble the outline of a boot).

Then as now, the well raised land formation rises steadily from sea level on the north-west to over three-hundred feet near Eastmoor and maintains a gradual slope to two-hundred feet and more through Newton to Caswell on the west, and to Thistleboon eastwards. This small tableland runs from north to south-west and south-east, and within its triangular shape possesses a triple watershed : on the east to Swansea Bay, southwards to the British Channel, and westwards through Caswell Bay to the bay itself. Geologically, the area could be divided simply into an upper third above the ankle, extending from Norton through Newton to Hesperlone, consisting of lower shales and clays of the Glamorgan coal bed; and a lower two thirds, containing underlying carboniferous limestone, and comprising the localities of Caswell, Langland, Castleton, Mumbles and Thistleboon. This geological distribution of impervious clay and porous limestone explained the presence of small streams which ran east and west in the northern section; and the absence of any but subterranean water which flowed on to the beach at Mumbles and at Langland and Caswell Bays, in the southern portion.

During the 1870's, the hilly terrain of small valleys, streams and sloping fields in and around this area was farmed by upwards of thirty families. As well as a water-course for their cattle, the tenant farmers utilised some of the more permanent brooks for irrigation purposes while the high ground accommodated the flocks of sheep.

The Boarspit Stream was once much used by the inhabitants of Norton for washing and other household requirements. Such activities here and elsewhere caused problems of pollution for the local authority. The intermittent stream on the eastern watershed which descended into the valley below Norton Village was a constant nuisance and health hazard. As a rule, it remained barely visible in the summer and autumn seasons, but during the winter and spring months it flooded the fields below Underhill with the unsightly washings and leavings of the farms and houses which overlooked this site.

Among those who worked the land throughout the last quarter of the 19th century, and for some time afterwards, were: John Ackland, Boarspit; David Bennett, Newton; Mrs. Margaret Bennett, Coltshill Farm, Norton; John Beynon, Thistleboon; John Bidder, Newton; Harry Clement, Long Ash; John Edwards, Newton; Charles Gammon, Newton; John Gammon, 'Ship & Castle Inn,' Newton; Philip Gwyn, Newton; Thomas Jones, Haslydd; John Matthews, farm manager, Norton; William Morris, farmer & butcher; David F. Nicholls; David Owens, Griffith Owens, John Owens, William Owens, Richard Parry,—Newton; Richard

Pike, Norton; John Tucker, Mayals; Robert Westcott, West Cross; and Richard Woollacott, 'Rock & Fountain,' Newton.

Some of the blacksmiths available in those days were: T. Bevan, 2 Church Terrace; John Davies, 3 Commercial Place; and J. Sanders, shoeing forge of the Dunns, listed in "Butcher & Company's Directory" for 1875-6. Richard Slocombe of "Bayswater Cottage," Mumbles Road, was a cattle dealer, and the miller, D. Morgan, managed Blackpill Mill.

At times throughout the 19th century, it was quite noticeable to visitors that some acres of land in Gower were subdivided into very small fields. According to tradition, these plots of land represented the lost stakes of those free-holders of land who had gambled them away in games of chance. Addiction to games of chance was fairly prevalent among the inhabitants at an earlier period of the peninsula's history.

Among the games in vogue were the five-card game and quoits; in the former, the knave was the best card, which accounted for "Knave's Acre." The Mumbles was not unaffected by such gambling habits of bygone days. In Greenslade, the valley that terminated in Caswell Bay, was a field entitled "Jack's Shoe's Land," for here Jack staked a pair of his shoes, rather rare items in those days, at cards, against the field, and won. By the side of the road from Caswell to Newton , was "Tailor's Park," which was staked in a game of quoits, as was also a smaller piece in the middle of Thistleboon Farm.

As elsewhere, various forms of card games, pitch and toss, and even, sometimes, illegal horse racing along stretches of the Mumbles Road, took place. In the first week of May, 1900, Farmer Richard Woollacott complained at an Oystermouth U.D.C. meeting about the number of youths who gambled on Sundays in the Thistleboon neighbourhood. As well as in secluded public places, some of them frequently hid themselves away on private land to hold gambling sessions, common enough practices which became more noticeable in times of depression.

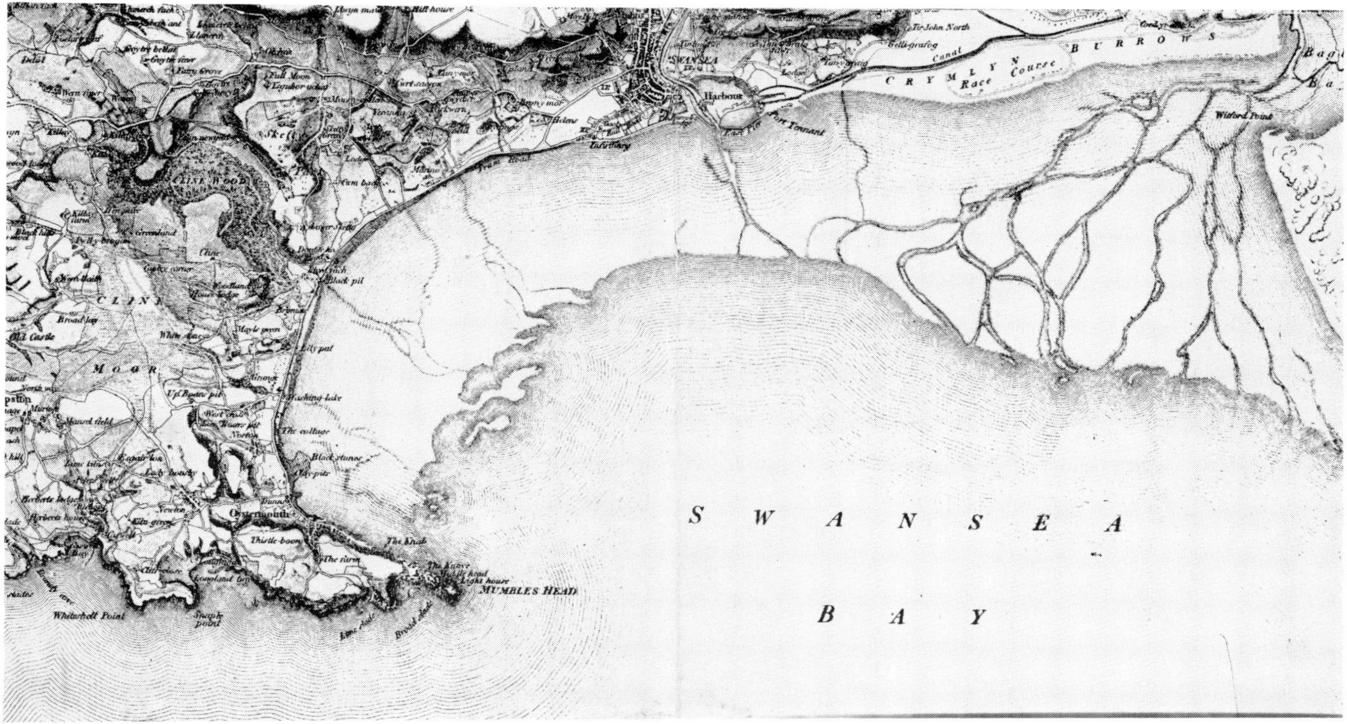

Swansea Bay 1825

Swansea Bay 1900

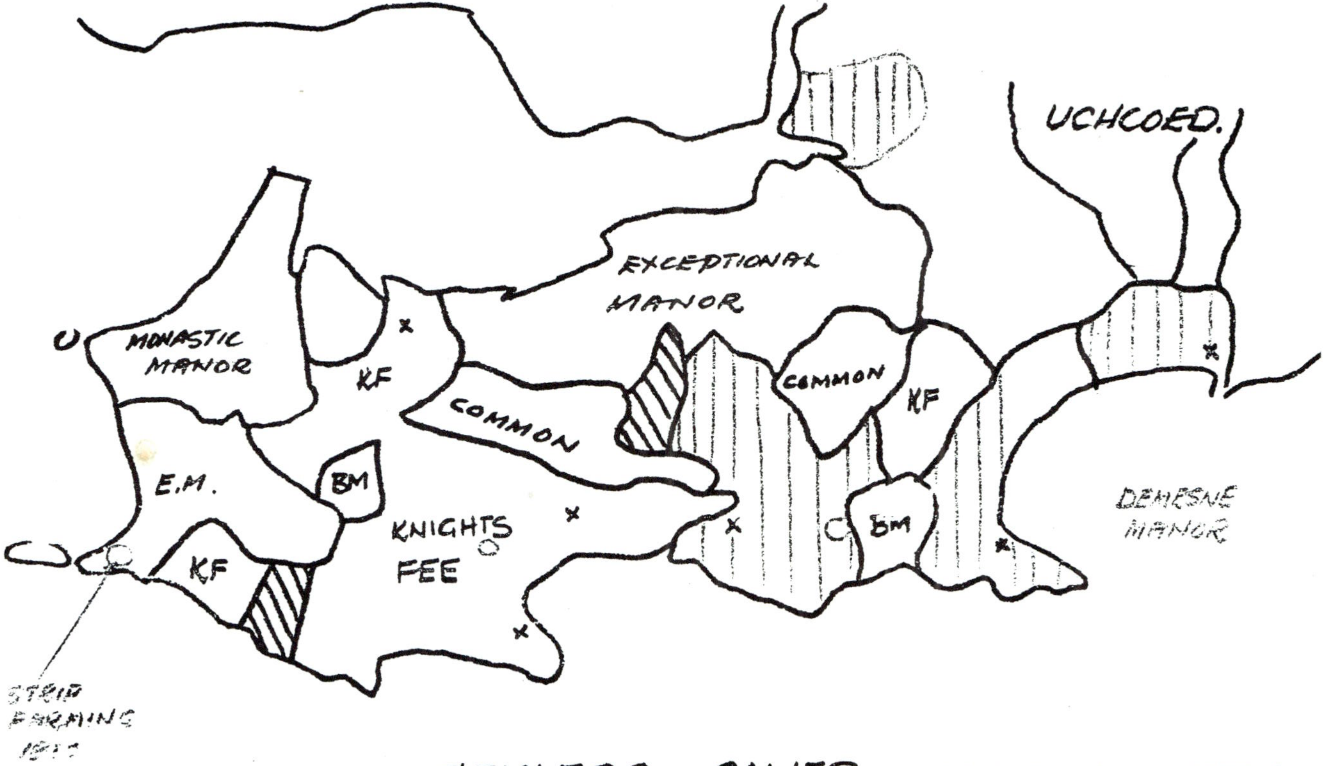

SEYLERS - GOWER. - MANORIAL SYSTEM

Circa 1869

By permission, Swansea City Council

Town Hall, Somerset Place, Swansea, erected in 1847; John Henry Vivian, M.P. bronze statue (now in Victoria Park) flanked by two Russian cannon taken at Sebastopol.

By permission, Roger David Studios

Mumbles, 1888   By Hannaford

By permission, Swansea City Council

Oystermouth 1892 *By permission, Swansea City Council*

William Goddard   Circa 1890
D. G. Bowden

CHAPTER TWO

TWENTIETH CENTURY DEVELOPMENTS

"The past is neither dead nor irrelevant. It has shaped us—our conventions, our practices, our environment, even our present mood: even as, we are repeatedly assured, our capacity to respond to our current predicament, will determine our future. To understand an individual one examines not, if one is wise, what he says but what he has done and the background from which he springs. So too with society. The relevance of history is evident enough."
Howell A. Lloyd. Hull University, 1965.

"On that fateful day in August, 1914, I walked with the Carpenter, who had received notice to report himself for service, and was leaving the next day for that purpose . . . In those early days the Censor was very busy and very strict. I gathered from the illustrated post cards I received that he was serving on board H.M.S. 'Hawke,' and was on coastal service, or something like it. We missed him sorely in the Chapel, Brotherhood and Class Meeting; and then, in October, came the fatal news of the torpedoing of the 'Hawke' and the consequent loss of many lives. Amongst those who were so sacrificed was the Carpenter."
C. W. Slater: "The Corner Pew." 1919.

". . . All the things we ought to do have been done and I'm afraid Mr. Wilkinson would say we haven't left undone a deuce of a lot we ought not to have done. Street Tea Parties, Dances (especially in Stanley Street), Bonfires, Lifeboat Trips for the kids, and now Fireworks. At midnight last night everything went on a bonfire in the Station Square and the policeman only missed a similar experience by goodwill—Southend went wild—parachute flares went up, and there were more nightdresses on parade between the Yacht Club and Sander's Corner than I imagined were ever worn. We didn't forget the boys who will not come back nor He who giveth us the Victory and suitable references were made not only in Churches but in Cinemas, Dances and Tennis Tournaments . . .
"To see all the lights on around the Bay and up on the higher reaches of Swansea has been a tonic; to realise that our Prisoners in Japan will soon be home is another; and to get basic petrol is a help."

Cllr. Harry Libby: Last of the Mumbles (Wartime) News-letters, 15th August, 1945.

Among some noteworthy Mumbles dates of the present century may be mentioned: the second Mumbles Lifeboat disaster which took place in 1903; the Oystermouth Urban District Council Water Act passed in 1911; Mumbles' contribution made to the First World War, 1914-18; Oystermouth U.D.C. brought into the expanded Swansea County Borough programme of 1918; small Coastguard Look-out Station placed on Tutt Head, 1921; electrification of the Mumbles Railway undertaken, 1927-29; war effort rendered by the citizens of Mumbles during 1939-45; the S.S. "Samtampa" disaster when the entire crew of the Mumbles Lifeboat was lost in 1947; the shut-down of the Swansea & Mumbles Railway line undertaken on the 5th January, 1960; the skilful, dramatic rescue of ten sailors from the burning motor vessel "Kilo" of Amsterdam, performed by Coxswain Derek Scott, M.B.E., and his crew who had to contend with a dangerous deck cargo of sodium under severe gale conditions, 1963; and the highly successful land and sea, summer programme of events, organised by the "Ostreme" committees annually throughout a major part of the 1970's.

A special event looked forward to among farming communities was the annual ploughing match organised by the Gower & District Farmers' Association. From timc to time, Mumbles was selected as the venue and the one held in 1900, for example, took place in the fields of Thistleboon Farm loaned by Richard Woollacott. Ploughing teams competed for awards in the champion class, first class and boys' class sections. The ploughing skill of W. Davies, 14 years old, "was much admired for one so young," reported "The Cambrian" dated the 2nd March for that year. Prizes were presented for the smartest team of horses, the best groomed horses and the finest turn-out. In the evening, the farmers attended the "Ship & Castle Inn," Newton, for the annual supper where speeches and a programme of vocal music were heard under the chairmanship of James Slocombe, West Cross. Today, farming activities have all but disappeared from the Mumbles scene in the wake of numerous property developments. However, some of the family names live on locally to serve, perhaps, as a tangible reminder of a bygone age. Tenant farmer, Mr. P. Griffin continues to cultivate currently a rising acreage of some nine fields worked formerly by the Woollacott family. This is that area overlooked by the Beaufort Avenue and Lambswell residences and which stretches upwards in the direction of Rams Tor.

Among the popular forms of entertainment attended by local residents in the early 1900's before the outbreak of World War I, were those held at St. David's Hall on Saturdays under the auspices of the Wesleyan Methodist Church. In this building, later renamed Victoria Hall, people listened to recitations, songs, pianoforte, solos and whistling solos and similar programmes were organised by other denominational groups. Additional attractions were provided by the Mumbles Management Pier's weekly and week-end summer engagements for well-known bands and vocal concerts. Performances were undertaken by such groups as Gittens' Carl Rosa Opera Singers, the Royal Strolling Players and Royal Bohemian Players.

Environmental change and contrast were evident in Edwardian Mumbles: the picturesque sea views and landscapes tended at times to overshadow those less salubrious features inland; while commercial prosperity outside the Urban District Council boundary frequently caused marine pollution within its own precinct. As elsewhere, whooping cough and scarlet fever were no respecter of guide books' eulogistic phrases describing the beneficial effects of the district's mild yet bracing, equable climate.

At the turn of the century, chemical salts in effluent form, among other obnoxious substances, released into the Tawe by factories sited on either side of the river, had begun to build up as foul deposits of black mud in the vicinity of the oyster beds. This situation combined with the primitive disposal of some sewage tipped directly into the sea off Southend, embittered the remaining skiff owners who had already lost most of the curved beach which had been replaced by a seawall built in connection with the Mumbles Railway Line's extension from Oystermouth to Mumbles Head. As a result, there arose the "oyster scare" of 1903.

More fields disappeared as private building developments progressed up to the outbreak of the 1914-18 War. These solid Edwardian structures were mainly terraced properties and emerged along Oakland Road, King's Road, Queen's Road, Victoria Avenue and Woodville Road. In 1902, the members of the Bristol Yacht Club Headquarters, based at the Treffgarne Private Hotel, acquired the land immediately adjacent to John Henry Libby's forge on the Mumbles Head side, upon which was erected the elegant Club Headquarters in existence today. At the opposite end of the village, the narrow thoroughfare through the Dunns of 1904 presented the appearance of a dirt track, its pot-holes or indentations being filled in with suitably-sized limestones.

Before the mass production years of motorbikes, the fastest machines on two wheels in wide circulation then, were, of course, bicycles: Singer Cycles' 1906-07 prices ranged from £7 to £14. 14s.; and the Premier Cycle (Coventry) Co. Ltd.'s models, £5. 5s. to £14. 14s. The latter's "No. 3 Helical" cycle at £12. 12s. finished in super-fine black enamel, lined crimson and silver, the bright parts heavily nickel-plated on copper, with Dunlop tyres, was considered the beau ideal by many enthusiasts in those days. Punctured tyres were attended to by the Maslens of West Cross.

Saturday walking races also attracted large crowds of onlookers and adherents. The champion walkers of Wales frequently took part in these competitions held between Swansea and Mumbles or the Parkmill route; participants were generally accompanied by groups of supporters who ran alongside them there and back while others rode on their bicycles.

The ground known as the Ballast Bank opposite Oystermouth Parish Church became an alternative site for the ever popular fairground with its coconut shies, penny-peep show machines, roundabouts and sometimes a kinematograph showing "moving pictures," as so well recounted by the late Cllr. Harry Libby. Within the area occupied by the present-day Tivoli Entertainments establishment, formerly the Tivoli Cinema, there once stood a Kursaal-type building; purchased in Ilfracombe, the fairly large, dismantled reception hall was shipped across to Mumbles and then unloaded near its destination and re-erected. With mixed success, it catered for a number of different entertainments such as a skating rink, concert hall and cinema. (At a much later date afterwards, the building was bought by a Mr. E. Merrells who promoted a rebuilding programme which produced the Tivoli Cinema premises of pre-War Two years. The small Regent Cinema in Newton Road was also acquired by him but it has been used for various business ventures since its original function).

Two interesting facets of Edwardian life in respect of the Mumbles are supplied by the 1908 edition of "The Cambrian." In early February, future trends in mechanical transport were under review by Mr. Hubert Monger, son of one of the departmental managers of the Hafod Copper Works. With others, he made a public proposal to operate six motor-cars for party return journeys from Swansea to Mumbles, Bishopston and Parkmill. If the trial period proved a viable undertaking the small fleet was to be offered to a local syndicate at an agreed price.

In constrast, the weekly issue for the 5th June served yet again to remind its readers of the continuation of an old, established Mediaeval practice, namely, the meeting of the annual Court Leet of the Manor of Oystermouth. This was a court of record held in the presence of the steward or reeve of a manor or lordship; originally, there was only one court for a manor, but during Edward I's reign it branched into two, the court baron and the court leet. A Marcher Lord, especially, used such a court, with its criminal jurisdiction, as a right or implied right bestowed upon him by his sovereign. By the 20th century, Court Leets had been practically stripped of their former, ancient rights. Such meetings, however, arranged at the will or pleasure of the Dukes of Beaufort, did sometimes have beneficial consequences for the community.

The 1908 gathering met at the Marine Hotel and among those who presided were: R. W. Beor, Miss Dillwyn, Hubert Plant, Dr. T. B. Griffiths, F. H. Glyn Price, (Duke of Beaufort's agent) and jurors. Farmer Richard E. Woollacott, the reeve, was also elected foreman of the jurors.

Among the appointments made were: ale taster, John Edwards; pound-keeper, John Phillips; and the haywards, John Gwynne (Mumbles Hill); R. E. Woollacott (Newton Hill); and Mr. Thomas (Mayals Green & Clyne Moor). A hayward in bygone times was one who herded the common cattle of a town. Later, the task involved the care of parish fences and enclosures by an elected official who also had to look after all strays, remove booths, order trespassers off hills as well as prevent people from taking away turfs.

On the 10th May, 1898, the Mumbles Pier and the new line of the Mumbles Railway, an extension from Oystermouth to Mumbles Head, were opened to traffic. These twin events widened the scope of Mumbles as a modest seaside resort and far beyond its much earlier image as a tiny fishing village or watering retreat. By mid-1899, the railway and pier undertakings of the Swansea & Mumbles Railway Co. and the Mumbles Railway & Pier Co. were leased to the Swansea Improvements & Tramways Co. for 999 years. A new line constructed along the seashore was then opened between Blackpill and Oystermouth on the 26th August, 1900, and the former line which previously ran alongside the road between the same points was abandoned.

From its inception , the pier proved an immediate success with the day trippers during the twilight period left remaining of Queen Victoria's momentous reign which was to be a little under two years, nine months. Its popularity increased throughout the Edwardian era onwards when at peak holiday times the railway's large double-decked cars conveyed hundreds of passengers per journey, sometimes well in excess of a thousand, en route for the Mumbles. Additional uncovered single-decked third-class coaches made of wood were provided; their seats ran down the sides and centre, being placed back to back. Passengers were also allowed to stand, so it was little wonder that these coaches became known locally as "The Cattle Trucks." The public thoroughfare alongside the line would also be crowded with holiday-makers travelling in horse-drawn carriages, on bicycles in their scores, while some were driving more sedately perhaps, the early automobiles.

Piers of the last century had much to offer visitors, even though these afforded less faddish pleasures than some do today. Apart from their original, practical purpose of keeping boat passengers dry, piers later became synonymous with fresh air and healthy exercise. For many people, there was a real sense of adventure then in walking the 800 ft. length of Mumbles Pier, built at a cost of more than £10,000. They were able to enjoy the sea without getting their feet wet as well as actually viewing the waves immediately beneath them through the wafer-line divisions of the platform's timbered planking. If visitors were not tempted to undertake a return trip across the Bristol Channel in such paddle steamers as the

"Normandy," alternative entertainments were to hand for the pier supported large refreshment rooms, a concert pavilion and band stand.

Regrettably, fewer than fifty of the United Kingdom's piers now remain out of the ninety that were constructed before the 19th century pier mania had reached saturation point in nearly every coastal resort. Much credit is due, therefore, to the Mumbles Pier Amusements owners for their maintenance and upkeep of the present-day Mumbles Pier. As such they own the land underneath the pier and for an area approximately thirty feet wide around it. The insurance cost annually is an expensive item, for it must be borne in mind that a pier is a possible fire hazard and is susceptible to corrosion and damage by heavy seas or even complete destruction.

Meanwhile, the pier still caters for the regular, enthusiastic groups of anglers; provides a landing area for departures or arrivals in respect of sea excursions to Ilfracombe etc.; and permits access to those who simply wish to enjoy a stroll and admire the compelling views. Opposite its entrance is the popular Pier Hotel. In addition, the narrow, short connecting platform to the Lifeboat Station provides an essential and quick way too for crew members dashing to answer the rockets' call to duty. Fortunately, the fun-palace placed near the entrance is not very large so that the overall scene presents a suitable balance.

On occasions, the annual pre-War One regattas did not always live up to public expectations due sometimes to the absence of entries by celebrated yacht owners of international fame, or when the events themselves were marred by days of inclement weather. In addition to previous events organised by the Bristol Channel Yacht Club, whose original Headquarters adjoined the George Hotel, Southend, further revivals of major regattas succeeded under the auspices of the Swansea Bay Sailing Club.

A contributor to the Gowerton County School's magazine, "The Gowertonian," volume 3, dated July, 1913, who adopted the pseudonym, "Mermaid," recaptures vividly the Mumbles Regatta scene for that year:

> "Swansea has been trying for some time past to revive interest in yachting in the Bristol Channel, and with such a beautiful bay as she has, it is no wonder that the thoughts of the people turn seawards. The Regatta took place on June 18th, and proved a great attraction for townspeople and visitors, Mumbles being invaded by many thousands of sightseers during the day.
>
> "Early morning prospects were in favour of a good regatta. The water was smooth, the wind was slight enough, but there was a probability of the wind increasing as the day went on. As keen followers of yacht racing were making their way to their respective places whence to view the races, scores of rowing boats and one or two motor boats were plying between the yachts (moored some distance off) and the shore. Soon after the large, silky sails

were hoisted up and everything got in sailing order. About half an hour before the first race was to start the majority of the boats were gracefully gliding here and there. Some of the larger craft were seen making headway towards the Committee and Mark boats, a good way up the bay. A few minutes later they reached there and manouvering for position were soon in progress.

"We heard the report of a gun. 'They're off!' was the popular cry; and so they were. Two 19—metre yachts, the *Norada* and the *Mariquita,* were quickly heading for a mark not far from our spot—the pier hill. As they rounded the mark nearby—the *Mariquita* having a useful lead—all had a grand view of the two 'white wings.' From stem to stern they looked beautiful—glossy, smart, and skilfully handled as they were. Before these two had gone far from us, two more loomed into sight. These were the *Istria* and *Mandrey,* each 15 metres long. For gracefulness the *Istria* could not be surpassed, and as her blue hull skimmed over the water, she was admired by all. She was leading but her rival was also a fast boat, and when they finished there was very little to choose between them. Fifteen minutes after, the *Lady Beatrice* and the *Hyacinth* started, but the latter after establishing a good lead passed the mark on the wrong side and after winning a well-earned race, was disqualified. The men on board were unaware of the error until the race was completed, and all together about £40 was lost; but such are the fortunes of yachting. Race 4 was between the *Eileen* and *Zimita* which the former won handsomely . . .

"In the afternoon the shore-sports were the attraction and the promenade was crowded, while along the shore hundreds of rowing boats were scattered about for the people in them to have a good view of the events. In the rowing races, both junior and senior *four-oared Mumbles* were seen to advantage against Penarth and Cardiff. The races for the whalers and skiffs of the warships evoked considerable interest, and the races were so well-contested that *H.M.S. Shark* and *Christopher* only won by a few feet in each of their races. Swimming races proved fast and exciting though the water was not very warm, but one of the most amusing events was that of the *coracles,* or as someone remarked, the 'chronicles.' They resemble a cockle-shell in shape and are made of cane and the speed obtained out of them by some of the professionals from Carmarthen was surprising. In the amateur coracle race the speed was more surprising because some did not even finish the course. Manned by some men attired in bathing costume, they sometimes spun round like a top and frequently went backwards.

"Many of the 'chroniclers' received a ducking and one member, in endeavouring to catch his shoes thrown to him from someone on the Committee boat, capsized his own and lost the shoes in the attempt. The Plank and Shovel race was amusing and so was the Greasy Pole, but the Polo match was rather tame . . . The latter ended the programme for the day, and on the whole the regatta passed off very smoothly and successfully."

In circa 1911-12, the much smaller Mumbles Sailing Club was formed, the first joint secretaries being Messrs. Albert Williams and Harry Libby. (Enthusiastic community support and the financial backing of Mr.

Frederick Ley, a noted potato merchant, ensured its continuity after the First World War. Subsequent pre-War Two and post-War Two revivals finally resulted in today's flourishing Mumbles Yacht Club and Headquarters situated a little above the Bristol Channel Yacht Club).

On the outbreak of World War One, a large number of military personnel was stationed in and around the Mumbles area. Troops who guarded the fortifications on Mumbles Head were housed in the requisitioned Bristol Channel Yacht Club and this end of "outalong" was classified as a prohibited zone. Temporary huts were built by the Army to accommodate those soldiers encamped on this hillside.

On the sloping terrain overlooking Plunch Lane, and beyond, there also emerged groups of small, circular-shaped dwellings, complete with cone-type roofs, constructed out of corrugated, galvanised sheeting, and used by the military authorities as additional accommodation. When viewed at from certain angles, their frames were a little reminiscent, perhaps, of the Mediaeval knights' tents pitched on a selected field of battle. (However, these temporary buildings far out-lived their original purposes for throughout the inter-war years, World War Two, and afterwards, they were utilised as holiday chalets or homes. There are but a few lcft remaining today).

Church committees of the various denominations and other civilian working parties concentrated their voluntary efforts towards supplying the soldiers at the front with extra clothing and gifts. Regular sewing sessions and Red Cross service were early examples of the women's contribution.

A tangible, grim reminder of the reality of war on the Western Front, and elsewhere, soon confronted the civilian population as the local hospitalisation of wounded personnel began to get under way. The continuation of the war now meant that the mounting numbers of maimed, crippled, shell-shocked and seriously injured men had to be nursed in different types of private and public buildings. An insight into this situation is recalled by C. W. Slater's revealing 1919 publication, "The Corner Pew," subtitled, "A Series Of Sketches of Mumbles Methodism." He writes:

> "Then the necessity for hospitals for the wounded and convalescent men, who were arriving in large numbers, became clamant, and the whole range of buildings (i.e. hall, church parlour, classroom, etc.) was handed over, free of rent, to the local Red Cross Society for use as a Hospital. The only condition laid down was, that when no longer required, it should be returned in 'good tenantable repair,' but in the meantime they could do what they liked with it. In a very short time it was fully and beautifully equipped, and a thoroughly efficient staff installed. Our own people took their fair share in providing the equipment, and many of the best members of the staff, both male and female, came from their ranks. It is only fair to say,

too, that they contributed largely both in cash and in kind, to the upkeep and provisioning part of the good work. It really was a splendid little Hospital, and one which won the warmest encomiums from every Colonel and General who visited and inspected it. The Hall itself formed an ideal Ward, the Culinary department was perfect, and the Boys' room made a most comfortable day room for the men, whilst in the summer time the lawn was an asset of great value.

"Soon, the poor wounded men began to arrive, and they were all tended with an affectionate care and tenderness, their appreciation of which was most pathetic. Many of them cried when leaving. They said, 'We were well treated in the other hospitals, but this is like a home.' Our own cooks, nurses and orderlies were second to none in capacity and sympathy . . .

"After a while, the need for hospital accommodation increased, and 'Head Quarters' asked that more beds should be provided. This meant the erection of another room, and the local Red Cross Society asked permission to erect a temporary one, which they undertook to remove when leaving. We agreed, but suggested that if they would erect a permanent room, according to an approved plan, we would pay the difference in the cost. They agreed readily, raised the money, built and opened the new room, and all within about two months. We paid them the difference, which amounted to rather less than one-fourth of the total cost . . .

"So the Hospital was carried on, until soon after the Armistice was declared it was closed, having from first to last received over 500 patients, as is recorded on the Brass Plate affixed to the wall by the Red Cross authorities when they restored the Building to us."

As in the case of other church communities, there occurred the inevitable, sad loss of life. Out of approximately sixty Methodist members who joined the Armed Forces, nine were killed and others wounded.

It may be sometimes overlooked that school-children too made their own practical contribution to the war effort on the home front and one is reminded of this significant fact in an excellent, historical booklet produced recently by the staff of Oystermouth Junior Comprehensive School entitled, "Oystermouth School Centenary 1878-1978." This was in connection with the making of knitted garments for soldiers on active service when "special knitting classes were set up. Prizes were given to the girls, and in 1916 the Oystermouth girls (i.e. Oystermouth Council School) won the largest number of prizes out of several hundred schools in England and Wales."

The last year of the First World War also coincided with the termination of Oystermouth as an Urban District Council. Together with the Parish of Brynau in the Gower Rural District, the Parishes of Cockett and Llansamlet, and parts of the Parishes of Penderry and Clase Rural in the Swansea Rural District, Oystermouth became an integral part of the 1918 Swansea County Borough extension scheme. Henceforth, Mumbles' status was that of a Ward, one of eighteen divisions formed within the town's land area which had increased consequently from 6,229 to 24,241 acres. A statutory obligation was now placed upon Swansea Corporation to undertake the completion of a major drainage programme for the extended borough and operations commenced in 1922. The main sewer, extending from the county borough boundary at Clydach to the Mumbles, was completed in the mid-1930's; its construction involved the placing of four parallel tunnels, each 2,000 feet long, underneath the Mumbles Head, and permitted the discharge of sewage at specified intervals into the true tide of the Bristol Channel at a point approximately 750 feet to the east and seaward of Mumbles Head. Proposals presented previously to Parliament by Swansea Corporation during the years immediately before 1914 for building a drainage system in order to release sewage off Mumbles Head encountered strong Mumbles opposition, especially from the fishing fraternity. Then the project had to be shelved, along with the boundary extension idea, due to the outbreak of the European War.

The Mumbles inhabitants of the inter-war years witnessed periods of social change and modest commercial progress interrupted by those depressive times of limited economic out-put nationally combined with mass unemployment associated with the mid-1920's and early 1930's. Nevertheless, a new row of shops appeared on the Castle side of Newton Road in the twenties and more private residences were erected gradually on sites in Newton, West Cross, as well as on rising ground overlooking Rotherslade, Langland and Caswell Bays. Reminders of the past persisted; oysters, for example, could be purchased until the 1930's from a number of small oyster bars placed along the sea front.

As part of the Swansea C. B., Mumbles acquired the benefits of a modern municipal water supply, via the Cray Reservoir link-up initially; shared in the improved sewage developments; and additional advantages were realised such as the widespread domestic and business use of electricity as well as better road surfaces. Such 20th century advances did not always meet with whole-hearted approval, especially from some of the more traditionally-minded, older inhabitants, who preferred the Mumbles of the Victorian-Edwardian times; others viewed with apprehension the possibilities of future rises occurring in their rate demands. One acquisition which pleased many Mumbles residents was the purchase of the private fields off Newton by the Corporation for £1,870. The venue of numerous annual sporting and social events before 1914, approximately 17½ acres of the Underhill site were converted into the present day park of the same name. One of three Ward Representatives of the 1920's, Cllr. John J. Jones, played a leading role in obtaining this attractive public amenity. Its official opening took place during June, 1925.

The steam service of the Mumbles Railway line up to early 1929, and afterwards, its electrically-powered tram-coaches, opened up the Mumbles still further as a popular holiday haunt for day-trippers and tourists, a process complemented by the operation of a motorised bus schedule between Swansea and the Mumbles. The relatively cheap, competitive fares issued by the South Wales Transport Company Ltd. in respect of its early workmen's day rates, weekly returns and monthly seasons on the double-decked tramway-type cars during pre-War Two years and onwards, prompted more Mumbles men and women to seek employment in the enlarged Swansea County Borough. Others remained, however, to work in those traditional occupations connected with hotels, guest-houses, family-owned businesses, market-gardening, limestone quarrying and some farming activities. Swansea Bay offered a livelihood for those engaged in inshore fishing to a certain degree but only a very limited few dredged the remaining beds for oysters.

With a rising population and a substantial influx of summer visitors during the thirties, the need for a Public Library became increasingly apparent. This was finally resolved when the 1935 Branch Library was built in Dunns Lane. The library's cream-coloured exterior, complete with flat roof, is pleasantly reminiscent of the uncluttered, straight-lined style of architecture which appeared on the 1930's scene. Above the two-columned entrance porch is an arresting, modernistic stone engraving of Swansea's official coat of arms. The building was opened on the 21st September, 1935, by the then Chairman of the Libraries' Committee, Cllr. David Richards; joint librarians at the time were Walter W. Young and D. Rhys Phillips, F.L.A. Messrs. E. Rich & Son were the contractors, while Mr. E. E. Morgan, F.R.I.B.A., Borough Architect, was responsible for its design.

The late Mr. Christopher Tucker and his wife, Mary, who both played a prominent part in the life of the area, were among those principally responsible for bringing the library to Mumbles. Mr. C. Tucker was the proprietor of the paper, "The Mumbles Crest," which chronicled local events from 1903 to 1937.

The outbreak of the Second World War and the subsequent air raids on the Borough became a testing time for the people of Mumbles. Even before the aerial attacks, the residents here were reminded early on of the enemy's activities seawards. In the very first month of hostilities, shipping in the Bristol Channel felt the effects of war at sea when the Royal Mail vessel "Loch Goil" and the Brocklebank-owned "Marwaree" were both mined in the channel, not far from the Mumbles Head. They were brought into the "Roads" and taken over by the Liverpool & Glasgow Salvage Association, acting as Admiralty Salvage Agents, and for whom T. H. Couch Ltd. of Swansea acted as local representatives.

Although the Mumbles did not sustain any direct, concentrated air raids such as befell the blitzed town centre and its adjacent districts of St.

Thomas, Hafod and Bonymaen etc., nevertheless, the Luftwaffe made its presence felt in and around the locality. The close proximity of Swansea's dockland, the Eastside oil installations, hinterland industries, dispersal of military encampments, (as at Thistleboon and Limeslade), and the movements of Merchant Navy and Royal Navy vessels in the Channel, engaged enemy aircraft in the expected reconnaissance flights combined with numerous probing or nuisance value raids. A brief summary of those attacks which affected the Mumbles area would include: fourteen high explosives and numbers of incendiaries dropped on the Mumbles foreshore shortly after eleven p.m., 2nd August, 1940; two high explosives and a number of incendiaries released into the sea off West Cross, 3rd August, 1940; a further ten high explosives dropped in the sea off West Cross, 6th August, 1940; approximately twelve high explosives released onto the foreshore between Mumbles and Swansea, 4th March, 1941; and an estimated eight-hundred incendiaries were unleashed on Limeslade and Thistleboon, 8th April, 1941. For a time, the hillside area around Limeslade was set alight but only slight damage resulted with no casualties involved. One high explosive hit a field adjoining Plunch Lane and some wooden bungalows were slightly damaged. No casualties or damage were recorded when two high explosives fell into the sea between Langland and Caswell Bays on the 28th June, 1941.

Personnel on Civil Defence duties in the Mumbles area during the fearsome three nights' blitz on the town centre of the 19th-21st February, 1941, witnessed an awesome sight across the bay. As the virtually unopposed, seemingly incessant formations of bombers flew over their targets, the skylines on those three, successive nights were vividly lit up by the glare from slowly descending parachute flares; from the fiercly glowing fires spread by the many thousands of incendiaries which rained down on people and buildings; and from the violent flashes of erupting high explosives. Devotion to duty and high courage were displayed by members of the Civil Defence Services, the National Fire brigades and fire-fighting bodies, A.R.P., military, police and medical staffs who faced this and subsequent air assaults. The Luftwaffe pressed home its February attacks for a period of very nearly fourteen hours' duration.

Throughout the war, the Borough underwent 44 air raids in which 1,494 high explosive bombs, four parachute mines and some 35,000 incendiaries were dropped; 387 people killed; 851 injured, of which 412 were seriously injured; 802 premises totally destroyed; 13,927 premises heavily damaged and 13,523 premises slightly damaged. These and other relevant facts are well recorded in an authentic booklet published by Keith Pryer & Co. Ltd., entitled "Luftwaffe Over Swansea."

The outstanding bravery and achievements of the Mumbles Lifeboat crews in saving lives at sea during the Second World War are, of course, splendidly recounted in Carl Smith's recent history of the Lifeboat Station from 1832 onwards. The arduous and expanded role of H.M. Coastguard Service locally must also not be forgotten; their wartime duties were considerably widened in addition to their normal rescue operations. Some coast watching posts supplemented the work of the main station; officers had to guard against possible landings on the beach, watch out for the dropping of mines by enemy aircraft and report on drifting mines out at sea. As an armed force, they organised daily coastal patrols which were put into effect in 1942, as well as night watches, connected with the safety of the realm.

A well-known personality and a former Mayor of Swansea, who represented Mumbles on the Corporation as a very active Independent member for 24 years, was the late Mr. Harry Libby, who died in 1964. He was the son of John Henry Libby, whose forge occupied the present site of the Bristol Yacht Club; Cllr. Libby's home adjoined the Yacht Club premises in Southend. After serving in the Royal Navy during First War I, he went to work for T.R.W. Mason's shipping concern, Swansea, where his first experience of the travel business was gained. On leaving this firm in 1922, he undertook a partnership in the tinplate side of the trade.

Following his success in the 1933 seven-candidate local election to represent Oystermouth on the Swansea Council, he decided to concentrate personal business activities within the Mumbles. Consequently, he founded his Libby's Agency in the Dunns and thereafter catered consistently for the travelling needs of local people. However, the travel agency adopted a much wider role and became a popular Advice & Information Bureau for visitors and residents alike as an early kind of unofficial Citizens' Advice Bureau. As his eventual business successor, Mr. A. C. Foy, recalls: "Harry Libby's whole life centred around the Mumbles, and he gave to it everything he had."

He took on an immense amount of public work in the wider Swansea sphere and for many years his colourful personality made its impression on town politics as well as where worthy causes were concerned. With others, he was involved in many voluntary duties throughout the last War, such as Civil Defence, National Savings and with the Y.M.C.A. Mobile Canteens operating at Swansea Docks and Fairwood Airfield. Another practical, self-imposed task, was the writing of monthly circular newsletters to Mumbles men and women serving in the Forces; a regular delivery service was maintained by a loyal band of helpers who distributed more than 67,000 stencil-typed letters.

The ever-increasing popularity of the Mumbles as a holiday resort of the late forties, fifties and early sixties, is due in large measure to the determined work of Harry Libby, who, among others, never missed an opportunity to publicize its varied attractions and the fact that this small township is a gateway to the scenic splendour of Gower. Some highlights of the Agency's summer season in past years were the annual visits to the Penrice Gower Show and tea tours of the peninsula; conducted train excursions to the London Ideal Homes Exhibitions or Boat Races; and the regular summer coach holidays to Summercourt Village, Cornwall, which created firm friendships in both places, being in effect, an early inception of the twinning system.

More ambitious ventures evolved afterwards, including Libby's Swiss Holidays. He was honoured by the visit of a Swiss delegation to Swansea during his mayorality, 1956-57, in recognition of his work for developing inter-travel between Wales and Switzerland. With the Mayoress, his sister, Mrs. C. R. Nicholson, he also paid an official visit to that country. In company with a former Director of Education for Swansea, Mr. L. J. Drew, another journey was made to Germany, and from this trip a successful link-up between Swansea and Manheim was commenced which has since produced beneficial results in both social and cultural exchange visits.

(Subsequent environmental improvements, tourist information offices and publicity booklets promoted by the Mumbles Chamber of Commerce and the Municipal Authorities from the mid-1960's onwards, have now helped to attract thousands of additional summer visitors annually, many of whom return again. Libby's Agency, now placed conveniently above the present day Co-operative Stores, and supported today by the extensive T. H. Couch Ltd. travel organisation, remains fully operative and deals with all public travel requirements by rail, airline, coach or shipping. Its long association with Campbell's White Funnel Fleet sailings between Mumbles and Devon continues as part of the Mumbles scene).

Ample evidence of Harry Libby's devotion to, concern for, and love of Mumbles, is revealed in his 1964 publication, "The Mixture: Mumbles & Harry Libby." Interesting aspects of Mumbles life abound in this valuable contribution to local history. Pages 83-87 in chapter eight, for example, make absorbing reading, for he proudly relates the wartime efforts undertaken by the people of Mumbles during the period 1939-45, on the homefront locally, and by those men and women who served in the Armed Forces.

> "The story of Mumbles at war during the period 1939 to 1945, should be, for all born here, a most essential part of their historical knowledge and background. Undoubtedly any small place in Britain could report with equal sincerity and with perhaps equal pride, but those of us who lived and had our being in Mumbles from start to finish can be pardoned for being mighty proud of nearly everything that happened during those terrible years . . . There was a wonderful improvement in all personal relationships, a standard of community and observance which never has been equalled

before or since. One thousand, three hundred and fifty men and women were away serving, a far greater number than that imported through the Services and temporary residents engaged on war work in Swansea and District. The same problems appertained here as elsewhere but there was a remarkable sense of oneness, and if the occasion for self-preservation had arisen from an invasion, Mumbles would have been left with Swansea cut off by a prescribed dividing line along the valley, the Clyne Valley, from the sea at Blackpill and Killay. We had stored here sufficient foodstuffs, drinks and small arms to ensure siege conditions for a fortnight being met with the essentials of life . . . Yes, everybody pulled together, and during the blitzing on Swansea, Mumbles housed and certainly slept freely for long periods, thousands of Swansea folk who nightly crowded the old train and the roads with their bits and pieces, seeking to get away from that anticipated devastation.

"From the casualty standpoint, whilst we had so many away, our losses were relatively light, thank God, and our collective effort could well be expressed by saying that we never failed, so far as I know, to meet all the demands that were made upon us. Folk in the Forces had a monthly letter from us, aggregating sixty-eight thousand from 1939 to 1945; the Comforts Fund sent regular parcels—Newton Road traders on one occasion sent a Christmas Box of a seven and sixpenny postal order. Combined voluntary efforts raised £1,300 in six weeks, Park Street's Petticoat Lane raised twelve pounds, and the Main Road's effort six weeks later brought in very many hundreds for the Red Cross and Comforts Fund. These were experiences shared with considerable pleasure by all concerned, the more pronounced in the knowledge that that pleasure was going to be shared by others. In addition, when we staked our claims for a separate effort to raise money on loan for investment purposes under the slogans of 'Warship Week,' and the rest, our crowning glory was to amass no less than one hundred thousand pounds in one week's effort during such a campaign. . . I broadcast to our folks away in the Forces on a couple of occasions, once on the programme, 'In Town tonight.' . . .

"What a mixture of 'joy and happiness, sorrow and sadness' did those War years bring us. I recall that a man called Slee was the first to lose his life on the 'Rawalpindi' and what joy there was in Gloucester Place years later when news came that Bryn Balsdon, missing from the 'Repulse' was found out East. One could carry on with many such stories, but alas space is limited, and incidentally, I must pay tribute to three ladies who were so active in connection with those news letters. Betty Howard wrote to the girls, Peggy Daniels cyclostyled the lot, and Amelia Brock was better than the deliverer of Parish Magazines in distributing hundreds to the homes of boys for the parents to send out with the next letter. I've just been reminding myself that by 1942, we had a thousand people in the forces, and in six weeks Mumbles raised no less than £1,300 for local charities in efforts in different parts of the village, stretching from Newton to Southend and along the main road up to 'the sidings.' . . .

"And so we ambled on, with plenty of visitors, including the boys of the Royal Sussex, led by Gerald Templer, then just an ordinary Colonel—and they were two a penny—now risen to great fame as C.I.G.S. and various other big appointments, including a Governor—Generalship . . . Later, we had a lot of coloured troops from America, and they were equally as welcome as their white compatriots; in fact there was a welcome in Mumbles for everybody, and we're always happy to note the acquaintances that we fashioned then, and have become moulded into a friendship as year succeeds year. The inevitable end at long last. In May, 1945, a nice day, a short service on the front in the afternoon, then short trips in the Mumbles Lifeboat from the foreshore for about four hundred local youths."

In particular, the late Harry Libby's monthly newsletters produced for the servicemen and women of Mumbles during the Second World War often served to cheer up the recipients in times of danger and stress. His chatty accounts referred not only to local events but also to the whereabouts of Mumbles personnel on active service. A brief extract from the typed edition dated the 27th November, 1943, is an example:

"On the Wednesday before Christmas, the children of Mumbles servicemen are being entertained at the cinema to a special show. That's the alternative to sending their Dads a Christmas Box, and also effectively winds up last year's Newton Road effort . . .

"This month's briefs, 'without coupons': Jasper Davies is a survivor of 'Charybdis'; Desmond Jones 'did a bunny' in Italy and is expected home; and the other escaped prisioners, Capt. Ken Bangham and S.Q.M.S. Trevor Thomas have arrived. Percy Maslen is en route after three years in the Bermudas. John Howard is in Morriston Hospital. Derek Jones has been promoted to Flt. Engineer, and his brother Roy, after being wounded, is sunning in Italy. Ernie Kift of Underhill is on embarkation leave, and Harold Smale arrived today."

In the last of the 'Mumbles Correspondence Committee' monthly letters issued on the 15th August, 1945, the joyous euphoria brought on by the 'V' and 'VJ' peace celebrations readily comes to light:

"Street tea parties, dances (especially in Stanley Street), bonfires, lifeboat trips for the children, and now fireworks. At midnight last night everything went on a bonfire in the Station Square and the policeman only missed a similar experience by goodwill. Southend went wild: parachute flares soared up, and there were more nightdresses on parade between the Yacht Club and Sander's Corner than I imagined were ever worn. We didn't forget the boys who will not come back nor He who giveth us the Victory and suitable references were made not only in churches but in cinemas, dances and tennis tournaments . . .

"To see all the lights on around the Bay and up on the higher reaches of Swansea has been a tonic; to realise that our prisoners in Japan will soon be home is another; and to get basic petrol is a help . . . War brought its trials. It also engendered in Mumbles a spirit of comradeship and brotherhood. Away went those little pockets of pre-war snobbery. We mustn't be pessimistic, but let's all be careful to ensure they do not return."

As elsewhere, the Second World War years brought in their wake periods of much inconvenience, excitement, danger, sorrow and relief for Mumbles' children and adults alike. School life throughout those anxious times, for one particular school, is well reflected by those descriptions recorded in pages 31-33 of the Oystermouth Junior Comprehensive Centenary Booklet, 1878-1978. However briefly, past events are reawakened by the following extracts:

". . . At this opening season (i.e. 18th September, 1939), 38 pupils were admitted, chiefly from the London Area, who had voluntarily come to reside in this district because of the war, the first evacuees. Various precautions were made in view of the danger of enemy air raids; for example, it was arranged for as many pupils as possible living more than seven minutes walk from the school to go to the homes of other pupils living nearer the school premises.

". . . On 4th July, 1940, declarations in support of the Government in the prosecution of the war were signed by the staff of the School. The Town Council had resolved that all conscientious objectors, members of the Peace Pledge Union, and those whose opinions were in conflict with the nation's purpose in the war should be suspended. Arrangements were made for the construction of Air Raid Shelters in school . . . Various air raid warnings disturbed the normal life of the school.

". . . It is also recorded for 21st April, 1941, that the number on roll had increased considerably, owing to an influx of people caused by the air raids on Swansea. Plans were also made for the evacuation of school children from Swansea, and in fact this was carried out for some Swansea pupils . . . It seems that only two pupils actually left Oystermouth and they went in a party of 40 pupils to Gwynfe, Carmarthenshire, on 8th July, 1941.

"On 21st January, 1942, the Headmaster was absent in the afternoon attending the funeral of an old pupil, John Humphrey Martin, R.A.F. who sadly lost his life in air operations. December 7th was a momentous day in many aspects since School Dinners were introduced for the first time, the number of dinners served being 191 at 5d. per head.

"On 3rd August, 1944, at a School Assembly, the forty London evacuees were presented with a holiday gift by the prefects on behalf of the scholars. The evacuees responded suitably and expressed their warm thanks for the splendid way in which they had been received into the school. In the following year, the Second World War finally came to an end, and the school was closed on the 8th and 9th May, 1945, for the Peace celebrations with the ending of the war in Europe. A School Thanksgiving Service was held on 10th May in the Mumbles Baptist Church, when the address was given by the Headmaster (Mr. R. O. Smith)."

For a variety of reasons, the 1939-1945 War years are not easily forgotten by some. There were those, lest we forget, who paid the final sacrifice as the war graves in Oystermouth Municipal Cemetery testify together with the fallen of World War One. In this connection, one of the most plain yet moving, telling memorial inscriptions is recorded on the small Mumbles Cenotaph, placed in Southend Gardens; it reads: "1914-1918 1939-1945. Mumbles Remembers With Gratitude And Pride All Who Fell In The Great War." It was a time, too, when people were drawn more closely together in a spirit of positive cooperation and comradeship which helped the nation to win through in the end. Today, as one walks along the pleasant stretches of Mumbles Hill or relaxes to view the grand sweep of Swansea Bay, Mumbles Roadstead and the Oystermouth scene below, wartime memories of military encampments, concrete pill boxes, anti-aircraft emplacements, mine-fields, barbed wire and the castellated pattern formed by large concrete blocks facing seawards, (a former anti-tank barrier in case of invasion), become happily blurred.

Nearly 35 years have passed by since the end of World War Two. As in other Swansea Wards, progress and change have inevitably made their mark within the Mumbles area; a period, perhaps, which calls for a little reflection and appraisal to be recorded in respect of the social and environmental aspects affected by the inexorable march of time.

Despite much public dismay, some of which was expressed in a petition of nearly 14,000 signatures, the Mumbles Railway line was finally closed on the 5th January, 1960, by its owners, the South Wales Transport Co. Ltd. Unsuccessful efforts were made afterwards in Leeds by the Middleton Railway Society to preserve electric car No. 2 together with the steam locomotive "Swansea," and, sadly, nothing remains of the original stock except the bogies from No. 2 and an end section of car No. 7, restored by the determined work of "Y Clwb Rheil Cymru," the Railway Club of Wales.

As described in a preceding chapter, during its existence the line provided a valuable, alternative means of public transport for the citizens of Mumbles and Swansea, which reached its peak throughout the war years of 1939-45, when petrol rationing drastically curtailed the use of private motoring as well as bus services. In its souvenir brochure published to commemorate the shutting down of the railway, the S.W.T. Company recognised that "there was a distinct feeling of personal loss" felt by Swansea citizens as a result of the closure.

Its abandonment was caused by a noticeable drop in the numbers of passengers using the line in the 1950's which resulted in a continued loss of revenue. As the Company's 1960 brochure, "The Chain Of Progress" recounts:

> ". . . More and more car owners meant fewer and fewer train passengers and naturally, a subsequent loss of earnings.

"Not only did the traffic fall but costs increased alarmingly. The railway began to lose money. It had to be subsidised by the rest of the South Wales Transport undertaking; in effect, the bus passenger.

"Just as steam had ousted the horse, just as electricity had ousted steam, the internal combustion engine was ousting electricity. The 1950's saw marked developments in the motor bus. It got bigger and bigger.

". . . The fact had to be faced, the Mumbles Railway could not earn its keep. With great reluctance, the Directors decided to close the undertaking and supplant it with services of modern, well-equipped motor buses."

However, the substantial increase in car ownership from the 1960's onwards, combined with rising, operative costs and inflation, has, in turn, posed a challenge to the profitableness involved in running a modern bus fleet. Nowadays, the Company receives a Municipal subsidy towards the upkeep of its present service. This is a very necessary and praiseworthy move on the part of the Local Authority which assists somewhat to maintain a public transport system for the benefit of the elderly and many others unable to drive or afford private motoring. Without it, some routes would be discontinued all together, while others would be drastically reduced again. In spite of the 1968 Transport Act whereby the National Bus Company was formed to bring about the better integration and organisation of existing larger bus companies, the South Wales Transport Company in company with other regional concerns, has had to contend with recurring rationalisation programmes and a consequent reduction in the number of buses serving any one particular route in the 1970's.

During 1978, the end section of No. 7 car housed formerly in the grounds of the Royal Institution of South Wales, Swansea, was transferred to the nearby City of Swansea Maritime & Industrial Museum for further display. However, before the close of the present century, we may yet witness the re-emergence of the Mumbles Railway as a kind of miniature railway system run by practical enthusiasts to provide an added tourist attraction for our City.

In future decades, local historians will doubtlessly refer to the former quaint, narrow road called "The Dunns" as the street that was cut in half during the Autumn of 1970. As part of a road-widening process, business premises on the left hand side of the Dunns leading into Oystermouth and near the Square, were demolished and the site afterwards transformed into an attractive landscape-gardening area. Buildings which disappeared then were the late Cllr. Harry Libby's Travel Agency, the first premises on the same side; Forte's Ice Cream Parlour at the opposite end, founded by the late Mr. Guiseppe Macari who will be remembered by many locals today for presenting every child in the Mumbles with an ice-cream cornet the day War ended in Europe; and, among others, the Eleanor Library Shop which also sold interesting novelty items and chinaware etc., to attract the constant attention of passers-by.

Between the turn of the century and 1970, the Dunns was the location of many family businesses such as Messrs. Samuel Harris, the toilet saloon; Harry Davies, fruit merchant; Eley's butcher shop; the Dunns Cafe of Mr. Leyshon; Buckmaster's the florist; Cecil Thomas, florist; and Thomas Morgan, grocer and baker. Again, there were Lee's the draper followed by Hawkes of the same trade; Christie Tucker's printing shop, the Mumbles Press; Jenkins the ironmonger and another draper's establishment nearby owned by the Thomas family. On the opposite side unaffected by the 1970 demolition project once stood Peachey's Livery & Posting Stables; Brayley's Forge and the Oystermouth Coffee Tavern.

A little more than a century ago, during the mid-1870's, small family business concerns within the Dunns included: Messrs. Clark & Son, grocers; Miss E. B. Evans, fancy repository; Herbert Lloyd, "Nag's Head"; Edwin Peachey, butcher; Mrs. E. Powell, fancy repository; J. Sanders, shoeing forge; and J. A. Taylor, jun., tailor. Others here in the mid-1880's were: J. F. Loney, chemist & insurance agent, Dunns View; Edwin Michael, ironmonger; and Miss Emily Michael, lodging house proprietress. Those premises lost in the path of the Dunns' clearance were, fortunately, compensated afterwards by the erection of four shops and a bank sited opposite the Tivoli and adjacent to the Mumbles Post Office. In their midst, Forte's Ice Cream & Coffee Parlour has re-established its business links within the community.

A fine example of a progressive community uniting together in order to improve the social life of its people, and thereby others, is truly portrayed by the "Ostreme" events of the 1970's. The original, decidedly successful nine-days' pageant took place in the summer of 1973. As well as bringing together hundreds of citizens, the well-planned project embraced a wide range of activities such as amateur dramatics, arts and crafts, discotheques, regattas, displays by the Women's Institutes, youth activities, community hymn singing and "old Swansea" slide shows presented by Mr. Rowley Davies. Four thousand pounds were then raised towards a Community Centre building while the entire event was vastly enjoyed by holiday-makers and residents alike and set the pattern for future pageants which have so delighted audiences and spectators throughout the current decade.

Among a number of exciting features is "M.O.A.T." i.e., the Mumbles Open Air Theatre's presentation of plays, operettas and Son-et-Lumiere productions held within the moat area of Oystermouth Castle. The walls are wired for sound and light effects on these occasions and a spacious amphitheatre created for the mutual benefit of performers and audiences. Since its inception, these festivals have received practical support, encouragement and donations from industrial firms, businesses, clubs and various associations within Swansea as well as from some others outside the City district, together with the co-operation of the Municipal Parks Department. In effect, the work of the Ostreme Community Association, a charity organisation, represents a practical crusade of service on behalf of the community at large, towards a betterment of life in social and environmental terms for all age groups. In many respects, their annual pageants have added a new dimension to the Mumbles scene and have certainly enhanced the summer season for its inhabitants and visiting tourists. The name "Ostreme," adopted for the festival, is reputed to have been given to Oystermouth by the Romans. It was provided by Mrs. Fiona Beynon whose home address contains this particular title.

Many Mumbles' family names or those possessing strong ties with the Ward were represented on the original 1973 pageant committees and these have reappeared in successive years. The President for that year was C. Methuen-Campbell of Penrice Castle. Vice-Presidents were: His Honour Judge H. Trevor Morgan, Q.C.; Cllr. A. G. Chilcott; H. Clements, Esq.; Vernon R. Davies, Esq., J.P.; H. J. Howells, Esq., J.P.; Cllr. Mrs. Megan Jones; Colin Maggs, Esq.; Cllr. Herbert Morgan; and Cllr. W. W. Sivertsen.

The principal organising bodies then comprised: *Administration,* Chairman, C. M. Edwards (currently Cllr. C. M. Edwards); Secretary, Malcolm Phillips; Hon. Solicitor, S. Batcup; Asst. Secretary, Dr. Barry Wood; *Finance,* Chairman, James Seagroatt; Treasurer, Alan Grocutt; Fund Raising & Sales, Wyn Loney, Gwyneth Swales and Ian Percival; *Producer,* Dr. Peter Thompson; *Theme Adviser,* Timothy Perkins; *Production Committee,* Regatta, Swansea Bay Associations, Ivor Bowen and Lincoln Allen; Churches' History, Lesley Vancura and Ken Pierce; Fete, Swansea Lions Club, Peter Dawson, John Davies, Owen Thomas and Brian Burgess; Military Pageant, Keith Harley and Peter Taylor; *Midweek Entertainments,* Sports, Peter Atkinson and David Williams; Arts & Crafts Exhibition, Gloria Thomas and Mrs. Wendy Noel; Old Mumbles Exhibition, Margaret Wingrave and Carl Smith; Competitions, Stanley Rooker; Plays, Merial Mathias; *Publicity,* P.R.O., Paul Chambert; Advertising, Christopher D'Arcy Jones; Editor, Alan Machin; Works & Decoration, Stuart Winks; Recording, Mervyn Price; Music , Stuart Price; Constructions, Alec Carter; Costume, Ann Winks; Production/Scripts, Jean Haines; Designer, Nancy Machin; and Usherette, Shirley Calloway.

Among others, the Mumbles Chamber Of Trade has long been associated with reasonable, forward-looking projects aimed at enhancing the attractions of Mumbles as a holiday resort for the benefit of residents, visitors and business people. Its members have featured prominently in cooperating with various bodies both locally and nationally which have involved themselves in promoting schemes for the well being of the community.

In co-operation with the City of Swansea Council, the Chamber has recently, 1978, pioneered a particularly imaginative, experimental scheme to reclaim a new two miles' stretch of sandy beach between the Mumbles and Swansea foreshore. On the Norton sands, approximately 150 yards from the shore, a pilot gabion has been placed filled with quarry stones encased in wire mesh to hold them together. If an accumulation of sand here proves successful it is planned to construct a breakwater at the furthest extremity of the gabion, the forerunner it is hoped of a series of breakwaters to run between Blackpill and Oystermouth. Such a breakwater, between seven and eight feet high, should, it is anticipated, create a greater build-up of sand than an ordinary groyne. Financial support has also been offered by the Chamber towards part of the costs connected with the first gabion test which is being fully-monitored by the City's Environmental Department.

Service on behalf of the community is, of course, very much part of a local police force's duties. Since 1973, Mumbles and Gower have come under the Swansea West or "J" Division of the South Wales Constabulary. Swansea Central or "H" Division controls the Swansea Central, Morriston and Swansea Valley areas. The Swansea West Division embraces a large area within a boundary which commences at Brynmill Lane, follows the coastline route around Mumbles, Langland and Gower to Penclawdd and the Loughor Estuary, continues along the West Glamorgan-Dyfed boundary to Garnswllt, and thence to Pantlassau, Llangyfelach, Treboeth, Brynhyfryd, Manselton, Cwmbwrla, Waun Wen, Mount Pleasant, Glanmor and back again to Brynmill Lane. Its Divisional H.Q. is situated at the purpose built premises facing John Street, Cockett, opened in October, 1976. Small residential stations are situated in Newton Road and Fairwood Road.

There are occasions, perhaps, when members of the public are not fully aware of the wide extent of a police force's obligations and responsibilities. Today, the nature of their work stretches beyond the basic requirements of maintaining law and order, protecting life and property. Co-ordination and co-operation with such bodies as Fire Brigades, Ambulance Groups, Armed Forces and Welfare Departments form a normal pattern of procedure for successful operations when speed is of the essence. On twenty-four hours' call, if required at any time, the police are often first on the scene of accidents in a variety of difficult situations which demand immediate first-aid. Sometimes, they may have to undertake preliminary rescue work inside collapsed buildings, burning premises and damaged vehicles before other help arrives on the scene. In all kinds of weather, motorway pile-ups, for instance, entail highly efficient, disciplined, operational tactics as witnessed by the development of their specialised units engaged in rescue, medical and control work. Professional assessment of a critical situation, the swift setting up of a communications site and the directing of key personnel from other public services to where they are urgently needed are the three immediate requirements in these circumstances. The police also frequently find themselves involved in air-sea-land rescue manoeuvres; in addition, further duties relate to crime prevention, road safety and juvenile liaison.

In most aspects of their work there is a high risk factor for it may be all too easily forgotten that those elements of danger, injury or even death are never very far away. Their role, therefore, is fundamental and of inestimable value within the framework of a democratic society.

Another rewarding community undertaking was completed during the summer of 1978, when members of the Mumbles & District Conservation Society restored to its original condition, the Prince's Fountain which stands at the foot of Western Lane and Myrtle Terrace facing towards the sea-front. This Victorian drinking fountain, of grey limestone construction and complete with iron railings, was built to commemorate the marriage of the Prince of Wales to Princess Alexandra in 1863; the foundation stone was laid on the 10th March of that year, the day of the actual marriage. Celebrations, however, took place a year later when the work was completed. Then, 200 old people were treated to a dinner while approximately 700 children were entertained on what were in those days open fields opposite the White Rose tavern in Newton Road.

By way of public contributions, the fountain was erected on land donated by the Duke of Beaufort and spring water used from the supply of a Philip Walter. On completion, it was handed over to the care of the Vicar and Churchwardens in March, 1864. The fountain provided a valuable public service at a time in Mumbles' history when cholera and other water-borne diseases frequently threatened as well as affected the health of the local populace. Its use supplemented the sources of the two existing public supplies at that period: the water pump situated near the Antelope Hotel, and the second one by the George Hotel.

Some funds were set aside by the Society to meet the costs involved of approximately £400; other donations came from the present Duke of Beaufort and the Swansea City Council. As a result, the fountain's stonework has been refaced, its inscriptions renewed and the water supply reconnected, a very worthwhile project accomplished by the Society's supporters as their particular contribution to the Queen's Silver Jubilee Year.

In addition to those organisations mentioned previously, Mumbles is the centre of many more active associations, clubs and societies, each one having its own history of achievements. Their continued existence is yet another reminder of a vigorous community spirit, whose inhabitants possess a diversity of skills in the professions, commerce, businesses, arts, sciences, cultural and sporting fields, much of which is often utilised, on a voluntary basis, for the benefit of the neighbourhood at large as well as outside areas.

Among these may be listed: the Mumbles Yacht Club; Mumbles Motor Boat & Fishing Club(housed within the renovated old Church School premises); Mumbles Amateur Rowing Club; Bristol Channel Yacht Club; Mumbles Water Ski Club; Gower Surf Club; Mumbles Concert Band; Mumbles Carnival Committee; Mumbles Railway Society; Mumbles Rotary; Victoria (Mumbles) Bowls Club; Mumbles Council Of Churches; Mumbles Rugby Club; Mumbles Cricket Club; Mumbles Rangers Football Club; Mumbles Rangers Boys' Club; Mumbles Cubs; Mumbles Guides; Mumbles Conservative Club; Mumbles Ward Labour Group; Mumbles Old People's Welfare Association; Royal British Legion, Mumbles Branch; Royal British Legion, Women's Mumbles Branch; Mumbles Darts League; Mumbles Town Women's Guild; Blackpill Women's Institute; Norton W.I.; Oystermouth F.C.; Oystermouth W.I.; Langland Bay Golf Club; Oystermouth Hockey Club; Oystermouth Bowling Club; R.N.L.I. Ladies Guild; West Cross Community Centre; and the P.D.S.A., Mumbles.

A highly popular rendezvous for yachting and other aquatic events, Mumbles remains today a noted centre for boat-owners, the "Cowes" of the Bristol Channel. During the height of the summer season, it is not unusual to see more than two hundred sailing craft of different sizes racing, cruising or lying to moorings in the bay. There has been a marked increase in boat ownership since the 1960's, and consequently, laying-up spaces along sections of the Southend and Village Lane Boat Parks has become very limited latterly. Apart from those afloat, vessels tied up ashore in summertime, from the tiniest tenders upwards, number, on occasions, well in excess of three hundred, especially when inclement weather limits operations. On the other hand, improvements on the Mumbles foreshore throughout the late 1970's have made launching procedures for a hundred or more vessels somewhat easier than in previous years.

Sailing dinghies, cabin cruisers and small inshore fishing boats provide hours of pleasure for those who sail in them as well as for onlookers relaxing on the promenade. The Mumbles Yacht Club with a membership of approximately one-thousand, two-hundred, is one of the largest in the U.K. Its committees organise a full, mixed programme of annual crew races, women's races, single-handed and class events; participants compete keenly for a variety of handsome trophies in the Osprey, Albacore, G.P. 14's, Handicap, Enterprise, Laser, Mirror and Cruiser championships.

As a body, the Club was formed shortly before the outbreak of World

War Two, at a meeting held at the ever popular Pilot Inn, Southend, on the 30th May, 1938; its aims were to encourage yacht and motor boat cruising, racing, and to provide a headquarters' base for members. Both the entrance fee and subscription rate cost 2s. 6d. in those days; cadets were charged 1s. 6d. Post-war sailing activities began to get under way during the Spring of 1948 in an era of shortages and austerity. Then, as a restricted class in the 1950's, the 18 ft. National appeared as the first dinghy, followed afterwards by the G.P. 14, Osprey and other small type craft which could be built up from sophisticated sections of plywood supplied in kit form. The Club's present premises were opened during March, 1959; kitchen, bar lounge and roof race control area extensions have been added since that date. The Mumbles Yacht Club is also affiliated to the Royal Yachting Association and the Bristol Channel Yachting Conference.

When held in Swansea Bay, the National Osprey Racing Dinghy Championship attracts a heavy quota of local and outside entries, well in excess of a hundred, when the Club acts as host to the two-man crews. The 17-foot designed Osprey is an extremely fast sea boat and to handle her demands great skill, strength and sheer determination especially in rough seas and high winds at speeds up to 16 knots. Such conditions arise in Swansea Bay with its fierce tides and changing winds and provide an exacting challenge to the experienced helmsman who must also depend on the expertise of his crewman. The latter balances the boat by standing on the side of the craft above the water supported by a special harness attached to the mast. Although the Osprey is designed for self-recovery, rescue vessels are to hand to render help swiftly if required.

Members of the Mumbles Motorboat & Fishing Club and the Mumbles Amateur Rowing Club also hold their own yearly competitions; in addition, there are swimming contests, water skiing, water jumps, towing displays and canoe regattas at Langland. In a "South Wales Evening Post" article dated the 3rd December, 1959, J. R. John appraises succinctly the trend of the post-War Two Mumbles sailing scene in the concluding paragraph of his feature entitled "When Mumbles Stopped At Southend."

> "The old beach interests, Southend—Inner Sound, (i.e. referring to former White Gate area) have disappeared, but Southend Beach is now the headquarters of the new armada of little pleasure craft whose great growth of recent years has shown that even in the age of the motor car and the jet plane, the itch to 'go down to the sea in ships' is reviving in the people—a most wholesome and pleasant sight, far more so than the old regattas with their exotic king's and millionaires' yachts, Britania, Meteor, Shamrock, Ailsa and others that were sea birds of passage in Swansea Bay."

Since the late 1950's, there has been an extensive growth in the numbers of private housing estates put up within the Ward and these stretch from Blackpill, West Cross, Thistleboon through to the Langland and Picket Mead areas. Attractive municipal housing schemes have also arisen in the West Cross district. In a small way, this urbanisation process commenced in the very early 1870's in that part of Newton Road which meets the junction of today's Chapel Street and at a time before the Dunns was fully developed. The erection of the terraced, three-storey fashionable residences of the 'Seventies stood out in sharp contrast to the cottage dwellings wherein most people then lived and brought up large families. Their appearance not only supplemented the large, detached, scattered villas of the very wealthy but was the beginning of a trend which gathered momentum at various stages throughout the subsequent decades to transform a village community into the flourishing dormitory suburb it is today.

Today's pattern of retailing has moved from the particular to the general: bookshops sell toys and pottery; gift-shops offer clothes; hardware shops display pictures etc., often out of economic necessity; and on the grand scale there are the efficient and all-embracing super-markets. Fortunately, the long-established tradition of shopping in the Mumbles has not yet been seriously affected by such trends which have manifested themselves elsewhere as in city centres. That is not to say, however, that a spirit of courtesy and helpfulness does not prevail within larger establishments, especially where the Mumbles is concerned.

On the other hand, an observer detects the feeling that residents and visitors alike appreciate the direct, friendly and personal service maintained by the Mumbles' proprietors and their staffs in the many, small family-owned or medium-sized businesses, whether these be well-established concerns or newcomers to the Ward, the population of which was recorded as 13,700 in the 1971 Census. This total is likely to increase noticeably by 1981 in view of housing developments latterly.

Whether one is seeking everyday necessities, looking for presents, or merely browsing, shopping in Oystermouth can be both interesting and rewarding on visiting Newton Road with its delightful sea views at one end, the busy Dunns section, along the Parade and Southend, and in and around the tiny square formed by the meeting place of Queen's Road, Gower Place, Woodville Road and Chapel Street. The area's commercial prosperity too is mirrored somewhat by the number of principal branch banks which have established themselves in new premises as a permanent feature of the present everyday scene.

And, as always, the sea is never very far away.

The Dunns 1906 (Postcard)
D. G. Bowden

Mumbles Cabbies' Fishing Club 1909

By permission, Roger David Studios

The Dunns 5th June, 1922 *By permission, Swansea City Council*

Circa 1922

By permission, Swansea City Council

Newton Road   Circa 1920's
Rowley Davies

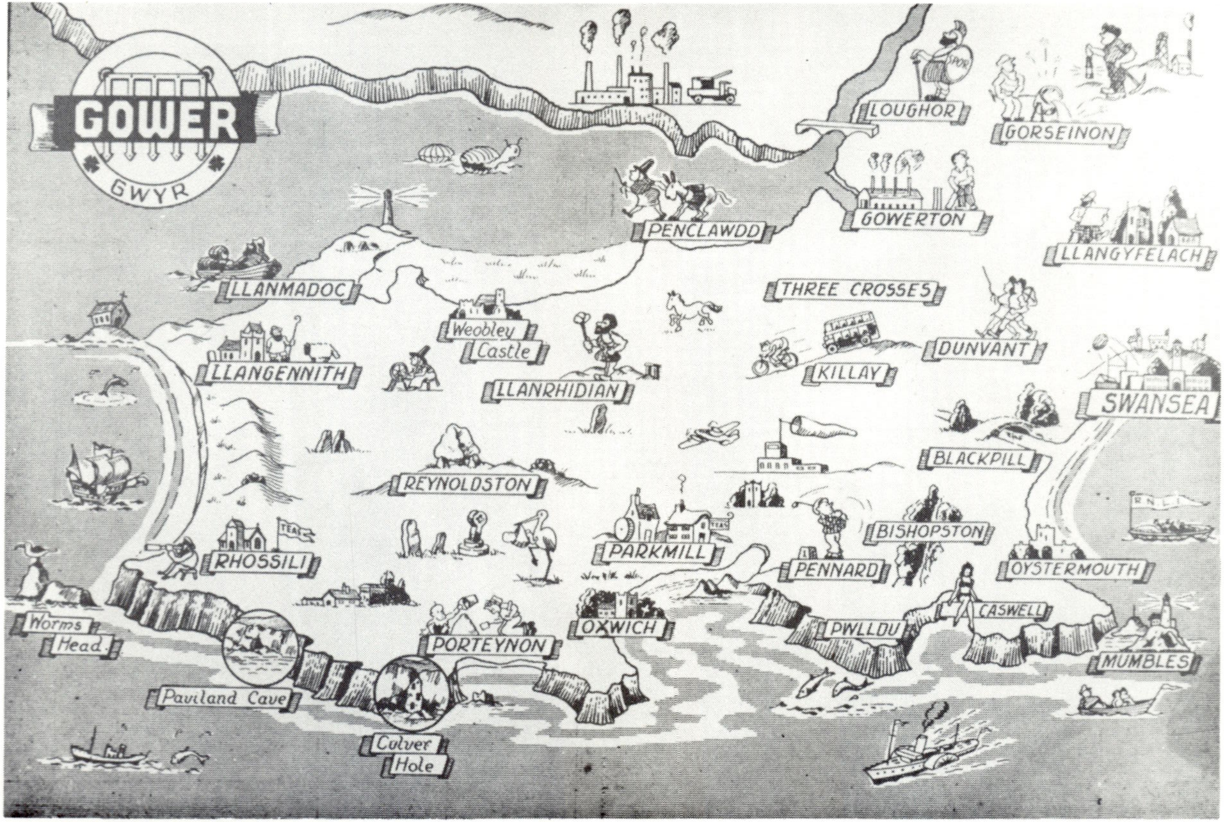

Courtesy of Robert W. May, F.R.S.A.

Mid-1970's

By permission, Swansea City Council

CHAPTER THREE

THE MUMBLES RAILWAY

"The history of the world is the record of a man in quest of his daily bread and butter."
H. M. Van Loon: "The Story Of Mankind."

"How beautiful was the sea shore covered with low roses, yellow snap-dragons, and thousands of other plants. That streak of black along the most beautiful coast in the universe will never succeed in rendering me indifferent to Swansea. Two years afterwards the detestable tram road was made along it. Besides, before this, thousands of small vessels covered the bay, laden with lime and whatever else is now carried in those train wagons. The Gulf of Salerno, I hear, is much finer than Naples, but give me Swansea for scenery and climate. I prefer good apples to bad peaches. If it should ever be my fortune, which I cannot expect, and do not much hope, to return to England, I would pass the remainder of my days in Swansea—between that place and Mumbles."
Walter Savage Landor (b. 1775 d. 1864): Letter written to his mother.

"In retrospect, the Mumbles Railway then helped to bolster public morale, for its familiar coaches were a source of comfort to many citizens who came to appreciate its dependable service and share in a kind of passenger camaraderied which existed throughout those anxious years." (1939-1945).
N. L. Thomas: "The Mumbles: Past & Present."

The history of the former Swansea and Mumbles Railway continues to provide compelling reading for many residents and visitors. It became universally famous as the first and oldest surviving passenger railway in the world.

The railway's construction began in the year before the Battle of Trafalgar, during the autumn of 1804; and the line was completed in 1806. Throughout its existence, up to 1960, numerous methods of propulsion were used: horses, sail, steam locomotive, electricity; and for goods traffic, petrol and diesel locomotive.

Mineral wealth in the form of coal and iron-ore deposits located in the picturesque Clyne Valley, as well as the stone and limestone quarries of

Oystermouth, engendered the commercial motivation behind Sir John Morris' scheme for promoting the establishment of the Swansea to Oystermouth tramroad in 1804. Sir John owned the Ynys and Rhydydefaid mines situated in this valley and he and his associates desired, naturally, to open up communications here by way of a tramroad to transport wagons.

The promoters of the tramroad plan met spirited opposition from a Mr. Edward Martin and his supporters; they advocated an alternative project whereby a canal from the Mumbles was to link up with the recently built Swansea Canal. Mr. Martin presented his plans to the burgesses in July, 1803, and on the 11th January, 1804, the portreeve was authorised "to subscribe the sum of Five Hundred Pounds for this Corporation towards making and maintaining the intended Canal from Swansea to Oystermouth." At the next following Common Hall meeting on the 20th March, 1804, the Swansea Corporation then agreed officially to the contents of a printed copy of a "Bill for making a canal and a Railway or Tram Road from Swansea to Oystermouth."

During the next ensuing weeks, a heated correspondence arose in the columns of the "Cambrian" in which Mr. Edward Martin was very prominent. Quite a number of anonymous correspondents supported him but there were those writers who opposed his scheme. In February, 1804, a petition was presented to the House of Commons which begged leave to introduce a bill for constructing a canal from Swansea to Oystermouth. Consequently, the issue was fought out in the House of Commons by the contending parties. Victory went to the tramroad promoters, for the Act of the 29th June, 1804, acquiesced to the railway plan but did not include the proposal for a canal being built.

On the 4th July, 1804, the triumphant railway projectors held the first meeting of the "Oystermouth Railway or Tram-road Company," in the "Bush Inn," High Street, Swansea. Sir John Morris announced the list of shareholders, the burgesses of the Borough holding five shares. The Act incorporating the railway was afterwards read out:-

> "An Act for making and maintaining a Railway or Tramroad from the Town of Swansea, into the Parish of Oystermouth, in the County of Glamorgan. 29th June, 1804.
>
> "Whereas the making and maintaining of a Railway or Tramroad for the passage of Wagons and other Carriages, to communicate with the Swansea Canal near a certain place called The Brewery Bank, within the Town of Swansea in the County of Glamorgan to, or near to, a certain Field called Castle Hill, in the Parish of Oystermouth in the said County of Glamorgan; and also the making and maintaining of a Branch of such Railway or Tramroad, to communicate therewith, from a certain place near the Mount in the said Town of Swansea, in the County aforesaid to, or nearly to, Swansea Pier; and likewise the making and maintaining of another Branch of

such Railway or Tramroad, to communicate therewith, from a certain place near Black Pill, to or nearly to, a certain place called Ynys, in the Parish of Swansea in the said County of Glamorgan, will open a Communication with several extensive Limestone Quarries, Coal Mines, Iron Mines and other Mines, whereby the Carriage and Conveyance of Limestone , Coal, Iron Ore, and other Minerals and Commodities, will be greatly facilitated, and will materially assist the Agriculture of the Country throughout the Line and Neighbourhood thereof, and will in other respects be of great Public Utility; but the same cannot be effected without the Authority of Parliament.

"And whereas the several Persons herein-after named are willing and desirous at their own Expense, to make and maintain the said Railway or Tramroad, and the Branches thereof, as aforesaid: May it therefore please Your Majesty that it may be enacted; and be it enacted by the King's most Excellent Majesty, by and with the Advice and consent of the Lords Spiritual and Temporal, and Commons, in this present Parliament assembled, and by the Authority of the same, That the most Noble Henry Charles Duke of Beaufort, the Burgesses of the Borough of Swansea, Charles Collins, John Charles Collins, John Edmund, Benjamin French, Thomas Hobbes Doctor of Physic, Calvert Richard Jones, Edward King, John Landeg, Roger Landeg, Thomas Lockwood, Thomas Loft, Thomas Morgan, John Morris, John Morris, the younger, Thomas Sylvester, William Vaughan, and their several and respective Successors, Executors, Administrators and Assigns, together with such Person and Persons as they shall nominate and appoint under their Hands and Seals, or the said Burgesses under their Common Seal, are and shall be united into a Company for the better carrying on, making, completing, and maintaining the said intended Railway or Tramroad, with the Branches thereof as aforesaid, according to the Rules, Orders, and Directions, herein-after expressed and laid down, and shall for that Purpose be one Body Politic and Corporate, by the Name of The Oystermouth Railway or Tramroad Company."

Preliminary work in respect of surveying, clearing and preparing the line commenced in the autumn of 1804. Old account books reveal that the actual rail laying operations took place during September, 1805, Messrs. Homfray & Company being credited with the sum of £2,794 0s. 6d. for tram plates and castings. As originally constructed, the rails consisted of three feet lengths of angle iron, dogged into blocks of granite, the wagon wheels being unflanged.

A detailed, standard work of reference about the history of this railway is, "The Swansea & Mumbles Railway," by Charles E. Lee, F.R.S.A., M. Inst. T., published originally in 1942. The second edition published by "The Oakwood Press" in 1954 included the whole of the text relating to this line, revised and supplemented throughout by Mr. C. E. Lee, together with most of the original illustrations and two new ones. A third, up-to-date edition has recently been released by The Oakwood Press.

Specific measurements are quoted by C. E. Lee, chapter 5, page 30, relating to the original rails laid down, some of which are in the possession of the Royal Institution of South Wales, Swansea. He states:

> "Mr. E. A. Forward has called attention to some very interesting additional particulars which were recorded by the Prussian mining engineers, Dechen and Oeynhausen, who visited England in 1827. They give a short description of the Oystermouth line, and also provide evidence of the gauge of the original plateway. Mr. Foward's translation of this reference is as follows:
>
> "Cast-iron Tramroad from Swansea to Oystermouth. The bay of Swansea is at ebbtide too shallow to permit vessels to enter Swansea Harbour, and they are accustomed to anchor off Oystermouth, a small fishing village 5 English miles from Swansea.
>
> "Also, there are extensive limestone quarries close to Oystermouth, which supply hewn stone and mortar, so that generally a large and vigorous traffic takes place between Swansea and Oystermouth.
>
> "In order to facilitate and increase this traffic, a tramroad has been laid between these two places, and is about 7 English miles long, and has a gauge of 47 in. The track follows the coast and is entirely level. The rails are 35 in. long, 3½ in. wide without the flange; ½ in. thick, except at the ends, where they are ⅝ in. thick; the flange is 2½ in. high, ⅓ in. thick at the top,and ½ in. at the bottom. The fastening upon the stone sleepers is the same as on the Portreath tramroad.
>
> "The line, also, is specially intended for the quick transport of travellers; in the summer a kind of coach runs on it, in which about 20 passengers are drawn by one horse, a peculiarity not exclusively offered by this tramroad.
>
> "Mr. Forward also comments that, as the length of the rails is, in this case, given as 35 in., it is evident that they were using their Prussian measures in which 3 English ft. = 34. 96 Prussian in., and therefore the gauge of 47 Prussian in. = 48. 4 English in. He assumes, therefore, that the gauge was actually 4 ft. between the flanges of the rails."

The original 1804-5 tramway commenced from the Brewery Bank adjacent to the 1798 Swansea Canal; proceeded along the busy Strand, a branch line of which terminated on land called Bath Lane after 1820, and close to a lime-kiln which adjoined the old ferry across the Tawe. The route entailed the pulling down of the town's ancient mount and its area of ground levelled off. This was Corporation land between what was once a road leading to the Ford, later known as Somerset Place, and the Oystermouth Tramroad opposite the Somerset Buildings. The line then continued across the Burrows, along the slightly levelled sand hills between Swansea and Oystermouth. The other branch-line at Blackpill was constructed to follow the Clyne brook route to Ynys.

Goods traffic started to pass over the line as early as April, 1806. However, one of the most important dates in the history of the railway is the 25th March, 1807, when passenger traffic was inaugurated. The service was started by Benjamin French, one of the company shareholders, who paid £20 to the Tramroad Company instead of toll money, so that he could be permitted to run a wagon or waggons on the line for a year to convey passengers. It was an unique, historical event, because the first public passenger service by rail in this country, and in the world, had been successfully launched. It is also worthwhile repeating that the Stockton and Darlington Railway introduced a public passenger service nearly twenty years after the Mumbles line was opened.

The poet and eminent man of letters, Walter Savage Landor, (b. 1775 - d. 1864), in a letter written to his mother from Italy, deplored the tramroad's early 19th century arrival on the Swansea scene. He declared:

> "How beautiful was the sea shore covered with low roses, yellow snapdragons, and thousands of other plants. *That streak of black* along the most beautiful coast in the universe will never succeed in rendering me indifferent to Swansea. *Two years afterwards the detestable tram road was made along it.* Besides, before this, thousands of small vessels covered the bay, laden with lime and whatever else is now carried in those *train wagons.* The Gulf of Salerno, I hear, is much finer than Naples, but give me Swansea for scenery and climate. I prefer good apples to bad peaches. If it should ever be my fortune, which I cannot expect, and do not much hope, to return to England, I would pass the remainder of my days in Swansea—between that place and Mumbles."

An early experiment in order to obtain motive power for the wagons by fixing sails on them was duly reported by the "Cambrian" edition dated the 18th April, 1807, thus:

> "An experiment of a novel kind was made on the Oystermouth Tramroad yesterday, to ascertain the practicability of a carriage proceeding to the Mumbles without horse, by the aid of the wind alone. Some Jolly Sons of Neptune rigged a wagon with a lug-sail, and the wind blowing strong and as fair as could be wished, set out from our quay, and after clearing the houses dropped anchor at the end of the tramroad in less than threequarters-of-an-hour, having come a distance of about 4½ miles."

Variations in daily wind speeds or the absence of them all together, were obviously bound to prove the commercial unsuitability of any similar trials in the utilisation of wind power.

The early passenger service, started from the Brewery Bank on the Swansea Canal to reach its terminus at Castle Hill, Oystermouth. An early conveyance appears to have been provided in the form of a four-wheeled horse-drawn dandy.

Meanwhile, in late February, 1808, Benjamin French with two others,

Simon Llewellyn and Benjamin Rose, offered jointly, the larger sum of £25 for a renewal of the passenger contract and this was accepted by the company.

There are a number of interesting references made to the mode of travel experienced by passengers on the line during the early decades of the 19th century. A Miss Elizabeth Isabella Spence, authoress, who also wrote about her travelling episodes in Great Britain, recorded the following account for her friend, the Dowager Countess of Winterton, in 1808:

> "I never spent an afternoon with more delight than the former one in exploring the romantic scenery of Oystermouth. I was conveyed there in a carriage of a singular construction, built for the conveniency of parties, who go hence to Oystermouth to spend the day. The car contains twelve persons and is constructed chiefly of iron, its four wheels run on an iron railway by the aid of one horse, and is an easy and light vehicle."

In sharp contrast, Richard Ayton appeared to have suffered a hazardous ride on the railway. In his "Voyage Round Great Britain undertaken in the Year 1813," he recounts:

> "We made an excursion to Oystermouth village near the western extremity of Swansea Bay, in the tram car, a singular kind of vehicle established for the accommodation of visitors to this place. It is a very long carriage, supported on four low iron wheels, carries sixteen persons, exclusive of the driver, is drawn by one horse, and rolls along over an iron railroad, at the rate of five miles an hour, and with the noise of twenty sledge hammers in full play. The passage is only four miles but it is quite sufficient to make one reel from the car at the journey's end, and in a state of dizziness and confusion of the senses that it is well if he recovers from in a week."

It is most likely that the car or coach used by these passengers and owned by Simon Llewellyn, is the one depicted in J. Ashford's painting of 1819. The original is housed within the Royal Institution of South Wales.

The journey there and back as "A Description of Swansea and Its Environs 1813" states, was undertaken at "the small expence of two shillings each person." "The New Swansea Guide . . . 1823" confirmed its continued use as a passenger service thus: "A car, capable of containing 16 people, drawn by one horse, generally goes from Swansea to Oystermouth, over this tramroad, twice a day; the charge 1s." The price of one shilling presumably referred to a one way journey.

As the line was situated originally quite close to the Swansea foreshore, it inevitably suffered periodically from inundations of the sea. The resulting damage sometimes necessitated repairs and relevelling work and ultimately parts of the line had to be moved further inland. A serious flooding took place in 1824 when the sea once again broke in and swept away a large section of the line. Consequently, Sir John Morris, who by this time was the principal owner of the enterprise following foreclosing procedures in 1815, moved the line still further inland and traffic was resumed. By the end of 1819, Sir John Morris had become the leading mortgagee in possession of the company.

In 1826, a turnpike road was built between Swansea and Oystermouth which Mathews' "Swansea Directory, 1830-1" described as an "excellent road . . . a finer piece is not to be found in the Principality." The railway line ran alongside the new road but its route remained on that side nearest to the seashore.

Proprietors of horse-drawn buses soon utilised the new highway's route commercially for the convenience of visitors to Mumbles, especially during the summer months, and consequently, the railway's passenger service was withdrawn prior to 1830. Mineral traffic had also declined markedly by this time; for almost thirty years the railway line lay practically abandoned, accommodating now and then a small amount of goods traffic.

Among others, in the 1830's, the Pilot Post Coach proceeded to and from the Mumbles, twice daily, at ten a.m. and three in the afternoon. Oystermouth Castle was then under the care of a W. Collier, Esq., who acted as its warden as well as being the Mumbles' postman and schoolmaster!

The railway line is not referred to by John Lewis in his "Swansea Guide" of 1851 but the omibuses which ran from the town to the Mumbles received special note. These commenced "from Rees's, the 'Horse and Groom,' College-street, twice a-day; from Barter's, 'The Rutland Arms,' and from the 'Bush Inn,' High Street, each three times a-day; and from the Railway Booking Office, Wind Street, several times a-day."

By mid 1847, George Byng Morris had become the sole proprietor of the freehold concern in connection with the Oystermouth Railway or Tramroad Company. He had, in fact, owned the railway since 1840 under a mortgage foreclosure initiated by Sir John Morris. The latter had also transferred ten of the Company's shares over to George Byng Morris who then contrived to keep the little used line open for limited goods' use during the 1840's and 1850's.

In 1855, a section of the Oystermouth line was relaid with edge rails to improve the transportation of coal between Clyne Valley's two collieries and the Strand. Five years later, George Byng Morris re-introduced a horse-drawn service for passengers from the town's Royal Institution to Blackpill at a charge of 3d. single, 4d. return.

The reopening of the Mumbles Railway line prompted the revival of the Black Pill Races as the following passage from the "Cambrian" dated the 27th July, 1860, indicates:

> "Some of our sporting readers will be glad to find that the above races are again revived, and are to take place on the 4th August next. From the very attractive programme got up by the indefatigable exertions of Mr. Abel Vivian of the "Red Lion Inn," Black Pill, a few hours good sport is anticipated. Since the opening of the Oystermouth Railroad for passenger traffic great facilities will be afforded to parties, as there will be trains running at intervals of half-an-hour on that day."

"The Cambrian" for the same date published a timetable alteration which further stated that cabs and omnibuses ran between Blackpill and the Mumbles. The journey took 21 minutes and involved five weekday trains each, six on Sundays.

Morris also caused the remainder of the principal line to be relaid between Blackpill and Oystermouth in 1860 along which a passenger service was once again put into operation by the 10th November of that year. From the latter date until the line's final closure in 1960, a hundred years of public transport was provided locally through man's application of horse-drawn power, steam and electric.

During 1864-65, a Mr. John Dickson, who was widely interested in various railway schemes in and around Swansea, attempted to purchase the Oystermouth Railway from G. B. Morris for the sum of £20,000. However, Dickson overreached himself in his financial affairs at the time and became bankrupt. As a result, the line remained in Morris' possession.

A timetable for May, 1869, revealed that ten trains ran in each direction on weekdays; eleven trains worked each way on Saturdays; and additional trains operated on the Whit Monday. The Sunday service was reduced to about half the weekday number.

A first class fare, single, to the Mumbles then cost 7d.; second class, 5d. Return ticket, first class, was priced at 10d.; second class, 8d. First class accommodation was covered but the second class passengers had to climb to the top of the horse-drawn cars. The halt stops for the "Down Trains" commencing with Rutland Street, Swansea, were placed at Water Works Road, Sketty Road, Black Pill Road, Bishopston Road, Lilliput Road, West Cross Road, Norton Road and the Mumbles.

Another interesting feature of the line at this period was the fact that it carried mail. There was a special mail coach which left Swansea at 6 a.m. and again at 12.30 p.m. On Sundays, only the former time applied. The mail coaches from Mumbles to Swansea, the "Up Trains" services, were at 9 a.m., 2 p.m. and 5 p.m. on weekdays, and 5 p.m. only on Sundays. The station master of the Oystermouth Railway Station, Mumbles Road, in 1875 was William Pressdee.

By 1874-75, the horse-drawn passenger service was operating a five miles' service from Rutland Street (i.e. on the opposite side to Swansea's present-day spacious Leisure Centre) to its terminus at Oystermouth with halts situated at St. Helen's Road, Sketty Road, Blackpill, Lilliput, West Cross and Norton. Seven trains daily each way were provided and a one way journey took approximately forty-three minutes. One or sometimes two horses were used to pull a single coach or more. An average annual return of receipts between 1863 and 1873, but discounting 1866, reveals a sum of practically £4,000; upwards of 5,000 passengers could be transported between Swansea and Oystermouth in one day. Total of receipts for the ten years quoted was £39,142. 5s. 10d. (C. E. Lee, chapter 2, page 15).

Meanwhile, the 1860's witnessed the passing of several Railway Acts of Parliament on behalf of some private companies who were increasingly interested in constructing steam railway routes in South-West Wales which would embrace in part or wholly lines extending along the Swansea Bay foreshore to Mumbles. One such example was an Act of 1871, for vesting the Swansea and Carmarthen lines, and Mumbles extension and pier of the Llanelli Railway & Dock Company in a new company to be called the Swansea & Carmarthen Railway Company. However, a subsequent Act in 1873 empowered the latter to abandon its Mumbles extension scheme.

A more positive form of commercial competition emerged by way of the Swansea Improvements and Tramways Company, headed by an astute business man and a leading, local antiquarian, Colonel George Grant Francis, who had been made Mayor of Swansea in 1854. This limited company had been incorporated as a statutory company by an Act of July, 1874, with powers to construct a system of horse tramways in the town. In particular, Colonel Francis and his associates desired to purchase the Oystermouth Railway which aim was disclosed, among other items, in the 1874 Act whereby, "The Tramways Company . . . might use the railways or tramroads referred to as the Oystermouth Railway for traffic of all kinds on terms to be agreed or failing agreement fixed by arbitration . . . and further might purchase or lease the railway."

However, the Swansea Improvements and Tramways Company failed in its bid to buy out the Oystermouth Railway; instead a legal agreement was resolved between the Tramways Company and G. B. Morris who permitted the former to work the Oystermouth line at the commencement of July, 1877. Morris was to receive an annual rent of £1,600 for a term of 21 years.

Then on the 16th August, 1877, an historic local event took place when the Swansea Improvements and Tramways Company introduced and operated successfully the application of steam traction on the line. Henry Hughes' tram-way type locomotive, "The Pioneer," travelling at a trial speed of 8 m.p.h. pulled two new, large tram-cars accommodating some 80 passengers.

Several prominent citizens of the town, such as Henry Hussey Vivian (later Lord Swansea), Lewis Llewellyn Dillwyn, M.P., and the Mayor for that year, Dr. James Rogers, were numbered among the opponents of the scheme. They maintained that the engine would frighten horses being ridden on the nearby, adjacent road and cause them to bolt or rear up suddenly as well as possibly endanger life and limb.

Dr. James Rogers, the Mayor, even brought the head of his lively horse to within a few yards of the locomotive but the animal remained unaffected by this action. His fears thus allayed, the mayor withdrew his objections and a regular steam traction service commenced working on the 17th August, 1877.

By the close of October, 1877, the Swansea & Oystermouth Railway, as it was then referred to, was sold by auction for £31,000, the buyers being staunch friends of the enthusiastic railway contractor, John Dickson, who had become very interested in the Oystermouth line back in 1865 as part of a larger scheme, but he had not been able to complete the purchase. As Charles E. Lee pinpoints, chapter 3, page 20, the money was found in particular by Frank Ash Yeo, to whom the railway was mortgaged for £15,000.

C. E. Lee further recounts:

> "The particulars and conditions of sale included a map showing the line running from a point alongside the Great Western Railway just north of High Street Station, to a terminus outside Oystermouth, with a branch 1,700 yd. long from Black Pill to Rhydydyfyd Colliery. The vendor was shown as John Stanley Blease of Liverpool, the trustee in the liquidation of John Dickson, and it was stated that the property was being sold by the Order of the Judge to whose Court the liquidation was attached."

In addition, C. E. Lee refers to an account from "The Engineer" of that same year:

> ". . . The railway, or tramroad, is 6 miles in length and there is power to work the same by steam, a very neat locomotive being in use, although horses are more generally used at this season of the year. The auctioneer described the property to be freehold, the permanent way in good order, and said that at present the line was worked by a company at a rental of $1,600 a year, but a buyer could probably have actual possession, and work it himself. The first offer was £10,000 and the biddings advanced but slowly

up to £20,000, when a somewhat more brisk competition set in, and the property was ultimately sold at £31,000."

Meanwhile, however, the Swansea Improvements & Tramways Company had been incorporated by an Act of July, 1874, with powers to construct a system of horse tramways within Swansea. Among other things, this Act provided that:

> "The tramways company . . . might use the railways or tramroads referred to as the Oystermouth Railway for traffic of all kinds on terms to be agreed or failing agreement fixed by arbitration . . . and further might purchase or lease the railway."

Within a very short space of time, a fierce clash of business interests arose between Dickson and the S. I. & Tramways Co. concerning the use of the Oystermouth line and a long drawn-out, legal dispute took place in the High Court. Dickson, who on the 31st March, 1879, had formed his business into the Swansea & Mumbles Railway Company Limited, did all he could to keep the S. I. & Tramways Co. from working over his line. With an authorised total capital of £101,000, the Swansea & Mumbles Railway Co. Ltd.'s directors were J. Beattie (Chairman), J. Dickson and J. Dickson, jr. The conveyance of the freehold from Dickson to this newly formed company was dated 17th March, 1881.

Dickson's strenuous efforts to baulk the moves of the S. I. & Tramways Co. proved successful at first in that the latter company had to withdraw its steam services from the Oystermouth route and then its horse-drawn trams. Eventually, the S. I. & Tramways Co. secured a Court Order in April, 1880, enabling it to resume working horse-drawn cars from the Slip to Oystermouth. The Railway Commissioners had also issued an award on the 20th April, 1880, six days previous to the Court of Appeal findings, which detailed precise conditions for the S. I. & Tramways Co.'s application to use its running powers on the Oystermouth line.

Of particular significance was the fact that the S. I. & Tramways Co. had to run its horse-drawn vehicles over the Oystermouth line immediately after the Swansea & Mumbles Railway Co. Ltd.'s steam trains. On the other hand, the latter company were legally bound to keep the surface between the rails in such a condition as would form a roadway suitable for horses used by the S. I. & Tramways Co. The latter firm was directed to pay the Swansea & Mumbles Railway Co. Ltd. 2s. 9d. for every hundred passengers it transported over the Oystermouth line.

Irrespective of the two companies' legal wrangles, the line continued to be a popular institution with the public who used it in ever-increasing numbers. The fortunate advent of favourable weather especially from early Spring onwards, brought out the crowds so that revenue returns for both firms benefited accordingly. Tentative business plans for further expansion schemes must have now occupied the thoughts of the rival proprietors. Indeed, the encouraging, early Spring weather of 1882, rather emphasised the need for an improved service when, on the 14th April, of that same year, the "Cambrian" noted:

> "We are informed that the actual numbers carried to and fro were, by the Swansea & Mumbles Railway Co. Ltd., 8,076; and by the Swansea Improvements & Tramways Co., 2,349 . . . total, 10,425."

Some of the day-trippers' behaviour in the Mumbles also caught the attention of the newspaper's reporter thus;

> ". . . The bulk of the visitors to the village, and the bays, were of course of the rougher classes, whose enjoyment is of the hearty and vociferous style . . . Some militia recruits and others did indulge in a parody of the marching of the Salvation Army, and chant the popular hymn about 'wearing a starry crown,' but good temper prevailed and so little harm seemed to be done."

However, the line's passenger service came in for censure:

> "It was to be regretted that the evening home trains did not run more frequently . . . Of course, the Swansea & Mumbles Company's *fine train of 21 carriages and two engines* was able to carry a great number of persons at once, but it was too long to leave the remaining crowd standing in the open roadway in the teeth of the east wind waiting for the train from eight until ten o'clock at night. In this awkward interval, as the steam train did not run, *the horse trams were not allowed to run either,* and so a great many persons were inconvenienced, and their health endangered, and many others had to walk home, or pay for a seat in one of the breaks plying along the road, although they had taken railway return tickets . . . the older system of running a train every hour is better."

This state of affairs underwent a change towards the end of 1884, when Sir John Jones Jenkins, a prominent figure in Swansea's shipping industry, and Robert Capper obtained a lease of the Swansea & Mumbles Railway Co. Ltd. and then invited the S. I. & Tramways Co. to work the line with steam power for six and a half years with effect from the 1st July, 1885, as a profitable undertaking for both parties. As a result, the S. I. & Tramways Co. operated a steam service from Rutland Street to Oystermouth while its horse cars plied through the Swansea streets to the junction point at the slip.

On the termination of this agreement, Sir J. J. Jenkins, who had meanwhile acquired a substantial fiscal interest in the Swansea & Mumbles Railway Co. Ltd., now took over the working of the line personally. Some three years prior to this action, Robert Capper had transferred his interests entirely to Sir John. This change of manoeuvre brought the two transport companies once again into legal dispute and a return to the situation of April, 1880, whereby a horse car of the S. I. & Tramways Co. followed behind every steam-hauled train of the Swansea & Mumbles Railway Co. Ltd.

However, the commercial warfare between these two rival firms was to cease finally by 1896 as a result of another business venture embarked upon by Sir J. J. Jenkins. He brought into being on the 26th July, 1893, the Swansea & Mumbles Railways Limited, registered, with a nominal capital of some £130,000 to purchase outright the older company of practically the same name. One of the original subscribers, incidentally, was a Mr. Ernest Arthur Watkins, who held the post of secretary to the company for half a century.

On completion of the 1893 transaction and the taking over of the working of the line, the new owners resolved to settle all outstanding business differences which had existed for some time between the S. I. & Tramways Co. and the former Swansea & Mumbles Railway Co. Ltd. Satisfactory legal and financial arrangements were eventually agreed upon between the both concerns; of added historical interest was the fact that the last horse-drawn mode of transport on the Swansea & Mumbles Railway ended on the 31st March, 1896.

The last decade of the 19th century witnessed quite a number of important developments in connection with the Mumbles Railway's further growth and expansion. C. E. Lee's painstaking research, chapter 4, pages 26-27, reveals the extent of these changes thus:

> "Thus far no extensions of the original line had been made, but the legal proceedings just recorded (although a continuation of long-standing friction) take on added importance in view of the fact that an important extension railway was under construction. On 26th August, 1889, an Act of Parliament was obtained incorporating a new company, known as the Mumbles Railway & Pier Company, with powers to build a new railway 1 mile 22 chains long from an end-on junction with the old line at Dunns (Oystermouth) to Mumbles Head, and to construct a deep-water pier at the latter place. Work was begun on Monday, 23rd May, 1892, and 61 chains of the railway from Dunns to Southend, along the beach, were opened for passenger traffic on Saturday, 6th May, 1893. After two further Acts, of 1892 and 1897 respectively, had been obtained, granting extensions of time for completing the works, the remainder of the new line and the pier were opened for traffic on the 10th May, 1898. Before the opening took place, further application had been made to Parliament for authority to extend the new line from Oystermouth to Black Pill, a distance of 1 mile 38 chains; this was granted by an Act which received the Royal Assent on 25th July, 1898.

> "Scheduled to the same Act was an agreement dated the 18th April, *whereby the Mumbles Railway & Pier Company worked the undertaking of the Swansea & Mumbles Railways Limited from 1st July, 1898.* The extension was completed and opened on 26th August, 1900, bringing the total of the new line up to 2 miles 60 chains. (At first this was a single line; the up line was brought into use at the opening, and the down line was approved by the Board of Trade on 3rd January, 1901). The old Oystermouth line between the same points, which had run upon the side of the narrow highway, was thereupon abandoned in favour of the new line constructed on the sea shore, a change which facilitated the traffic on the railway, in addition to effecting a great public improvement. The abandonment was legalised by the Oystermouth Railway or Tramroad Act of 1899, which Act it will be noted was the first to be obtained by the original line subsequent to that of incorporation in 1804; this is probably the only case of a railway conducting its affairs over so long a period as ninety-five years without a subsequent Act of Parliament."

Furthermore, in 1899, negotiations were initiated between the two railway undertakings and the S. I. & Tramways Co., in which a controlling interest had by then been acquired by The British Electric Traction Company Limited, a pioneer of electric tramways in many parts of the country. The result was that the railway line and Mumbles Pier of approximately 800 feet in length were leased to the Swansea Improvements & Tramways Co. for 999 years and which meant in practical terms that the S. I. & Tramways Co. were virtually the owners of these two valuable acquisitions.

Again, C. E. Lee relates the events behind these moves:

> "The Swansea & Mumbles Railways Limited formerly had a large interest in the Mumbles Railway & Pier Company, but in June, 1899, the majority of these shares was distributed to ordinary shareholders in the Swansea & Mumbles Company at the rate of 1 Mumbles share for every 5 Swansea shares; the latter were then written down by £2 each. This rearrangement was made in consequence of the lease for 999 years of both undertakings to the Swansea Improvements & Tramways Company as from 1st July, 1899. The lease was sanctioned by the Oystermouth Railway or Tramroad Act of 1899 (mentioned above), but the actual agreement was dated 16th December, 1899. The rent began at £10,000 per annum and increased to £13,000. The old owning company, the Swansea & Mumbles Railways Limited, and the statutory company which built the extension (the Mumbles Railway & Pier Company) still exist as freeholders collecting their rents under the terms of the lease (i.e. up until the closure of the line in 1960).
>
> "The S. I. & T. had passed into the control of The British Electric Traction Co. Ltd. early in 1898, and inaugurated electric traction on its street tramways on 20th June, 1900. Electrification of the Swansea & Mumbles

line was often considered but not undertaken, and for thirty years the S. I. & T. group worked the line with steam traction. Shortly after the S. I. & T. took charge, a programme of improvements was begun and during the next few years the line was almost entirely relaid with 85 lb. rails, and additional rolling-stock was provided."

The new route of 1900, constructed between Blackpill and Oystermouth, now ran along the sea-shore while the old line previously placed alongside the road between these two localities was abandoned. Lilliput Hall's site, a quaint old building referred to by Mathews' Swansea Guide of 1830 as originally "measuring twenty feet by sixteen," a little above Blackpill, was now by-passed at this point by the Mumbles steam trains which ran to the rear of its location whereas before the engines proceeded in front of the premises on the Mumbles Road railway track.

During the early part of the Edwardian era, additional improvements were made to the original £10,000 Mumbles Pier which, on completion, embraced large refreshment rooms, a concert pavilion and band stand. The expenditure involved amounted to nearly £40,000, but it was a worthwhile investment for the Mumbles had now become a highly, popular holiday resort visited by thousands of day-trippers in the summer season as well as others who stayed for longer annual vacations.

Guide books and topographical publications of the era were full of laudatory descriptions of the Mumbles scene. A journey on the Mumbles Train too, no doubt, enhanced visitors' anticipations of the day's forthcoming attractions. On alighting at the pier station they would crowd eagerly onto the pier itself or embark aboard the waiting pleasure boats, such as the passenger steamship "Brighton" (Pockett's Bristol Channel Steam Packet Co. Ltd.) or the "Normandy" which would take them to the Bristol Channel resorts.

Others preferred to enjoy the Mumbles' amenities, views, amusements or shows, and in this respect "The Mumbles Railway Centenary Souvenir" of June, 1904, highlighted some of these:

"The pier has become without doubt the most popular resort in the locality . . . The attractions provided thereon by the Company comprise all that the pleasure-seeker can wish for. Amongst the most attractive features during the season are the vocal and instrumental competitions which bring forward the cream of the musical talent of South Wales. Splendid bands are engaged, whilst an accomplished troupe of troubadours give concerts twice daily. The Sacred concerts held on Sunday afternoons and evenings are well patronised, enabling as they do the busy worker to enjoy his rest listening in the open air to sweet music whilst inhaling the health-giving ozone from the Atlantic Ocean."

In July of the same year, King Edward VII and Queen Alexandra came by yacht to Swansea and then travelled in a special, decorated coach of the Mumbles Railway to the town's dock area, where his Majesty cut the first sod of the King's Dock. The royal coach operated originally on the stored system of electric traction, the current being obtained from accumulators, but this method proved unsuccessful.

Oystermouth and Mumbles were one of a number of local districts absorbed into the Borough of Swansea in 1918 under the town's borough extension programme. The horrors of the First World War behind them, people flocked to use the ever popular Mumbles Railway and its passenger traffic of the early 1920's increased noticeably, especially at the height of the summer season. Another royal visit occurred on the 19th July, 1920, when King George V and Queen Mary visited the railway when officially opening the Queen's Dock for oil tankers on Swansea's Eastside.

Its long, crowded trains consisted sometimes of 20 double-deck cars which carried upwards of 2,000 holiday-makers in one journey, a total rarely, if ever, equalled by any other British railway company. As Dan Morgan's ballad of the day recalls:

> "No matter the number, the Guards ne'er refrain
> From finding 'em room—on the old Mumbles Train."

In either direction, some journeys provided sightseeing passengers with a view of amusing happenings outside, on par with Robert L. Stevenson's famous poem, "From A Railway Carriage." On other occasions, in contrast, travellers experienced somewhat more uncomfortable situations and even a few dangerous moments. As elsewhere, first, second and third class seating arrangements made up the usual division of passenger accommodation at this time.

Along sections of the Mumbles Road, in years past, children would perform antics, such as cartwheel turns etc. as the trains passed by and passengers frequently rewarded their endeavours by throwing coins out to them. Again, cyclists would sometimes hold impromptu races or overtake a train between halts. Ahead, between Brynmill Lane and adjacent to Sketty Lane, near the present King George V Playing Fields, once stood a camping site for gypsies, the Gypsy Green of the last century onwards.

Apart from squally showers of rain, a particularly annoying hazard was frequently endured by those passengers huddled together on the top decks of the roofless cars when they became enveloped in clouds of billowing smoke and cinders thrown up by the locomotive's funnel. Other more rugged individuals clung tenaciously to the sides of the vehicles as they perched themselves awkwardly on the two or three tier layers of running boards attached to the coaches. Such incidents, however, as well as unexpected delays, were all part and parcel of enjoying a very pleasant if not exciting day's outing to the Mumbles.

The joys, tribulations and atmosphere of a ride on a Mumbles Railway steam-driven train of yesteryear are surely best recalled by Dan Morgan in his revealing "Ballad Of The Old Mumbles Railway."

BALLAD OF THE OLD MUMBLES RAILWAY

The Station

When we wished to partake of excitement,
That would fill us with joy—more or less
We would save up our cash and prepare for a dash,
On the wonderful Mumbles Express.

The station we start from is striking,
The roof is the sky—overhead.
And flat on the ground—the "Platform" is found
The oldest design—so 'tis said.

The booking hall is round in a sidestreet,
A shelter from sunshine—and rain.
And all rushed pell-mell, at the sound of a bell,
For then—it was time for our train.

The Train

Our train is a wonder of wonders,
The coaches are gorgeous and grand,
For the dainty design—of the train on this line,
Is easily the best in the land.

The engine—my word! what a beauty,
As slowly she snorts from her shed,
Then crosses the road—to take up her load,
And waits for "The full-steam ahead."

Some coaches are "First Class"—some "Second"
And "Third Class" and Workmen's as well,
Queer trucks at the rear—all open and bare,
And "no class" at all—I've heard tell.

There are carriages nicknamed "The Toast Racks,"
With leg room for sitters—so slight,
That to sit at one's ease, we've to dove-tail our knees,
With the lady's or gent's opposite.

And that wonderful Van—for the workmen,
If ever we found ourselves there—
With the fumes and the smoke—we would jolly soon choke
And be gurgling and gasping for air.

The Start

The train-load is ready and eager for starting,
And steam from the engine is hissing,
The smoke from the funnel causes lots of eye-smarting,
There's hardly a thing that is missing.

The guards—in a row—with their shrill whistles blowing,
The engine bell dismally tolling,
When all are impatient to see the train going
More passengers—up we see strolling.

They are then got aboard with shouting and shoving,
And crosswords and swearwords and grunting,
But just as we think to the Mumbles we're moving,
The engine must yet do some shunting.

We hear lots of creaking and bearings a-squeaking,
As backwards and forwards we're bumping,
With pistons a-clanking and whistles a-shrieking,
Soon o'er the first crossing we're jumping.

And this is a picture that's true more or less,
The starting away of the Mumbles Express.

On The Way

We're off at last—the great adventure started.
A tolling bell tells all—we're on the way,
From sleepy Swansea Town we'll soon be parted,
To reach—in time—the Mumbles,
'Cross the bay.

We leave behind the advertising station,
And row of cottages that flank our right,
Then pass the grimy gasworks—with elation!
For soon our pretty (!) prison looms in slight;

And prisoners within are much elated
To hear the great express—and that is all
Whilst we are swiftly passing
So 'tis stated
The "longest stone," built in the prison wall.

By school and yards and church we're quickly flashing,
And see the waiting people at the "Slip,"
Then by the railway arch you see us dashing,
But "pull up" for more shunting—on this trip.

They hitch on coaches from Trafalgar Siding,
To lengthen (in short time) this great express.
Impatient are some passengers—there riding,
We'll reach the Mumbles in an hour or less.

At The Slip

At the Slip—what a sight
'Twas a mystery quite
How the thousands of passengers vanished,
From the road—all aboard
On the train they were "stored."
By a magician's wand they were banished,
No matter the number, the guards ne'er refrain,
From finding 'em room—on the old Mumbles Train.

At Brynmill

On once more—to the "West,"
At a speed—near its best,
Brynmill Station our express approaches,
Thousands more—for this train
Which I'm sure must contain
Some invisible extending coaches.
For if hundreds or thousands the guards ne'er complain,
They'll find 'em all room—on the dear Mumbles Train.

Speeding Along

Off—off again on that long(!) stretch of line,
Where each express is proud to show her pace,
From Brynmill Lane to Gipsy's Green is fine,
Here cyclists oft the Mumbles Train would race:

The speed (!) we reached by some was deemed a crime;
Yet back-bent cyclists by us sped,
And reached Blackpill before us many a time
For that's the way our racing men are bred.

An "L. & N." we passed with sweet disdain,
We simply "left it standing," as they say;
(But here I think it best that I explain
It was a train that ran the other way).

Of course we had to "meet" the up-town train
At Blackpill Links—where all good golfers play.
Though every "waiting"—goes against the grain,
We saw two play four holes—'twas worth the stay.

Our trains now pass—the golf house points we reach
Something's gone wrong—as oftentimes they will.
Folks are much shocked—and passengers—they screech
"We're off the line,"—but much too slow to spill.

With levers, spanners, chains and then a jack,
The guards and driver work with eager zest,
With bump and jolt we soon regain the track,
Then reach Blackpill—to take a little rest.

In The Bay

The half-way reached, we're in the bay,
The most superb in Britain's Isle.
At Lilliput we do not stay,
But dash along the western mile!
The passengers inside—on top,
On stairs and platform look aghast,
And wonder when and where we'll stop
For we are travelling mighty fast.

Our driver knows what he can do,
And that the brakes will surely work!
So, for a test—without ado,
He pulls the train up with a jerk;
Folks' heads are bumped, some *are* upset,
Words to express they're at a loss.
No need to flurry—fume—or fret,
The station-master cries "West Cross."

On With The Mad Flight

We soon are on the move again,
The rollicking, rumbling Mumbles Train,
And at the speed our engine runs
We pretty soon will reach the Dunns.

That's if our train with such a load
Can keep the rails at Norton Road.
She keeps the track—though speeding fast,
And Oystermouth is reached at last.

Here crowds of passengers detrain
Some for their homes—lots for the bays,
To roam the sands beside the main,
Where they oft spend such happy days.

And in the station yard you'll find
Many a horse trap waiting there
Our old friend Peachy—ever kind,
Lifts whip to hat—he seeks a farc.

The engine bell is heard once more,
And on the move—swift ! as of yore,
And leave behind dear Oystermouth,
No station like it—north or south.

Upon our right a glimpse is seen
Of tennis courts and bowling green,
Hotels and shops—along the bend,
Leads to the sea of Southend.

The End—At Last

Now patient passengers prepare
To leave the train in just a while,
The terminus is very near
We end our journey with a smile.

And those on top—wipe out their eyes
To clear them of dust and grit
That from the engine's funnel flies,
(For years we've all endured it).

So we've had our share of excitement
On the wonderful Mumbles Express;
Though we say it with smiles, it has covered six miles
In an hour or so—more or less.

And the pier station, too, is striking,
For the roof is the sky overhead,
But the view all around, is the finest e'er found
In the world—anywhere—so 'tis said.

A further amusing reference to the days of steam on this former line is contained in H. Libby's "The Mixture: Mumbles & Harry Libby," chapter four, page 34:

"... The Mumbles Train did its stuff. On Bank Holidays it could carry, and did carry, some 2,000 people in one journey, more indeed than on many an express train these days. Thirty-odd coaches of different categories, first class, second class and 'the Dummy.' The Dummy was the workmen's transport of old, and one had to possess a weekly ticket to claim the right to travel in it. It had no windows that would open, and no other ventilation of any kind, and between start and stop it would become literally smoke-filled, the smoke being undoubtedly from old shag tobacco, and some of the authorities of the day (the lay authorities of course) justified travelling in that atmosphere by suggesting that that was the way to kill all the germs. Then the Second Class coaches were for the workers, and the First Class for the 'gentry'. That, of course, is a rough and ready description."

The "Dummy" was, of course, that "wonderful Van" referred to by Dan Morgan in his ballad, verse eight.

C. E. Lee, chapter 5, page 36, also relates:

"On occasions during the steam-traction days eighteen or twenty loaded cars were included in one train, conveying as many as 1,800 passengers (and without double-heading). Incidentally, this is a total but infrequently conveyed by one train on any other British railway. Of course the gradients are very easy—the line is practically level with the exception of a down grade from Black Pill to West Cross—and the steam locomotive speed never exceeded 20 m.p.h. with an average of about 7 or 8 m.p.h. Thirty minutes were allowed for the single journey of about 5½ miles. Eighteen trains on weekdays and twelve on Sundays were provided in each direction, at irregular intervals of roughly one hour. Taking 1925 (the year before the general strike) as typical, we find that 682,108 passengers were carried, made up of 140,814 first class, 278,528 second class, 14,804 second class excursion, and 247,962 workmen. The goods conveyed during the same period amounted only to 8,994 tons and consisted of 8,462 tons of coal, 63 of lime and limestone, and 469 of merchandise."

Efficient as the steam locomotives were for carrying the large crowds of holiday-makers and business people, and for the conveyance of mineral traffic, the increase in the passenger traffic, created largely as a result of new housing schemes developed within the Borough's extended area, made it increasingly apparent that the capacity of the line with its long trains running at comparatively infrequent intervals, did not meet sufficiently the requirements of the travelling public. Consequently, electrification of the line was decided upon in order to modernise the railway route by providing a more frequent, faster and certainly a more comfortable service. The growing importance of the motor-buses' contribution to public transport also had to be taken into consideration.

Application was made to the Ministry of Transport in July, 1924, under the Railways (Electrical Power) Act, 1903, in consequence of which the Minister made the following order in May, 1925:

> "The Oystermouth Railway or Tramroad and Mumbles Railway (Electrical Power) Order, 1925. An Order made under the above-named Act to facilitate the introduction of electrical power on certain railways or tramroads worked by the Swansea Improvements & Tramways Company."

In order to bring about a meaningful, binding co-operation between the proposed electrified line and the local bus services, the lease of the Mumbles Railway and Pier was transferred in July 1927 to the motor-bus associate of the Swansea Improvements & Tramways Co., under the same management, the South Wales Transport Company Limited, with effect from the 1st January, 1927. This move ensured the co-ordination of all Swansea-Mumbles road and rail services, and so avoided unnecessary and uneconomical competition between the two forms of transport. Prior to the electrification project, the South Wales Transport Co. Ltd. had already commenced to run omnibus services along the Mumbles Road route as far as Oystermouth, primarily to serve districts which were not adequately catered for by the Mumbles Railway.

The South Wales Transport Co. Ltd., (Lessees of The Mumbles Railway & Pier) then took in hand the electrification of the line between 1927 and 1929. An agreement was made with the Swansea Corporation for the supply of electric power from its generating station and arrangements completed for the erection of the Blackpill Sub-Station which was also built and equipped by the Corporation's Electricity Department on behalf of the Company.

The electric power or current was conveyed by overhead trolley wire; alternating current at 6,600 volts was passed from the Corporation's generating station to Blackpill Sub-Station, situated midway down the line, where it was converted to direct current and supplied to the line's various feeding points at 650 volts.

The Sub-Station's equipment was supplied by the Metropolitan—Vickers Electrical Co. Ltd. and consisted of two rotary converters, each of 500 kilowatt capacity; provision was also made for the installation of a third rotary converter set when required. The supply of power was an automatic operation via the automatic control protective gear provided by Metrovick.

With the completion of the electrification programme in 1929 came the inevitable end of the steam era in the history of the line. On St. David's Day of that year, the last steam train was driven along the route by four of the Company's employees. The "Black Gang" were Mr. W. Williams, a mechanic for 34 years on the railway; Mr. H. Davies, a driver for 30 years; Mr. W. Veale, fireman; and Mr. Owen Davies, the conductor.

In recognition of the change-over from steam to electric traction, the South Wales Transport Co. Ltd. published a short, illustrated, historical souvenir booklet in 1928. Directors of the firm at that time were Messrs. C. G. Tegetmeier (Chairman), C. H. Dade, S. E. Garcke, E. R. Soames and David James, J.P. (Managing Director).

Suppliers of the rolling stock were the Brush Electrical Engineering Company and in the beginning eleven double-bogie two-deck covered top type cars went into service. Two more were added in 1930. The 30 ton coaches, installed with British Thomson-Houston two-motor electrical driving equipment, platforms and staircases at each end, were, among other features, equipped with sliding bows instead of the more usual trolley wheels and possessed pneumatic power brakes in addition to hand brakes. With the commencement of electric traction, on the 2nd March, 1929, the South Wales Transport Co. Ltd. abolished the former system of separate passenger classes' status for seating accommodation on the coaches.

The reconstructed track now possessed additional passing places which permitted a service of coaches, when required, from seven to ten minutes intervals and a large depot-shed housed the vehicles at the Rutland Street terminus of the line. (After the 1960 closure, this building was purchased by Swansea Corporation; it was demolished later during June, 1978). The completed electrification programme entailed a cost of approximately £125,000.

Apparently, there has been no account of any signalling or other safety devices employed prior to the electrification of the railway line. By 1929, such a situation was bound to be changed in order to meet the requirements of any proposed speed restrictions likely to be imposed upon the Company by the Ministry of Transport. Therefore, an automatic block signal system was installed: the signals which were set by the car's pantograph touched a contact-maker and thereby energised the signalling circuit. At the same time, other light signals were brought into use which indicated whether the points at passing loops were securely locked.

In their day, the thirteen double decked cars were easily the largest electrically-driven tramway-type vehicles built for service in the United Kingdom: each car accommodated 106 passengers; 48 on the lower saloon and 58 on the upper deck. There was an entrance platform and staircase placed at each end of every car; both entrances faced the landward side. When two coaches were coupled together a maximum seating capacity for 212 passengers was provided for any journey. Moreover, during exceptionally busy days, a limited number of passengers were permitted to stand along the lower saloon of a packed car so that the figure of 212 was exceeded somewhat on occasions.

On the hot summer days of the 1930's onwards, it was a common sight, especially during week-ends or Bank Holidays, to witness many hundreds of people queuing patiently, in turns, at the Rutland Street terminus, in order to board the "down" trains for a typical day's outing to the Mumbles. Some others, however, individually, or in very small groups, would stand apart from the main throng in or around the ticket office towards the Gasworks' end. Whether season ticket-holders or no, these regular daily travellers from the Mumbles district would enter any available coach ahead of the day-trippers in order to get home for lunch and again after finishing work in the afternoons and evenings. It is to the credit of British patience, commonsense and the generally good-humoured nature of the conductors and drivers who knew the genuine residents that this unofficial practice was allowed to continue without outbreaks of physical violence or abuse, although from time to time, heated arguments arose from less tolerantly-minded members of the waiting public.

Among other changes, the electrification of the line made a noticeable difference to the time undertaken for one journey for now, under normal conditions, it took only nineteen minutes. Norton Road Station was reopened and a new one placed between Brynmill and Blackpill named Ashleigh Road. In all, there were ten stopping places: Rutland Street Terminus (Swansea), St. Helen's or the Slip, Brynmill, Ashleigh Road, Blackpill, West Cross, Norton Road, Oystermouth (The Dunns), Southend and the Mumbles Pier Terminus.

Some arresting figures of pre-War II and post-War II days in respect of passengers and goods transported on the electric line are recorded by C. E. Lee, chapter 5, page 37:

> "The pre-war summer timetable provided for about sixty journeys each way on weekdays and forty on Sundays. During the year 1938 the passengers totalled 1,192,922, made up of 972,244 ordinary one-class, and

220,678 workmen. The goods conveyed during the same period amounted only to 457 tons, of which 491 tons were coal, coke and patent fuel. In the later years of the recent war, when petrol rationing made it impossible for business men to use their cars and bus services were restricted, passenger figures on the Mumbles Railway reached unprecedented heights. In 1945 they totalled 4,995,000, and in 1946 4,237,000. Even today the traffic is nearly three times that of pre-war days, for the 1953 total of passengers was 3,150,000."

As a heavily-used public transport service, therefore, the Mumbles Railway made a significant contribution to the war effort on the home front locally. Several million passengers were carried yearly between 1939 and 1945, a period when the population of the Mumbles had risen because of the influx of bombed-out families and the encampments of essential military units within the district. Daily, the Company catered for the travelling needs of members of the armed forces, temporary residents, school-children, regular season ticket-holders and others of long-standing together with numbers of people who travelled nightly from Swansea to the Mumbles in order to escape any likely Luftwaffe raids on the town.

In retrospect, the Mumbles Railway then helped to bolster public morale, for its familiar coaches were a source of comfort to many citizens who came to appreciate its dependable service and share in a kind of passenger camaraderie which existed throughout those anxious years.

The railway's 150th anniversary was celebrated in the last week of June, 1954. In honour of the occasion a special procession took place on the line, complete with crews and passengers dressed in period costumes. At the head of the parade was a replica of the old Simon Llewellyn horse-drawn coach, followed by a steam engine pulling a carriage and an electric car. This colourful event was recorded on sound and television as well as being filmed; newspapers in such countries as Canada, Australia and Switzerland acknowledged the line's unique status in transport history.

At that time, the Company revealed that a quarter-of-a-million train miles were run each year and more than three million passengers transported between Swansea and the Mumbles. On exceptionally busy Bank Holidays, as many as 40,000 people had been carried by its coaches in a single day. It was also the only railway in the United Kingdom which was controlled by a bus company, the South Wales Transport Company Limited. The Company's directors then were Messrs. W. T. James, O.B.E. (Chairman), R. W. Birch, P. G. Stone Clark and J. S. Wills; and the General Manager was Mr. W. M. Dravers. Company Secretary was Mr. I. M. Smith.

In 1954, the Mumbles Pier, which had been sub-leased to the Amusement Equipment Co. in 1938, was barred to the general public for reasons of safety as its condition had seriously deteriorated since the early

1950's. However, the sub-lessees repaired the popular structure at a cost of some £75,000 and the renovated pier was officially reopened on the 9th June, 1965, by the then mayor, the late Cllr. Harry Libby.

Within six years of the 1954 celebration, the Mumbles Railway service was discontinued and the line eventually dismantled. The railway was running at a loss maintained the Company: rising costs, the competition rendered by the Company's extended or new bus routes within the area, as well as a growing trend towards individual car ownership, caused an inevitable decline in passenger traffic. In addition to these circumstances, an immediate sum of £350,000, at minimum, would have been required to keep the line in operation by the close of the 1950's.

Nearly a quarter of a century previously, an indication of a possible early future decrease in the conveyance of passengers suggested itself with the passing of the Swansea & District Transport Act, 1936. This provided for the abandonment of the Tramways & Light railways, and any legal rights related to these undertakings were assigned to the South Wales Transport Company together with the lease of the Mumbles Railway. Swansea's old trams passed into history, replaced by the Company's smart bus fleet; but, for the time being, the Mumbles Railway remained intact.

It was the outbreak of World War Two and the subsequent rationing of petrol supplies which effected an extended lease of life for the line. In some respects too, the nation's protracted post-war economic recovery programme of the late 1940's helped somewhat to prolong its existence.

Unfortunately, the passing of the South Wales Transport Act, 1959, for the abandonment of the Mumbles Railway, ended the hopes of those who looked for a last minute reprieve. On the 5th January, 1960, a large crowd gathered outside the Rutland Street Depot to see the privileged passengers take a last return journey down to the Mumbles. Mock mourners in appropriate attire attended the closing ceremony.

Consequently, on that date, the oldest surviving passenger railway line in the world ceased working to the genuine dismay of many Swansea citizens. Throughout its existence, various methods of propulsion were used: horses, sail, steam locomotive, electricity; and for goods traffic, petrol and diesel locomotive.

However, it may be sometimes overlooked that the Oystermouth Railway or Tramroad came into being during the period of the Canal Age, when "railway" then referred to some kind of timber or metal track for horse-drawn wagons to run on. As recorded previously, the original line which used horses as the normal form of motive power for some time, developed out of a proposal to extend the Swansea Canal, nearly two decades before the opening of the Stockton & Darlington Railway.

Although, therefore, fully entitled to its name on historical grounds, the

Mumbles Railway was not a "railway" in the modern meaning of the term. Even during the steam era on the line, its trains were double-deck, open-top tramcars; these ran on unfenced trackway under low speed limits and in accordance with street tramway practice. With electrification, the Mumbles "train" was for all practical purposes a tram similar to such vehicles in other parts of the United Kingdom as the Sheffield's "Roberts," and the true character of the line has always been that of a street tramway.

In this connection, it is of further interest to recall that the men employed by the South Wales Transport Co. Ltd. and who worked on the Mumbles Railway route, were classified as railwaymen by the National Union Of Railwaymen. This was accepted by the Railway Authorities and, as a result, they were given the privilege of reduced and free travel on the national network. In return, personnel from the latter employers were granted reduced rates of travel on the Mumbles Railway and a privileged return fare cost them one-quarter of the full rate. In 1956, for example, they could travel from Rutland Street to the Mumbles Pier for 4½d. Moreover, when the South Wales Transport Co. Ltd. bus crews were on strike, the Mumbles Train service continued to operate because of the different Union arrangements.

After the closure, most of the original track-bed went into road widening and other works. However, with the accent on tourism and leisure in recent years, various ideas have been proposed for restoring a section of the former route alongside the present seafront walk.

Two organisations of late have emerged to champion a possible restoration of part of the old Mumbles Railway route, namely, the Mumbles Railway Society, Swansea, and the Mumbles Railway Company Limited based at Cheltenham. Both undertakings organise exhibitions relating to the Mumbles Railway Story and steam engines in general. The Mumbles Railway Society has presented a number of particularly interesting displays which have attracted railway enthusiasts and others from a wide area. Past relics such as the bell and lamp from the old steam train dating back to 1877, a small section of the original line, two flintlock hand pistols thought to have been carried on the first horse-drawn passenger journey, old signs and advertisements, steam and electric passenger tickets, and other pieces of equipment have been placed on display at the widely attended annual Models' Exhibitions held at The Guildhall, Swansea, and the Leisure Centre, Bridgend. Items from the more recent post-electrification days have included a lamp and number plates from the last carriages in use, a set of drivers' keys, a "dead man's handle," and one of the blue leather seats. Other material supplied on loan were old photographs, postcards, together with facsimiles of documents and modern artists' impressions of past scenes on the line.

The 170th anniversary of the railway was celebrated on the 25th March, 1977, at Ashleys Restaurant, Mumbles, via a buffet and exhibition. At the end of the day, more than 1,500 people had visited the display and others had to be turned away by the Society's organisers. Such exhibitions readily reveal that the Mumbles Railway is still alive in many people's memories while Local History is certainly enriched on these occasions.

The Mumbles Railway Society was formed in the Autumn of 1975 as a voluntary organisation by Messrs. Tony Cottle and Ron Lawson, with the specific aim of reviving a part of the historic railway. The original Management Committee, as recorded in the Society's first Newsletter dated February, 1976, were: Chairman, Tony Cottle; Hon. Secretary, Ron Lawson; Hon. Treasurer, John Pile; and Leslie Evans, John Llewellyn, Christopher Morton, Peter Tremewan & Mrs. Tremewan.

Between 1975 and 1977, the Society mounted an enthusiastic and well-prepared restoration campaign which received invaluable publicity in the local media as well as further afield in the U.K. Originally, it was proposed that a new railway should be laid from St. Helen's to Oystermouth Square, following the route of the former L.M.S. main line as far as Blackpill, and thence along the old Mumbles Railway track to Oystermouth. One of their brochures, "Bring Back The Mumbles Train," stressed the fact that, "This 4-mile journey would offer the people of Swansea and visitors to the city, an unrivalled opportunity of viewing this magnificent Bay, and of going back for a while to the great age of steam. A live steam railway of such historic importance would be of considerable publicity value to the Swansea area." In their first meeting with the Swansea City Council Policy Committee, a deputation from the Society emphasised this latter aspect as one of their three principal aims in that the revival of part of the first passenger railway in the world would prove to be an immense attraction as well as a financial asset for Swansea. Secondly, it was maintained that a narrow-gauge railway could be laid along the foreshore without detriment to the existing picturesque, landscaped walk; and thirdly, the Society was not seeking financial support from the Council.

Newsletter No. 1 reveals the system favoured by the Society:

> "What we are proposing is a 2 ft. gauge railway, modelled on the very successful 'Great Little Trains' of North Wales. Motive power would be provided by small steam locomotives, oil-fired for cleanliness, and requiring no facilities for coal storage and ash disposal. Though originally designed to work in the slate quarries, many of these fascinating little engines have been rebuilt and 'promoted' to hauling passenger trains on the thriving narrow-gauge railways of the Principality. The kitchen-maid has become a star.

"'Pixie' is a good example of the type of locomotive we would like to see puffing along the new Mumbles Railway to revive a part of Swansea's heritage nearly 170 years old. Though much smaller than the original pannier tanks which worked on the line—she is only 8 ft. high and 10 ft. long—'Pixie' is capable of hauling up to 100 passengers. This engine worked in the Northamptonshire iron-ore mines for many years, but is now owned by the Rev. Teddy Boston, and runs on the Cadby Railway in the grounds of the rectory. She was built in 1919."

As an immediate practical measure, the original St. Helen's to Oystermouth length of route was amended; a reduced section from Blackpill to Oystermouth is currently the principal goal in mind. The proposals are as follows:

"A narrow-gauge railway operating between Blackpill and Oystermouth would be a viable unit, similar to the 2-mile Llanberis Lake Railway in North Wales. Your committee ruled out from the beginning any question of going beyond Oystermouth to the Pier, because of the extensive use being made of this section by the sailing boats which add so much charm and interest to Mumbles.

"By contrast, the foreshore between Blackpill and Oystermouth has few demands made upon it. Access to the beach would not be cut off by the kind of railway we envisage, and the leisurely passage of a small-scale train at hourly intervals during the summer is unlikely to disturb the composure of any angler.

". . . Blackpill is the obvious starting-point for the construction of the new Mumbles Railway. There is an existing recreational complex, to which the railway could be regarded as an additional attraction, and there is space for the modest facilities needed to operate the line. These amount to nothing more than the equivalent of a small petrol filling-station.

"A length of about 1,000 yards from Blackpill to Lilliput Lane is the first stage of track-laying planned, and with volunteer labour this could be completed in about ten week-ends. Out-and-back rides should be available as construction continued in stages via West Cross to the final terminus near Oystermouth Square.

"As with the old steam trains, the complete journey from Blackpill to Oystermouth would take 18 minutes, at a speed of about 7 m.p.h. giving passengers time to enjoy the unrivalled scenic attractions of Swansea Bay and Mumbles.

"In the longer term, it would be a fairly simple matter to bridge the small stream at Blackpill for such lightweight locomotives, and extend the line to St. Helen's, or even perhaps to the new Leisure Centre, following the old L.M.S. route. The selective development of tourism means more jobs for Swansea people, without damaging the environment, and the new Mumbles Railway is a forward-looking project. Our aim is to use the best features of the past to create something of great benefit for the future."

Meanwhile, the Society engaged the services of Messrs. W. S. Atkins & Partners, Civil Engineers, to undertake a feasibility study of the whole project. Their report confirmed that the laying down and operating of a narrow-gauge railway between Blackpill and Oystermouth was a practical proposition. The firm's recommendations were outlined in the Society's second Newsletter of November, 1976. Members were also informed that the Committee had worked "hard on plans, costings, and also the setting up of a Company for the Mumbles Railway Society." By that date, the Society was in a position to approach the City Council in order to seek permission for the use of their land and obtain outline planning permission for the railway.

Of three alternative routes available in constructing a new railway along the original route, W. S. Atkins & Partners recommended the one on the sea side of the existing footpath. One problem area was recognised in respect of services between Harris's, Blackpill and Fernhill, but here, fortunately, the difficulties were seen as less severe because of the existing wide verge avilable which would allow track location with the avoidance of any manholes. Interference, annoyance, etc. to pedestrians could be reduced to a minimum along the selected route which was also thc case in respect of disturbance to existing services and footpath as well as the landscape areas at Blackpill.

Although the speed of the proposed train would have been limited to approximately 7 m.p.h., and the danger aspects seen as relatively insignificant, it was recommended that, "a low, simple, fence is erected between the footpath and the railway route to provide a physical separation between the train and pedestrians. Warning signs should also be erected at each access point to the beach to warn pedestrians and to instruct the engine driver to take extra care and to sound the engine whistle." A special study of current safety precautions was undertaken by the Committee and, among other reports, particular attention was paid to the "Safety Legislation Relating To Railway Preservation Societies," by J. L. Alexander, H.M. District Inspector of Factories, Bradford South.

In the meantime, Mr. Ron Lawson, co-founder of the Mumbles Railway Society, resigned his position as secretary on the 30th November, 1976. A difference of opinion had arisen in respect of subsequent policy related principally to the question of fencing requirements. Present day legislation demands that any steam-operated line of 15″ gauge or more must be fenced along its whole length to a minimum height of 3 ft. On environmental grounds, Mr. Lawson felt that he could not support such an arrangement on the seafront. An alternative project of his, the proposed construction of a narrow gauge railway built through the Clyne Valley on the old L.M.S. track bed, as an additional tourist attraction, was not considered appropriate at the time by the Society.

The subject of fencing was the cause of the main objection voiced against the proposed railway project at the meeting held between the City of Swansea Council's Policy Committee and the Mumbles Railway Society's Committee in the first week of February, 1976. The Director of the Environment said he was opposed to the scheme because it would prevent free access to the seafront. Another objection that the intended railway would interfere with the boating at Southend proved invalid as the M.R.S.'s plans did not embrace a section along the stretch of the Mumbles seafront.

It was also in November, 1976, that The Mumbles Railway Company Limited came into being, of which, Mr Ron Lawson, the former M.R.S.'s secretary, became a director. As a private company, it was incorporated to carry on a famous name in the history of passenger transport, and, when a suitable opportunity presented itself, to bring about the restoration of part of the old line, "in some suitable form," as an amenity and tourist attraction. Currently, the Company seeks to secure its success and permanence by trading on a commercial basis in other directions.

While, therefore, the two separate organisations appear to hold similar basic aims for Swansea, they differ in the choice of motive power to be adopted. The Mumbles Railway Society members have clearly opted for the installation of a two ft. gauge railway, from Blackpill to a point near Oystermouth, upon which would run a small steam engine, oil-fired for cleanliness. The Society feel confident that once the initial cost of laying the track has been met, from grants and public subscription, the railway would prove a considerable tourist draw and would pay for itself.

Initially, The Mumbles Railway Co. Ltd. seek to lay down a length of unfenced tramway between Blackpill and Oystermouth, flush to ground level and involving no new buildings or structures on the seafront, as being the most suitable form of preservation. This is to be operated by horse-drawn cars similar to those running at present on the promenade at Douglas. Such a scheme reverts back to the original type of motive power used on the Mumbles Railway which spanned most of the 19th century.

In 1976, Mr. Lawson also commissioned a firm of railway construction experts who prepared an alternative feasibility study. From their conclusions, he published a four-sheet survey complete with large O.S. map and seven photographs entitled, "A New Role For The Mumbles Railway." The report envisages two schemes in respect of the seafront and the possible introduction of a steam line service in the Clyne Valley as revealed in the following extracts:

> "Given the right kind of restoration, the Mumbles Railway could be re-opened from Blackpill to Oystermouth bus station without any detriment whatsoever to the amenities. There are special environmental factors which

have to be taken into account on this $1\frac{3}{4}$ mile stretch of the foreshore, but they can all be fully satisfied by narrow-gauge, *battery-operated trams.*

"Travelling at a maximum speed of 8 m.p.h., these vehicles are safe and clean. They do not need overhead wires or continuous fencing of the track. What is more, trams bear a marked resemblance to the red electric cars most people remember with affection as 'The Mumbles Train.' The photograph shows the grass verge running from Blackpill towards Oystermouth, on which a tramway could be laid quite unobtrusively, with no effect on the path and no restriction on access to the sands.

"The project would benefit the people of Swansea without making any call on the rates because, like the original Mumbles Railway, it can be financed on a commercial basis. The approval and goodwill of the City Council, as owners of the land, are of course essential. However, it is the policy of the Council to promote Swansea, Mumbles and Gower as a tourist area, and nothing could further this policy more than to have an electric tramway, unique in Wales, operating at Blackpill.

"Earlier this year, local public opinion was shown to be very much in favour of restoring a part of the Mumbles Railway. A recent feasibility study by a well-known firm of consulting engineers, undertaken for the M.R.S., has confirmed that a narrow-gauge line between Blackpill and Oystermouth bus station is practicable. Such facilities as car parks and conveniences already exist at both of the proposed termini.

"The electricity sub-station at Blackpill was designed for the Mumbles Railway by the Borough Architect, Mr. Ernest Morgan, A.R.I.B.A. and completed in 1927 . . . The Mumbles train could run again from here, taking 15 minutes to reach Oystermouth over what is still the most attractive part of its former route. By arrangement with the City Council, the sub-station building (now a store) might be used as a booking office and *small tramway museum.* As the first place in Wales to have electric trams, Swansea is not an inappropriate location, further historical interest being added by the Constitution Hill Tramway, 1896-1903. This was cable-hauled like the colourful San Francisco trams which significantly are seen so often on TV and in American airline advertising."

The opening paragraph of "Steam In The Clyne Valley" notes:

"Across the road from the Mumbles Railway at Blackpill, there was an L.M.S. station on the former main line from Swansea (Victoria) to Shrewsbury and Crewe via Central Wales. The photograph shows the remaining bridge abutment where the L.M.S. turned inland to cross over the Mumbles Railway, after running parallel with it from Swansea. Originally opened through the Clyne Valley in 1867 as 'The Llanelly Railway' . . . the establishment of a tramway between Blackpill and Oystermouth would build up sufficient demand to justify laying a narrow-gauge railway into the Clyne Valley, to be worked by steam. The two systems could be connected for passengers by means of a footbridge at Blackpill . . .

"A narrow-gauge railway into the Clyne Valley from Blackpill would open up picnic sites which are otherwise inaccessible, relieving some of the pressure on the existing picnic areas in Gower at peak periods. And there is at least one possible location for a summer adventure centre in the valley.

"Expanding a new Mumbles Railway system from Blackpill towards Gowerton has the immense advantage in the long term of taking the railway closer to the M. 4 motorway, so that a proportion of the traffic visiting the system could be accommodated at some point between Gowerton and Dunvant. A tourist centre here would be the ideal terminus for the narrow-gauge line from Blackpill . . .

"Huge capital outlay is not necessary to get this project going. A start can be made simply by laying the first $\frac{1}{2}$ mile of tramway (i.e. the proposed line from Blackpill to Oystermouth as the essential first stage) and operating it as a temporary measure with a single horse-drawn car."

Eventually, on the 31st March, 1977, the Swansea City Council agreed to a suggestion put forward by Cllr. G. Chilcott that representatives of both railway organisations should meet their Policy Sub-Committee for discussions and to investigate the possibility of an alternative railway scheme placed in the Clyne Valley. Later in the same year, however, after an examination of all the schemes submitted to them for consideration, the City Council decided by a majority vote, on the 25th August, "not to consider proposals for the restoration of the railway on the seafront."

The restoration issue, as part of a conservation project, will doubtlessly become a subject for further debates and revised investigations in the years ahead. Meantime, the continued existence and activities of the Mumbles Railway Society and The Mumbles Railway Co. Ltd. help to keep the story of the famous line very much alive locally and elsewhere. Any successful re-establishment of part of this historic railway, therefore, as an acceptable amenity, would have to meet the following requirements: a concensus of opinion largely supported by the citizens of Swansea; the official consent of the local authority for the use of the land selected; the careful maintenance of the line as a viable concern; judicious distribution of necessary newspaper and magazine advertisements annually within the United Kingdom; and the much-needed support of railway enthusiasts from a wide area of the country.

Meanwhile, the flat-roofed Electricity Sub-Station, still stands today as a tangible reminder of the railway's former existence. As part of the Blackpill scene, the building's exterior displays a pleasing design of architectural merit. Its five long-arched, church-like windows facing the busy dual-carriageway, present an elegant appearance, which is, perhaps, not readily appreciated by passers-by. On the seaward side, the colonnaded porch of seven pillars continues to provide shelter for people using the pleasant Blackpill Lido as it did for a travelling public of yesteryear. The future may yet see it become the starting point of a newly-restored Mumbles Railway.

Horse-drawn passenger coach on the Oystermouth Railway circa 1865.

Courtesty of Robert W. May, F.R.S.A.

0-6-0 side-tank locomotive. *Courtesy of Robert W. May, F.R.S.A.*

106-seat B.T.-H. electric car 1929-1960.

Courtesy of Robert W. May, F.R.S.A.

Circa Mid-1860's. *By permission, Roger David Studios*

Edwardian Days. *By permission, Roger David Studios*

19th July, 1920. *By permission, Roger David Studios*

1950's *Courtesy of Gordon Johns*

Artistic Impression, 1959.

Edwardian Advertisement.
(Author's Collection).

Photo by D. G. Bowden

Caswell Bay Early 19th C. Print.
Mumbles Railway Anniversary, 1954.

Courtesy of the Mumbles Railway Society

The Mumbles Railway Co. Ltd. (Cheltenham) Badge

By permission, Mr. Ron Lawson

CHAPTER FOUR

THE LIMESTONE INDUSTRY

"What is a Local Historian? . . . To begin with he is a person who is imbued with a strong interest, a keen love and an ardent desire to set on record, facts, true and legendary about a certain place, generally where he is living or with what he is associated. He must be the possessor of a great deal of tact, infinite patience, and above all he must have a nose like a ferret, for it is surprisingly true that information is to be found in the most unlikely places."
C. F. Shepherd: "Sidelights On Some Glamorgan Parishes." 1946.

"At the Mumbles, in Gower, limestone is raised by the ton, to be shipped off to the coast of Devon, & c. When the quarrymen meet with approved marble slabs, they preserve them for Messrs. Wallace and Gubbins, who have erected machinery on the Sketty brook, north of Oystermouth Castle, for the sawing and finishing of the marble. The quarrymen are induced to be careful, by having for the marble slabs about six times their value as limestone for the kilns . . . This marble is variegated of white, yellow, and liver colours, and some dark beautifully with white."
Walter Davies: "General View Of The Agriculture And Domestic Economy Of South Wales," Vol. I, 1814.

"Before the wars, the quarry provided the only industrial work available in the Mumbles. The grim importance of winning yearly contracts, for example, affected workmen and shopkeepers alike and they would wait around sometimes for the results like an election day count down. If unsuccessful, the firm's contracting section would be practically closed down for an entire year. During the busy years, however, approximately fifty men were employed and retailers in the village, and elsewhere, benefited accordingly by supplying those orders received for tools and materials."
Norton Limeworks Limited.

As in other parts of Glamorgan, the Gower Peninsula is well endowed with deposits of soft and resistant limestone. In centuries past, the economic motivation behind the quarrying of limestone was related to the common use of lime as a manure or fertiliser by farmers from the 16th century onwards and particularly throughout the 18th and 19th centuries. As a fertiliser, lime was and is used in the present century.

The cliffs and high grounds of the Mumbles area possessed ample limestone deposits which were quarried and burned in limekilns by the inhabitants, who built up, gradually, a fairly sizeable, thriving industry. In addition, the existence of numerous, small coal mines, located at such places as Llanmorlais, Penclawdd, Clyne Forest, Sketty, Landore and Llansamlet, provided a further boost to the industry: coal was used in the burning of the lime prior to its utilisation on the land. It was once a common practice for Gower farmers to mix lime with proportions of earth to produce what was termed marl.

The farmable terrain situated near the Gower coastline also benefited by its close accessibility to the seashore which provided man with alternative forms of fertilisers in the shape of sand, shells and especially seaweed. However, their usage was overshadowed by the extensive application of lime manure in the agriculture of South Wales and elsewhere.

The close proximity of some local mines in relation to the limestone quarries of Gower tended to reduce labour and transport costs and the Oystermouth quarries prospered accordingly. In the 16th and 17th centuries, Oystermouth not only supplied farming communities landwards but shipped quantities of lime over to Neath, Baglan and Margam in lighters, open boats useful for short trips although some ventured across the Bristol Channel to the West Country.

Pinnaces which were small vessels with oars and sails as well as barques of limited capacity served in the coastal export of lime throughout the 17th and 18th centuries to supply both the urgent needs of Welsh vale and foothill farmers afflicted with the short-comings of over-shaded, rain-soaked, acid-polluted acres. As a result of the ever-increasing passages undertaken by these same vessels to the South-West Peninsula, the limeless soils of Somerset and Devon were enriched yearly as supplies of this precious manure began to make an impact on cultivation yields. Later, and noticeably in the 19th century, it was the turn of the smacks to participate in this trade, small decked or half-decked coasters, most rigged as cutters, sloops or yawls. Coal would be exported together with lime, while limestone rocks were shipped out, often as ballast, as was the case with the rigged schooners and brigantines of the later decades of the last century.

By the turn of the 19th century, two significant advantages helped towards the growth of the limestone trade. At sea, in company with men-of-war and fishing vessels, boats carrying limestone of ten tons burden or more which entered the harbour or the river were exempted from paying the port dues of 2d. per ton as laid down by the first Harbour Act of 1791. Ready use therefore could be made of the numerous limekilns available within easy access of the Tawe for the burning of limestone into lime.

On land, the opening of the Oystermouth Railroad provided another commercial incentive. Apart from passengers, in the Spring of 1806, the line catered for the conveyance of goods and raw materials; while it remained in operation, Mumbles limestone was brought directly to the river area in horse-drawn waggons.

There were, of course, several other practical, commercial uses made of limestone in addition to its basic exploitation as a fertiliser. The stone was utilised for building purposes, dry-walling and adapted as a substitute for marble ware. The lime-washing of houses was once a widely practised custom. After referring to Swansea's principal manufactures and the mineral deposits of Glamorgan, an 18th century writer, in his 1774 book, "A Gentleman's Tour Through Monmouthshire And Wales," writes that "lime is the general manure of the whole country; and there are few estates, either here or in Monmouthshire, without the advantage of limepits for that purpose. The houses, walls, and out-buildings are commonly whitewashed, and there is scarcely a cottage to be seen which is not regularly brushed over every week."

The limestone quarried in the Mumbles and other parts of Gower was found sufficiently hard enough to be able to sustain a lustrous polish. As a result, during the early 19th century, limestone was used in the manufacture of handsome chimney pieces at Swansea. As a substitute for marble it was also utilised to make mantelpieces, monumental tablets and other articles. Numerous descriptions bear testimony to these activities. Reference is made to the working of limestone in this area by the "Cambrian Visitor" of 1813:

> "The limestone of Glamorganshire furnishes several beds capable of being worked as marble; that at Mumbles is at present worked by Mr. Wallis, Architect of Swansea, who has a mill for sawing and polishing it near the Village of Norton. It is an extremely neat marble, grey of various shades, veined with white, and takes an admirable polish. Very elegant and highly finished specimens may be seen at Mr. Wallis's wareroom in Frog Street, Swansea."

Another 1813 publication, "A Description Of Swansea & Its Environs," printed and sold by a David Jenkin, Castle Street, lists Mr. Wallis together with two other architects, Mr. Powell and the noted Mr. Jernegan. Oystermouth Village is mentioned as being situated near the shore, "under a vast rock of limestone, which from the beauty of its veins has been converted into chimney slabs, and other purposes for which marble is commonly used, and is not inferior in appearance to foreign marble."

The commercial significance of Mumbles limestone, at times, as a suitable replacement for genuine marble is noted by Walter Davies in

Volume I of his 1814 work, "General View Of The Agriculture And Domestic Economy Of South Wales," Chapter III, p. 153, thus:

> "At the Mumbles, in Gower, limestone is raised by the ton, to be shipped off to the coast of Devon, & c. *When the quarrymen meet with approved marble slabs, they preserve them for Messrs. Wallace and Gubbins,* who have erected machinery on the Sketty brook, north of Oystermouth Castle, for the sawing and finishing of the marble. *The quarrymen are induced to be careful, by having for the marble slabs about six times their value as limestone for the kilns.* Poor is the bargain where gain attaches to no side; but here the benefit is mutual. This marble is variegated of white, yellow, and liver colours, and some dark beautifully streaked with white. An elegant specimen of this marble is to be seen at Newfont, at Margam Church, made from an antique model in Lysons' collections."

Farming methods and the application of lime are also referred to by Walter Davies in the same volume, chapter VII, pp. 328-9:

> "In Gower, west of Swansea, sound soil on limestone; *some rich land near the Mumbles,* letting for 3 l., 3 l. 10s., and 4 l. per acre. The Duke of Beaufort grants three lives' leases, esteemed here the best preservatives of land, 'as the farmer finds a warmer interest in the soil.'
>
> "Course of leaseholders for three lives—I. Wheat on fallow, *limed* on the first ploughing with from 50 to 100 stacks or horse-loads (150 to 300 bushels) per acre, and as much dung on the third tilth; 2. Barley; 3. Oats; 4. Barley, with dung and coal-ashes, and lay down for four years without seeds.
>
> "Course of tenants at will, in the same tract—I. Wheat on fallow, *with half the above quantity of lime* and dung, or less than that; 2. Barley; 3. Oats; 4. Barley; and lay down for four years; or as some do, 5. Oats, and oats as long as any can be had.
>
> "On enquiring why turnips and clover were not cultivated? The answer by tenants at will was, 'We are stinted in our tillage; landlords will seldom permit old pasture to be broken; and our arable is so scanty, that we cannot be without a field for a year for turnips or clover. We must have as much corn of one kind or another, as will supply our families and workmen; and corn in the market brings in immediate money for common occasions; without it, we should be obliged to sell our cattle at an improper season, and to disadvantage. Turnips or clover would deprive us of a fourth part of our corn land, already by far too little.'"

"Were those honest farmers able and willing to give credit to turnips and clover only for one year or two," Walter Davies maintained, "they would soon be able to furnish the market with as much corn, and themselves with more money than by their present practice."

In Volume 2 of his "General View . . . of South Wales," published 1815, Walter Davies, A.M., records a detailed account of the limestone trade along the Gower coastline, chapter XII, p. 182:

> "A great trade in limestone is carried on along the coast of Gower in Glamorganshire; several hundred cargoes being shipped off for the coast of Devon, &c. during the summer. The vessels employed in this trade are from thirty to eighty tons burden. The people of the country get a good livelihood by this means; the men dig the stones both winter and summer; and as the vessels trade only in the summer, they get together several cargoes by the commencement of the trade: the men break the stones, after blasting the rocks, to a size easy to be lifted up; the women then, having a horse, and a little staked car made for the purpose, convey the stones to the shipping places within low-water mark; and at high water the vessels are moored alongside the heaps, which are known by poles being fixed in them, and there wait till the tide begins to ebb, when they are thrown into the vessels (by means of a temporary stage) by men and women, who receive a good hire from the captains, with an allowance of beer. The stones are sold by the quarrymen at *the rate of 1s. per ton,* or so much the cargo; there is also a *duty of 2d. and in some places 1d. in each shilling,* paid by the captain to the lord of the manor, for permission to raise the stones.
>
> "Near the *Mumbles,* several perpetual kilns have been erected by Messrs. *Yalden and Pemberton,* who ship off great quantities of lime for the county of Devon: and as coals are here procured at a cheap rate, and *no duty being paid for the lime carried across the channel,* they are enabled to sell their lime to the merchants of Devon cheaper than they can burn it themselves there; especially as the expense of carrying the limestone and coals (for the latter of which they pay duty), is very great . . . Rev. J. Collins."

There were some occasions, however, when limestone was actually shipped back to Swansea, as ballast, from the Plymouth area. Walter Davies recounts:

> "Not withstanding much limestone and lime being carried over the channel from Glamorgan to Devon, yet in return, limestone from the vicinity of Plymouth is brought as ballast to Swansea, and Neath, &c. and from thence, by the canals, up to the lime rocks of Brecknockshire. *This is carrying coals to Newcastle:* but the looseness of the Plymouth limestone in its stratification, and cheapness of ballast carriage, must account for it. Some of the Plymouth stone is beautifully variegated, and has a magnesian feel, very different from the primitive limestone of the middle range, which it here approaches."

Again, in 1823, "The New Swansea Guide" noted the fact that near Oystermouth was "the marble manufactory of Messrs. H. Griffiths and Co. equal in beauty and durability to any in the Kingdom." Norton was mentioned as a hamlet which belonged to Oystermouth.

During the early part of 1850, the quarrying of limestone at the inner sound of the Mumbles Head, below high water mark, came under public scrutiny. For some time previously, the Swansea Harbour Trustees, among others, had filed official complaints to the Admiralty Board that such quarrying operations by certain private individuals posed a serious threat to the security of the Mumbles Roadstead and part of Swansea Bay. In mid-April, 1850, a public court held at the Townhall, Somerset Place, investigated the matter in some detail and heard evidence for and against the allegations in respect of the possible injurious effects likely to be caused to the Mumbles Roadstead by the unchecked quarrying of limestone on Mumbles Hill.

Leading citizens of the day, such as P. St. Leger-Grenfell, chairman of the S.H.T., quarry owners, and other port officials, attended the hearing under the direction of the Tidal Harbour Commissioners' inspectors, John Washington, R.N. and James Abernethy, C.E. Throughout the resulting proceedings, a number of facts came to light. These related to the amount of limestone quarried annually; the shoaling of the inner roadstead caused by the dumping of ships' ballast; the undermining of sections of the cliff edges caused by blasting for limestone; and the effects of sea erosion.

Several observers had witnessed various quarrying activities carried out along the hilly terrain before the commencement of the enquiry. Captain John Edwards, the Swansea Harbour Master, who had been acquainted with the port for some 40 years, had frequently reported back to the Swansea Harbour Trustees about limestone quarrying carried on at the Mumbles below high water mark in the inner sound. The particular work in question had started up during the early 1840's, in about 1844; at the time, Capt. Edwards visited the person responsible, Mr. (Capt.) Phillips, tenant to the Duke of Beaufort, and asked him to cease working any more below the high water mark. This was agreed to and work was curtailed along the edge of the rocks westwards, but afterwards, operations were resumed periodically in other adjacent sections.

The Harbour Master was supported in this contention by a Dr. Bird; both had watched quarrying work in progress along different points which, in their opinion, was undermining the ridges of the inner sound despite what Mr. Phillips said to the contrary. James Abernethy maintained that the men were quarrying "as near the ridge to the east as twelve feet and about twenty to thirty feet westward."

Capt. J. Washington declared himself satisfied that many vessels engaged in the limestone trade discharged their ballast on the Mumbles Beach below high water mark. Such action, he affirmed, was the chief source of the shoaling of the inner roadstead.

Mr. Phillips, a principal witness present at the enquiry made several statements in reply:

"There are two acres of land joined to the Mumbles within the 20 years. None of it goes to the eastward. This accumulation comes, all of it, from the quarrying of the limestone. About 20 years ago, I remember the sea was within 11 feet of my own door; it is now between 50 and 60 feet off. I don't think that a particle of the deposit goes out into deep water.

"I believe that the quarrying does no harm whatever; it is rather an advantage than otherwise. About 3,000 or 4,000 tons are quarried annually at the Mumbles. The limestone is valuable for lime-burning and is sent principally to Swansea, Neath, Port Talbot and the coast of Devon. I have rented the quarry since 1814. Quarrying has been going on at the Mumbles for centuries. There has been more activity displayed there of late in quarrying. About 40 men are employed in the work. There are about 12 quarrying in the sound. There has been very little carried away from the top of the hill for the last three years. I have given instructions not to go very near the ridge. They are not undermining as has been stated today. Some time ago, one of the men did fire a rock in the middle-head, but I immediately discharged him, as he did so contrary to my instructions. That was, in my opinion, the very circumstance that caused all the proceedings that have led to this enquiry. In 1847, the ground was marked off at the request of Mr. Hooper; not a stone has been removed from the top since that time.

"A man might shift about 5 or 6 tons a day by quarrying, but they are not quarrying all the year round. They are dressing 8 months in the year. Upon the whole, I think that the quarrying at the Mumbles has proved a good thing rather than a bad thing for Swansea Port."

George Abernethy was particularly concerned about the possible future likelihood of further damage or silting-up of those waters, close to the shore-line, which normally permitted anchorage of vessels within the Mumbles Roadstead. His account, therefore, bears evidence of a detailed, on-the-spot inspection:

"I observed the men quarrying in two places below the high-water mark; in fact, they were undermining the crest on which the boundary rods were placed by the Duke of Beaufort's agent. They were also quarrying away, below high-water mark, at point F (i.e. marked on a map plan) taking away the jagged points elevated about seven feet above the bottom of the inner sound. They were quarrying so near the crest on the western side of the inner sound, that it must be so severely shaken as to fall down in a short time, and so open the sound as to expose the roadstead very much to the south-west gales."

He was also of the opinion that "the silt carried through the sounds is very prejudicial to the roadstead."

Several conclusions were eventually arrived at after numerous discussions and proposals. Despite Mr. Phillips' protestations, as the sole lessee of the principal quarry under scrutiny, that he endeavoured to confine the quarry-men within the prescribed boundary limits, Capt. J.

Washington reminded him, as well as the Swansea Harbour Trustees' members, of the current penalty for depositing ballast etc. below the high water mark. Each and every separate offence incurred a fine of ten pounds. As a matter of urgency, he maintained further that the Green Grounds should be well buoyed either by the Trinity House Board or the Swansea Harbour Trustees. Others present supported his statements for the despoilment of the Roadstead presented a possible threat to a future expansion of the shipping trade locally and at the port. James Hall, a long standing engineer of the S.H.T. and a layer-keeper to the Duke of Beaufort, also stressed that if the inner sound was widened in any form, such a move would most likely damage the Roadstead. The latter area had to be kept in as effective a state as possible for the sea trade of Swansea and its harbour. In the following year,* a sizeable part of the rocky ground and breastwork of the Mumbles Headland broke away and slid into the sea as a result of blasting activities connected with limestone quarrying.

Within twenty months of the enquiry the North Dock or "Town Float" was realised; it was followed by the South Dock of 1859, the "Swansea Docks" on the west side of the Tawe, as was the North Dock Basin, before the larger docks were established east of the river. In 1858, a Royal Commission on Harbours of Refuge examined the Mumbles Roadstead and produced a report for Parliament which further emphasised the site's importance to the the trading interests of the Bristol Channel at that time.

In addition to other South Wales ports which numbered the export of limestones as one of their shipping interests throughout the 1860's onwards, the Mumbles quarrymen had to compete with two formidable rivals relatively close to hand, the important Pwlldu and Oxwich Quarry localities. By now, Capt. Phillips, of "The Ship & Castle," had died, but his representatives maintained the lease of the Mumbles Quarries from the Duke of Beaufort.

There was little margin left, if any, whereby quarry proprietors of the Gower Peninsula could lower charges per ton loaded aboard ship. Prices offered by the Mumbles tenant-owners, such as Wm. Stephens, averaged from 1s. 3d. to 1s. 6d. per ton; the more durable , finer specimens of limestone, however, fetched higher prices when accepted by the Marble & Stone Works of Rogers & Son, Swansea, for carving into handsome mantelpieces or chimney slabs etc.

Mention may also be made of the medicinal properties of lime itself. These were known to apothecaries in previous centuries; quoting numerous sources, Abraham Rees in his 1819 Cyclopaedia, Vol. 21, declares:

> "Experience has shewn lime-water to be an excellent medicine in many cases; in the gravel and stone particularly. And it has also been found very

serviceable in the gout, in habitual relaxations of the bowels, and in other cases of relaxation. In some kinds of the scurvy likewise it is of use; and is often applied with success externally to ulcers, &c."

The "London Pharm. 1809" outlines one method of preparation thus:

> "Lime-water . . . is prepared by pouring twelve pints of boiling distilled water on half a pound of lime, and stirring them together: let the vessel be immediately covered, and left to stand for three hours; then keep the solution upon the remaining lime in stopped glass bottles, and pour off the clear liquor when it is wanted for use. Lime is soluble in about 450 times its weight of water, or little more than one grain in one fluid-ounce; hence the proportion here directed, is in fact more than is required for the saturation of the water."

Limestone exports fluctuated between 1880 and the mid-1890's as recessions in agriculture made life difficult for farmers. Eventually, some Gower quarries, like Pwlldu, ceased working more or less by the close of Queen Victoria's reign. Those at the Mumbles managed, however, to remain an operative undertaking.

During the latter half of the last century, loading limestone into the small vessels continued to be an arduous, physical occupation. After the limestone was extracted from the quarries, it was piled up in large heaps on the open beach by men, women and youngsters. Then, in the spring, when weather and tide permitted, the ketches or smacks of between 60 and 100 tons burden, arrived from the other side of the Bristol Channel to ship the stone away.

A smack would be beached and moored broadside on, as near to the limestone heaps as possible, and at a point which permitted refloating activities after the craft was fully loaded. Next, a gangway of planks, with supporting trestles, was connected up to the vessel's side and this structure sloped down in the direction of the heaped up piles of limestone rocks. Six or seven hundredweight of stones were then manhandled by individual loaders, placed into large conical barrows, wheeled along the gangway and tipped into the open hold of the vessel.

Loads of 60 tons or more of rough stone for one smack meant a heavy, long day's toil for men working in small groups. The stones had to be lifted from the heaps into the barrow as well as being wheeled upwards to be tipped over the side of the vessel. In addition the gangway would have to be moved from time to time. Short breaks were taken by the loaders, the "lowance time," but it was strenuous work even for strong men.

A true story written by C. W. Slater relates how one loader resolved publically to become a teetotaller if he could load up a smack entirely on his own without the aid of alcoholic refreshment. Failure meant that he would continue to carry on with his usual consumption of strong drink.

Supported by his wife, who supplied him with meals and non-intoxicating beverages during the short rest periods, he successfully completed the self-imposed, Herculean operation to the amazement and admiration of onlooking neighbours and friends. By evening, this personal victory for teetotalism had entailed the loader concerned in about 180 loading and tipping activities before he finally finished filling the vessel's hold with some 60 tons of stones.

In effect, the 20th century history of limestone quarrying in the Mumbles area is principally the story of one local firm, Norton Limeworks Limited, especially from 1918 onwards when the Mumbles Ward was created a part of the Swansea County Borough. With the rising terrain of Coltshill's former quarries in the background, the Company's site of approximately sixteen acres of land at about 125 feet above sea level, overlooks Castle Road or Limekiln Road as it was known in previous years. It was their successive plants which ensured the continuity of trade in this specialised field of industry for more than 50 years.

Norton Limeworks Ltd. was originally formed in 1914 under the ownership of Messrs. Bennett Brothers, Heathfield Yard, one of three noted Swansea building contractors at that time. (The well-established business of Bennett Brothers, Contractors, the builders of the Second Oxford Street Market, 1897, still operates from its Heathfield Yard location). Among previous owners of the limeworks was Thomas Lloyd who was succeeded for a time by his son-in-law, Thomas Thorne, a native of Minehead. Butcher & Co's 1875-76 Swansea Guide refers to the former as the manager of the Norton Lime Company, Coltshill, and a William Belton as manager of the Norton Lime Works Company, Norton.

The pre-War One directors of Bennett Brothers were John, William and Hugh who lived in three adjoining houses they had built for themselves in Montpelier Terrace. Upon the death of Mr. John Bennett, grandfather of the present director of Norton Limeworks Ltd., Mr. David Bennett, his estate in Bennett Brothers was credited with the shares of Norton Limeworks and the family connection with the building firm ceased.

After the return of Mr. David Bennett's father, Mr. Hubert Bennett and his two brothers, Arthur and Benjamin, from active service in World War One, they inherited Norton Limeworks, as did their sisters, Emily and Ethel. The new owners then invested their entire capital in the purchase of two experimental Millars' coal fired Asphalt Plants in order to compete efficiently for an y asphalt contracts won in the growing road development programmes of the 1920's onwards.

Apart from the quarry's deposits of limestone, its proximity to the Swansea Foreshore meant that additional, surplus supplies of sand could be obtained, an economic asset while it lasted. (Afterwards, the denudation of some parts of Swansea Sands and post-War Two preservation schemes, curtailed any exploitation of the beach for commercial reasons).

A Mr. Ernest L. Reynolds, from London, was also engaged as a control chemist and technical adviser to guide the Company in the early days of asphalt road-laying techniques. One of the first persons to welcome him to the Mumbles on the Sunday following his arrival in the early 1920's was the late Cllr. Harry Libby. Mr. E. L. Reynolds, a founder member of the Gower Society, remained with Norton Limeworks Ltd. until his retirement in 1962. Mr. Hubert Bennett became Managing Director of the Company; Mr. A. Bennett promoted to the post of Deputy Borough Estate Agent; and Mr. B. Bennett served as a Bank Manager at Llanelli and Cardiff.

After the installation of the asphalt plants, the firms secured eventually several important contracts, and in particular, those tenders obtained to lay asphalt roads within the borough. On occasions, technicians from Europe would visit the Company to study the current methods of road-surfacing procedure. Business competition was very intense in those days, when frequently, one penny per square yard in excess of other rival bids was sufficient to loose a contract.

Between the wars, the quarry provided the only industrial work available in the Mumbles. The grim importance of winning yearly contracts, for example, affected workmen and shopkeepers alike and they would wait around sometimes for the results like an election day count down. If unsuccessful, the firm's contracting section would be practically closed down for an entire year. During the busy years, however, approximately fifty men were employed and retailers in the village, and elsewhere, benefited accordingly by supplying those orders received for tools and materials.

Quarrying for limestone, more than half a century ago, was a dusty, rough, arduous occupation: men were not paid then for "wet time" but toiled on with sacks wrapped around their shoulders. As was often the case elsewhere in industry, employees worked on Good Fridays and holidays were granted without pay.

A large kiln and a small one were originally maintained on site; drilling was once a hand-operated job undertaken by men working in pairs. Before motorised transport was adopted, horses pulled two-wheeled carts; each cart took a load of up to 20 cwt. Afterwards, local contractors began to use motor lorries, a number of which had been purchased from army surplus World War One sales and in an age of solid tyres, the American "Peerless" and British "Dennis" models, among others, were much in evidence. Norton would hire lorries from such local firms as Messrs. F.

Williams, Hill & Bennett and the Nordhoffs. (The latter, as W. Nordhoff, serves the Company today).

There were a number of practical purposes whereby limestone was used commercially in the past and within more recent times. In graded quantities, loose, broken limestones served as rough and ready road surfaces for many 19th century and early 20th century thoroughfares locally. Tarred roads, for example, were not laid down in Gower until after the First World War.

Block limestone had long been used for building purposes, although, prior to the implementation of legislative directives on the subject, the absence of damp courses presented health hazards for householders. Garden walls were made up from suitably-sized pieces and the craft of the stone mason in the building trade of yesteryear was very much in demand.

As a rule, there was little wastage experienced in the limestone industry. Large mesh-wire rotary screens were used to grade the broken stones into various, assorted sizes. The quarter-inch, half-inch and three-quarters-inch chippings once found favour with many residents who covered their garden pathways with these particular sizes. On occasions, pathway chippings served as inexpensive burglar alarms at night when unwelcomed prowlers gave themselves away as their feet crunched noisily on the tiny stones.

The 1½ in. and 2½ in. grades were, of course, laid down as base foundations for roadways; the 4 in. and 6 in. sizes burnt to produce lime for fertilising purposes; and lime was also utilised in the making of mortar. The lime was mixed with sand and slaked with water until the desired strength or slack was obtained. Years ago and up to pre-War Two times, the lime-seller with his cart was one of a number of street vendors. Lumps of lime purchased for a few pennies were dissolved in water, stirred and used to paint the exterior and interior of many a dwelling or applied as a disinfectant.

The original two asphalt plants at Norton were assembled by Messrs. Millars who obtained parts and sections from other firms based on plans taken from America. This was, therefore, an experimental contract undertaken by Millars whose main occupation at the time was timber importing. Later in the 1920's and 1930's, Millars' standard hot asphalt plants became well-established and were manufactured in four sizes. These possessed outputs of 5/7 tons, 10/12 tons, 15/18 tons and 20/25 tons respectively per hour. Portable models were also available while the dryers could be fired with either solid or liquid fuel. From their early trial plants of nearly sixty years ago, Millars Machinery Co. Ltd., Bishop Stortford, Herts., a member of the Braham Millar Group, has become one of the U.K.'s largest builders of civil engineering and plants concerns.

In circa 1960, Norton's two plants were dismantled for scrap and replaced by more up-to-date machinery. At maximum, it is estimated that each of the former was capable of producing around 10/15 tons output per hour with a 600 lb. mixer; but today's modern plants can average 100/200 tonnes per hour with a 2/4 ton mixer.

Prior to the more universal use of electric power by the close of the 1930's decade, the plants were worked by steam-traction; the drams pulled along by horses; and the crushers operated by gas-engines as were once the drills. Normal daily working hours then commenced at 6-00 a.m. and ended at 5-00 p.m.; two half-an-hour breaks only were permitted for breakfast and lunch times. There were those occasions too, when the plant employees had to work overtime after the quarrymen had finished in order to meet the requirements of a particular contract. Bitumen supplies, for example, used to be delivered in drums; therefore, their contents had to be chopped up the night before and placed in the tanks ready for heating on the following morning. In a rush period, this frequently necessitated some men starting the task at 4-00 a.m. At one time, the drums were conveyed by the Mumbles Railway line's freight section and deposited at its Blackpill sidings to be picked up later by the Company.

It was an era when the average weekly wage amounted to £2. 5s.; overtime rates brought in about an extra 1s. per hour. Foremen did not earn much above these sums, while differentials were measured in pence, generally 1d. more for the drillers and those who wielded the 14 lb. and 16 lb. sledge-hammers. An hourly rate, 1920-30, was around 1s. 2d., but slack periods in the industry could reduce this to 10d. per hour.

Blasting operations were not permitted at night between sun-down and sun-up. Firing took place mid-morning and last thing before finishing in the evening. The explosive charges were inserted into the limestone rock by way of prepared holes of 6 feet lengths; small, stepped terraces were deliberately formed at four, six and eight feet levels down the selected rock face which helped to trap any subsequent loose or falling stones weakened by explosions. The larger, loose stones were drilled and fired, a procedure known as popping; the remainder were hand sledged, hand loaded and conveyed in drams to the plant.

First of all, crushing machines would break up the limestone rocks into various pieces and men loaded these again by hand into a chute system. From here the rocks were dropped into large, steel buckets suspended on a moving conveyor. This "bucket feed" proceeded by way of a rotating drum which was subjected to a specified coal-fired heating process. Eventually, the contents of the buckets were emptied into large wire mesh screens below designed to trap and grade the crushed limestones into ¼ in., ½ in., ¾ in., 1 in., 1½in. and 2½ in. sizes. The graded pieces were then despatched downwards through more shutes to the hoppers beneath.

Rejects, i.e. those too large to drop into the hoppers were collected up and redirected via another chute to the "Devil"... Within an enclosed area, the latter machine consisted basically of large flywheels, the rims of which possessed projecting edges powerful enough to shatter the "misfits" and reduce them to $\frac{1}{8}$ in. sizes if required. The end of the operation involved the heated limestones being weighed and mixed in a mixer to which hot bitumen was added by being hand tipped to form bituminous macadam.

When Norton Limeworks undertook a road surface contract on behalf of the Swansea County Borough, the latter's work force generally made up the road levels beforehand. This was not always the case, however, in respect of private contracts for similar work.

A new limestone pitching road was blinded with fine limestone and dust. This was well-watered afterwards and the resulting composition worked itself into the top surface to form a grouting or cementing cover. Then a base coat of coated material was laid down and rolled by the Company's workers. Next, the wearing or "topping course" of fine, coated material was applied which generally consisted in those days of three parts sand, one part dust and bitumen mixed at Norton in 500 lb. mixes. At times, a mixture of cement was prepared as part of the composite material.

As the hot base material was spread, a lorry, in its turn, would slowly follow along the untarred section and deposit the coated limestone chippings along prescribed lines as directed for the gangs of workmen engaged in the laying process. The man responsible controlled the movement of the lorry and the angle at which its contents were tipped, a skilled procedure, prior to the final levelling work undertaken with forks. When laying the topping or wearing course the material was worked off the back of the lorry. Specific amounts from barrows would be tipped neatly over the bottom part of a man's rake which he held ready in position to spread deftly and evenly between wooden battens. Clumsiness on the part of the lorry personnel or barrow-men caused irritation and prolonged the work in hand.

Steam-rollers of the period rolled in the chippings; small petrol-driven rollers were used on the pavement sections. Today, when slag deposits from steel blast furnaces have replaced limestone chippings which produced slippery road surfaces, large precision-moving machines of ten tons capacity, or more, as those of the "Blaw Knox" organisation, are capable of laying and compacting bitumen tarmac into very even thicknesses on present-day highways, at the rate of up to 100 tonnes per hour on motorways.

Unfortunately, most ot the pre-War Two records were destroyed when the Company's office moved to a new block during the 1960's. Norton's estimate that their pre-War tonnages were around the 20,000 tonnes a year mark, of which, one-third was burnt lime and sold mainly to the Cwmfelin Steel & Tinplate Works, Cwmbwrla, and the remainder as lump lime to farmers. There is, incidentally, a thirty per cent loss of weight from burning limestone into lime.

Output increased sharply with the advent of the 1939-45 War. At the commencement, limestone and lime were rushed daily to the Cwmfelin Works where, at its wartime peak of production, some three thousand people were employed. Lorries transported, on average, 50 tons of block limestone to Cwmfelin; and throughout the war years the Company produced around a hundred drams per day. Each dram, managed by three men and controlled by electric winches, could be filled with between 20 and 25 cwt. of limestone daily. Among other improvements, electricity was used to work the crushing apparatus.

As in other industries, the war brought about a rise in wage rates; working seven days a week, a plant foreman then earned £16 per week and one week's holiday for all employees became a reality. A worker had one week-end off in five, i.e. a Saturday and Sunday; and there was no such thing as a clothes' allowance paid in those days.

During the war, Norton's undertook the essential surfacing of roadways, runways, etc. at Fairwood Aerodrome. On one occasion, a fighter aircraft pilot forced to make an emergency crash-landing, hit one of the Company's steam-rollers which was shattered by the impact. It proved a blessing in disguise at the time, for the plane was heading directly in the path of the Control Tower building. A diesel-roller replacement was supplied afterwards.

The quarry tonnages dropped noticeably after the war when it became cheaper to obtain outside supplies of limestone and steel slag. The production figures fell to around 10,000 tonnes yearly, and it was not long before the entire limestone order was brought in and manufactured at the Norton Works.

The reduction in the use of manpower may be viewed, consequently, as somewhat dramatic when compared with the pre-War Two days of drams, horses and hand sledging work. The opening of a roadway down to the quarry pit during the middle of World War Two replaced the rail and dram system by means of road haulage. (While in existence, the route was referred to then as the "Burma Road," an evocative reminder of the Far East Theatre of Operations). Mechanical loading routines made up for the loss of employees in wartime and with the return of peace former workers here were not substituted by others.

On the plant production side, there were, fortunately, compensatory features. In the post-War Two years, the Company continued to undertake, as it still does, the laying of asphalt roads on contract, and supplied Cwmfelin Steel with lime until that works was closed down, 1957-58, a victim, among others, to the strip mill quality sheets of the S.C.O.W.'s Abbey Works, Margam. Meanwhile, the asphalt plants had been converted to oil-fired heating.

After the passing of Mr. Hubert Bennett, his son, the late Mr. John Bennett, became Managing Director between 1963 and 1971. He was succeeded by his brother, Mr. David Bennett, in 1971. Previously, Mr. D. Bennett had been on the permanent staff of the Swansea County Borough Estate Department as a Chartered Surveyor and Departmental Head.

The loss of the Cwmfelin market was made up for somewhat by supplies being maintained for Bynea Steel and later, Briton Ferry Steel, until it was discovered that the quality of the old, continuous draw type of limekiln did not prove satisfactory enough for the new, swift steel-making processes. Firstly, smaller lime lumps were required, free of all fines; and afterwards, grains of lime were needed to blow directly into the furnaces in order to speed up the heating times now demanded by the steel industry. Consequently, it proved far more economical to purchase the more expensive, high quality lime produced by the gas or oil kilns from as far away as Buxton in Derbyshire.

Furthermore, with the approach of the 1960's, the burning of lime for agricultural purposes had become very much a secondary sales incentive but continued as long as the farmers obtained a grant from the government of the day. When the grant was changed to cover ground limestone only instead of lime, the demand ceased. In addition, a large fault was located in the rock bed which would have entailed the removal of a heavy overburden of clay. Part of the land then owned by the Company was also classified as a zoned area and set aside for cemetery extension. Moreover, limestone could no longer be used for the wearing surfaces of main roads; its application inevitably caused slippery road conditions brought about by the polishing effect created by the chippings. As a result slag chipping replaced limestone.

The combination of these circumstances hastened the quarry's final closure with a working force down to three men. The two kilns discontinued production and were filled in during the early 1960's; these remain today as two stone buttresses within the landscape on Castle Road. The refilling of the quarried area also caused the disappearance of the "Burma Road" and at least half the quantity of rock excavated in years past has been replaced by the filling-in process.

Past and present, the Mumbles families were well represented at the works, and among others, these included: Messrs. Alfred, George and Ivor Baglow; Clifford, Frederick and Sidney Bales; Gilbert and Kenneth Colliers; J. Davies; Alfred Evans; Cyril and Sydney Gammon; Albert, Charles and John Harris; James Manning; Harold Peachey; Frederick

Rogers; Harry Smale; Phillip and Thomas Taylor; Phil. Taylor; and Arthur Williams.

As a result of a £550,000 business merger during April, 1977, the Norton Limeworks Company became a part of the huge English China Clays' Group. Currently, the Company functions under the same name but co-operates with E.C.C. Group's subsidiary, Associated Asphalt, as they are in the same line of business. Norton retains a work force of approximately 60 personnel who are engaged in manufacturing and laying more than 30 different types of coated materials on private and local authority contract works.

The asphalt-making process is a far more sophisticated procedure than hitherto. While limestone, dust and sand are brought in as usual by lorry loads, supplies of bitumen and butane gas arrive in lorry-tankers. Nowadays, within the two plants, an operator sits in a control room overlooking the very large rotating drum and directs the correct intake of mix. He is guided by three large measurement dials headed "Aggregate," "Bitumen" and "Filler," which are worked automatically to produce the desired proportion and flow of ingredients laid down.

Mr David Bennett remains in charge of Norton Limeworks Ltd. and at the same time is a Director of the Company. As an important employer of local labour, the firm's continued presence represents a natural extension today of the surfacing side of business on behalf of E.C.C. in respect of their South Wales market. However, with effect from 2nd October, 1978, the name of Norton Limeworks and the identity of the Company will cease. Instead, it becomes part of the South Wales Section of Associated Asphalt which introduces a new chapter in the history of the plant.

* * * * * *

Recent newcomers to Castle Road are Messrs. Rogers Industrial Equipment Limited, a specialist concern. They are distributors and spares stockists for industrial boiler plants, water coolers, incinerators and pumping equipment. Another service to industry is rendered by the Mumbles Plant Hire Co. Ltd. in Queen's Road.

View from Norton Limeworks Quarry, 1925.

CHAPTER FIVE

THE OYSTER FISHERY

"Further, it may be submitted that local history gives a sense of reality to the study of the past. Otherwise, it may be conceived as a tale that is told. Local history provides evidence other than documentary or written evidence. You can see it around you, if you have eyes to see. There are 'remains'; genuine 'visual aids', as, for example, Earth Works, Castles, Abbeys, Parish Churches, Works, Mills, Factories, siting of towns and villages; the road system; lay out of fields, etc. All these are things you can see. Local history also provides the means of a practical correlation between history and geography."

Sir J. F. Rees: "The Appeal Of Local History In Glamorgan."

"Some dispute has recently arisen as to the claim, by the Lay Impropriator, to certain tithes for depositing the oysters. By an understanding some years ago, the dredgers agreed to pay to the tithe owner thirty shillings a-year each, as a quittance. The collection was not vigorously made, and those of the fishermen who could least afford it, did not pay. In 1860, however, a claim was put in by the impropriator, who maintained his right to levy the oyster tithes—namely, a tenth of the labour of each dredger. This claim is disputed, and the matter still remains unsettled."

"Guide To The Mumbles & Adjacent Bays." Swansea: Published By Pearse & Brown, 22 Wind Street. 1860.

"The smaller yachts did not arouse great interest but their races were good, in fact better than most of the larger races. The local fishing skiffs were not seen to much advantage but the Emmeline *which won, was far and away the fastest boat in the last three or four races."*

"The Gowertonian" Magazine For July, 1913: Regatta Day.

As far back as the late 17th century, the Oystermouth Fishery was stated to possess the best bed of oysters in Great Britain by Thomas Dineley who accompanied Henry Somerset, the first Duke of Beaufort, on his official tour of Wales as Lord President of the Council in 1684. Archaeological excavations at Caerleon and Caerwent revealed that oysters obtained probably from the Bristol Channel were eaten by Roman garrisons. The proximity of their auxiliary fort at Nidum (Neath) and the possibility of a villa once sited in Oystermouth itself, would suggest that the oyster beds of the Mumbles and Gower coastline were not unknown to the Roman forces.

Throughout the 17th and 18th centuries, a trade in oysters had been built up between Mumbles and Swansea, Bristol and Bath; sometimes, barrels of pickled oysters were shipped coastwise to London. Gabriel Powell, lawyer, town burgess and the Duke of Beaufort's steward, also made reference to the oyster beds off Mumbles in his Gower Survey in 1764. Again, their existence is referred to by Walter Davies' 1815 publication, "General View Of The Agriculture . . . Of South Wales," volume, Chap. XIV, pp. 307-8:

> "The limestone coast also of Gower, in Glamorganshire, abounds in oysters. Porth Einion, 16′ W.. by S. of Swansea, employs about 20 boats, four men to each, during the season: those of the Mumbles (Ystum Llwynarth) near Oystermouth, 5′ S. of Swansea, are deemed the finest, and those of Porth Einion the largest. When the fishermen return from dredging, the oysters are deposited, within low-water mark, upon beds which are pointed out by buoys; and when a sufficient quantity are got together, they are shipped off for Bristol, Bath, and the interior counties along the Severn. Dredging begins the 4th of August, which the dredgers keep as a festival: it being the Eve of St. James's, O.S.; that Saint may have formerly been considered as the patron or protector of fishermen.
>
> "The sea shore in Gower is in many places heaps of oyster shells, and the sands full of fragments of them, and broken and abraded limestone: but here, lime being so convenient, little or no notice is taken of these circumstances.
>
> ". . . Other fish abound on the coast of Gower, of the most favourite varieties. The lobsters are uncommonly large, 18 inches in length; and some, they say, two feet and more."

Oyster shells were used by 18th century physicians as a medicine, and recognised by them as probably "in reality much better medicines than many of the more costly and pompous alkalis of the same class." The hollow shells of the oysters were cleaned, dried in the sun, and grounded into tiny pieces in a marble mortar. Dried again thoroughly in the sun, the powdered remains were sifted through a fine sieve. This medicine was especially recommended for stomach ailments. Patients took between 20 and 30 grains of powder once daily within a three or four weeks' period.

As an established staple, the Mumbles oyster trade rose to prominence during the 19th century and in particular between 1850 and 1873. Among other outlets, local dealers found ready markets for their oysters at Bristol, Gloucester, Liverpool and London. Inevitably, the fishery's fame attracted many outsiders who, in competition with local skiff-owners, over-fished the grounds. Such intense fishing activities caused a drastic depletion of the oyster beds to the eventual detriment of the Mumbles, Port Eynon and Swansea boat-owners from the mid-1870's onwards.

In the early years of the last century, the dredgers used heavy, open rowing boats, undecked, and carrying one dredge. These, in groups of two or three, were often pulled by women as they went out to the oyster grounds. Sometimes, when a favourable opportunity occurred, a lug sail was set, namely, a square sail bent upon a yard that hung obliquely to the mast; but the physical toil of rowing these rather clumsy boats, with a heavy dredge trailing behind, was very demanding. Nevertheless, on occasions, the catches were enormous when compared with some of those of later years. Even 20,000 was not an uncommon catch for a single boat.

The men would go out in the morning and take two boatloads before nightfall, but the then relatively low prices, between three and five shillings per thousand oysters on average, restricted great profits being obtained by the fishermen. Within approximately the first forty-five years of the 19th century, about thirty open boats were engaged in oyster dredging operations at the Mumbles.

In his publication, "The Cyclopaedia; Or Universal Dictionary," of 1819, Vol. 25, Abraham Rees records some general observations about oyster breeding and fishing in the U.K., wherein one section states:

> ". . . In the month of May, the dredgers, by the law of the admiralty court, have liberty to take every kind of oyster, whatsoever be their size . . . After the month of May, it is felony to carry away the clutch , and punishable to take any other oysters, except those of the size of a half-crown piece; or such as, when the two shells are shut, will admit of a shilling to rattle between them . . . There are great penalties, imposed by the admiralty court, upon those that fish out of the grounds which the court appoints, or that destroy the clutch, or that take any oysters that are not of the proper size, or that do not destroy a fish which they call the five-finger, the common sea-star, because that fish gets into the oysters when they gape, and sucks them out."

According to an authoritative account written by W. Ll. Jarvis, in 1896, about oyster dredging at the Mumbles, outsiders to the fishery were not uncommon prior to the 1850's. Smacks, generally those small decked or half-decked coasters and fishing vessels, rigged mostly as cutters or sloops, used to arrive here from London or the east coast, and take away cargoes, selling the large oysters and planting the smaller ones on the artificial grounds round the mouth of the Thames. In 1845, one of these smacks took away 200,000 oysters, and often, there were five or six at the same time waiting to be supplied. Later, during the mid-1860's, numbers of French luggers, small vessels with two or three masts, running bowsprits and long or lug sails, used to trade between the Mumbles and St. Malo and Arcachon, and take immense quantities back with them to lay down there where they developed into new, flourishing beds.

There were also sailing skiffs based at Swansea in the 1830's used for dredging purposes; but it would appear that the Mumbles dredgers only operated the old open row-boats until about circa 1845, when a certain Captain Phillips had one of these boats decked and rigged for sailing. This system did not prove too successful maintains W. Ll. Jarvis, and then, circa 1849-50, the first of the early type of 19th century skiffs, the "Pearl," was brought to the Mumbles from Bristol. This type of skiff was cutter rigged, i.e. a small vessel with one mast, a mainsail, a forestaysail, and a jib set to bowspritend; it was of narrow beam and deep draught, registered about seven tons, sailed well and was quite adequate for dredging work. S. C. Gamwell's "Guide & Handbook To Swansea And District," 1880, refers to the arrival of the first skiff as "The Seven Sisters," so named in honour of the Mumbles owner's fair daughters, but this statement cannot be verified.

Doubtlessly, the sailing qualities of the English East Coast smacks impressed a number of the Mumbles boat-owners. Consequently, as Carl Smith, local historian and member of the Mumbles Lifeboat, in his concentrated, three-part history of the Oyster Industry, ("Ostreme' 75" booklet) relates:

> "In the early 1850's a group of Mumbles men travelled to Essex and ordered a number of cutter rigged craft from the boat builders of the area. They were about forty feet long with a bowsprit projecting over 15 feet. The mast was stepped forward and reached forty feet off the deck. These new boats carried about a thousand square feet of canvas."

More skiffs of the Essex style of design appeared on the scene, many now Mumbles-owned, and by 1863 the total of oyster dredging craft numbered 144; of these, between 70 and 80 belonged to the Mumbles, while the remainder came under Swansea and Port Eynon. Among the 144 craft, a few could not be classified as skiffs because they were the old open rowing boats still being used in the trade, some rigged for sailing as in the late 1840's. With the pre-dominance of the oyster skiffs by the 1860's, the majority of the old lug boats fell into disuse and were subsequently beached on the sandy seashore.

A "Guide To The Mumbles & Adjacent Bays" published by Pearse & Brown, 22 Wind Street, Swansea, in 1860, also noted that between 50 and 60 skiffs as well as boats were engaged in the oyster fishery which gave employment to upwards of 250 hands during the season. The dredgers received an average of 9s. per thousand oysters from the retailers at this time; these were resold in England at prices ranging from 6d. to 8d. per score, or 2s. 6d. per hundred up to 25s. per thousand. The oyster season commenced on the 1st September and ended on the 31st April; between the months of May and August, dredging activities were not permitted, a ruling which could be enforced, whenever necessary, by the watchful eyes of the Mumbles Coastguard service.

A local custom celebrated for many years in the last century, the Oyster Fair, took place on the inauguration of the oyster season. At the skiffs' owners' expense, the dredger crews were liberally supplied with bread, cheese and beer; it was a truly festive occasion and a profitable one too as far as the tavern-keepers were concerned on the day. Afterwards, this time-honoured custom fell into disuse brought about probably by economic necessity and the eventual decline of the industry during the last quarter of the 19th century.

Pickled oysters provided another retail outlet and served as an additional source of food for local consumption. After being stewed and pickled, the oysters were preserved in jars; many were purchased by summer visitors or despatched as appropriate souvenirs of the neighbourhood. Larger quantities were stored in barrels and shipped coastwise as in the previous century.

Oyster dredging was an arduous occupation in which accidents at sea occurred along with the occasional fatality. An example of one dredging death was reported by the weekly "Cambrian" dated the 9th May, 1856, in respect of one, Thomas Jenkins, aged 34. The inquest was held at the "Ship and Castle" before C. Collins, Esq., Coroner.

> "Thomas Williams, mariner, stated that on Tuesday, the 29th April, the deceased and a man named William Howell went out dredging for oysters in a small skiff belonging to Mr. Wintle of Bristol. The skiff was under his charge. They were in Oxwich Bay and the deceased and William Howell were raising up the dredge by means of a winch, worked by two iron handles; one was at each handle. I was holding on the rope. The dredge caught in the ground which caused the winch to reverse, and the men were compelled to let go the handle, but the one which the deceased had hold of struck him in the forehead and he fell insensible on the deck. There was a severe wound from which a great deal of blood flowed; the bone was fractured near the left temple. We bound up his head and placed him below and then made for the Mumbles. Deceased did not survive and scarcely spoke a word up to the time of his death, Tuesday, 6th May. Verdict, accidental death."

Throughout the 1860's and early 1870's, when more and more vessels were dredging the bay than the natural increase of oysters could really support because of the over-fishing activities, the demand for Mumbles oysters increased apace with a subsequent rise both in prices charged and wages earned. The early 'Seventies was a time when upwards of 600 men were employed in the industry; and often one boat would catch 6,000 or 7,000 oysters in a day. Men earned £3, £4, £5 and sometimes £6 a week during the successful seasons.

Regrettably, many a hard-earned week's wage was squandered away in the Mumbles public-houses of the day. The evils of excessive drinking during the second half of the 19th century were much in evidence here as elsewhere locally, and were to engage the fervent attention of Temperance campaigns for many years to come. One somewhat upstanding anonymous citizen recorded the following impression of his visit to the Mumbles during the winter of 1865-66:

> "The staple traffic is in oysters which are dredged from the sea outside the bay. The main bulk of the villagers are employed in this dredging and the trade is a lucrative one. Everybody connected with it seems circumstanced and we are assured that no class of working-man have a better chance of being comfortable in life than the fishermen of Mumbles. Drunkenness seems to be the bane of the village; vacancy of mind being the consequence."

There were periods throughout the 19th century when oysters were consumed daily by Mumbles families as part of their normal diet. We are reminded of this fact by Dr. P. E. King and A. Osborn in their detailed dissertation, "Oyster Dredging," published in 1969. They reveal that:

> "During the years of peak production, oysters were almost the basic food of many Mumbles households and almost the earliest food of many Mumbles-born youngsters. The oysters fried in an omelet; oysters in breadcrumbs or in a 'carpet bag,' a steak an inch or an inch and a half thick, sliced inwards, filled with oysters and grilled. The most unusual combination however, and the one usually eaten on the skiffs whilst dredging was fried with bacon. These would be prepared on the small stove in the forecastle. This compartment, situated in front of the mast, had benches or lockers, but no specially built bunks, and the crew would sleep in these quarters during trips away from Mumbles. Some skiffs used to work off Stackpole for a week during August and would shelter for the night in Tenby, the crew remaining on board. During the summer months five or six skiffs made the voyage to Whithorn in the Clyde, to dredge for oysters. It normally took several days to get there and the season lasted for six weeks. Usually a telegram reporting safe arrival would be sent to one family who would then pass on the information to the others."

The period 1864-1872 witnessed the emergence of those skiffs which survived into living memory. The maximum number of skiffs working between 1870 and 1912 was 188, in the year 1871. This figure included the Swansea, Mumbles, Port Eynon and Porthcawl dredging craft. In all, there were 225 registrations listed on the Custom House Fishing Vessels' Register at Swansea from first to last, that is, from 1869, when the 1868 Sea Fisheries Act came into force, and up to 1939, when the dredging ceased.

In the first "Ostreme '73" Pageant's booklet, Carl Smith refers to the prosperous times thus:

> "At the peak of the trade in 1871 nearly 16 million oysters were landed and were sold for nearly £50,000. At that time the industry supported about six hundred people, apart from a number of owners who didn't work in the trade themselves. Over five hundred crewed the one hundred and eighty skiffs, forty men and women worked the perches and plantations, and then hauliers carried the catch to Swansea."

However, the ill effects of millions of oysters being taken away or destroyed without regard to age or fitness began to be felt before the mid 1870's. Until 1871 there was no public control of the fishery. On the whole, the Mumbles dredgers observed fairly well a closed season of the three summer months but the locals maintained that the Swansea craft and other vessels dredged during these months which resulted in a great deal of friction and ill-feeling. Finally, after the passing of the Sea Fisheries Act in 1868, measures were taken to obtain its protection and the Swansea Fishery Order, 1871, was obtained for "regulating the Oyster and Mussel Fisheries in Swansea Bay."

This order fixed the close period to the months of June, July and August, and, moreover, prohibited the taking of oysters of less than two inches in diameter. It also decreed that all oyster skiffs should be licensed. The Corporation of Swansea at that time were appointed to enforce the order.

Among the leading supporters for stricter dredging operations was the "Cambrian" newspaper. Frequently, its columns had drawn attention to the serious situation then developing as well as pinpointing different types of offences. Its edition for the 21st August, 1874 stated:

> "The Conservators of this Fishery have resolved to close a portion of it, namely, that shut in by an imaginary line drawn from the Mumbles Head to the Sker Weather Lightship, for the space of two years. This may be roundly stated as including the whole of Swansea Bay. We cannot say that this severe sentence is wholly undeserved on the part of the skiff owners. Many remonstrances have appeared in the columns of the Cambrian against the folly and injustice they were perpetrating in fishing the Oyster all the year round.
>
> "The poor bivalve was allowed no time for breeding and mothers with countless millions of young were destroyed in the summer months to fill the

> hands of the greedy and tickle the depraved palates of bibulous pleasure-seekers. *We acknowledge in this matter that the public are as blamable as the dredgers* . . . in eating oysters out of season they are virtually eating carrion. A breeding oyster is a thoroughly unwholesome fish."

Condemnation was also directed against those professional breeders who constantly sought after the "parent oyster and the ill-developed youngster" and the newspaper urged and supported any energetic action undertaken by the Swansea Town Council. Some skiff owners countered by suggesting that the sea area under scrutiny should be closed only for nine months in each year.

The harsh realities of a worsening situation were unhappily felt by the Mumbles fisherfolk during 1874-75. In its edtiion for the 25th February, 1876, the "Cambrian" brought to light the misery then prevailing in the village.

> "For years past, the oyster fisheries have been wretchedly bad, and, when the late precarious weather is also considered, it will be seen how slender has been the means of obtaining anything like a livelihood.
>
> "Families averaging from seven to ten persons, have been unable to earn more than from 8s. to 10s. per week and may not even earn this amount; and much poverty and distress consequently abound; in fact, we have been credibly informed that many familes have been compelled to live upon bread and water, and even of that scarcely enough to sustain life . . . a few benevolent gentlemen have inaugurated a soup kitchen, from which some 50 gallons of good, nutritious soup are weekly distributed amongst the more necessitous. It is intended to continue this Christian work until the end of March, if not later . . . Mr. R. H. Hancorne of the Mumbles will gladly receive subscriptions."

The heyday of the trade had passed by never to return on the same scale again. The depletion of the oyster beds bears witness to this fact as the following figures reveal: 1873 saw 9,050,000 oysters landed at Mumbles, nearly half the 1871 total; and by 1875, the year of the great depression, the numbers had slumped dramatically to 3,810,000. During 1876 onwards a large number of skiffs were either laid up or sold to other ports as fishing craft, yachts, etc., and this reduction continued up to cira 1888.

From 1880 onwards, the fishery declined still further after which prices fell markedly. The lowest ebb was reached in 1886. Then a day's catch of 200 oysters was considered a good amount at a period when the total force of skiffs had fallen to under twenty vessels. Boats that had cost originally between £200 and £250 to build were sold off gladly for £30 or £40. Many were bought at firewood prices and broken up while a few were up-ended and converted into temporary sheds.

By 1883 there were 47 skiffs working in the oyster industry at Mumbles; 24 skiffs in 1888; 25 in 1898; 18 in 1908; and 14 in 1914. For those remaining in the trade, a limited revival suggested itself during 1891-92, due principally to the small number of skiffs then engaged in dredging operations which permitted some of the exhausted beds to pick up again. Even so, by the mid 1890's a man was fortunate if he averaged £1 a week for a season.

As a rule, the Mumbles skiffs, when not working away, dredged within the vicinity of Swansea Bay and could soon seek the safety of the Roadstead anchorage if a gale sprang up. The latter was exposed, however, to the effects of any severe south-easterly winds but provided a natural refuge for vessels if gales hammered the coastline from a south-westerly direction. On occasions, a fleet ran into difficulties at sea as was the case on the morning of the 29th April, 1882. The skiffs' predicament on that particular day was described by "The Cambrian" edition of the following week:

> "On Saturday morning last, the Mumbles and District felt the effects of the severe gale which continued throughout the day veering from SE to SSW. The Mumbles fishing fleet left Stackpole fishing grounds on Saturday morning and long before reaching the Mumbles Head had felt the full fury of the gale; yet they struggled on for the Mumbles and ultimately got to the bay, having lost a portion of their canvas etc. Some got to their moorings in safety, while others had to throw out their anchors but to no effect, for they would not hold on, and the boats were soon drifting towards the dangerous shoals off the Mumbles Head.
>
> "The lifeboat crew seeing the perilous condition of the boats went off to their assistance, and took out sails, spars and men to those that were in peril, and put them on board boats. The boats were re-rigged with the canvas . . . and they were eventually brought to their moorings."

In his "The Men Of The Mumbles Head," Chap. 1, p. 15 Carl Smith identifies the three particular skiffs in trouble as the "Gertrude," "Gladstone," and "Shah," and that the gallant "Wolverhampton" lifeboat, under coxswain, Jenkin Jenkins, was manned by some of the dredger-men who had only just landed safely from the accompanying skiffs. The newspaper's dramatic conclusion noted that "the continuance of the danger was heart-rending, by reason of the agitation of the wives and children," who formed part of a large crowd who witnessed the rescue operations from the hillside.

This alarming event contrasts sharply with a far more peaceful scene viewed from the Mumbles hillside ten years earlier. Instead, a relatively calm, colourful panorama is recorded by the Rev. Francis Kilvert in his diary dated the 18th April, 1872:

"This morning we drove to Mumbles, the Westhorps, Miss Brown and myself . . . A tramway runs along the road side from Swansea to Mumbles upon which ply carriages drawn by horses.

"Oystermouth Castle stands nobly upon a hill over-looking the town and bay. The lurid copper smoke hung in a dense cloud over Swansea, and *the great fleet of oyster boats under the cliff was heaving in the greenest sea I ever saw.* We had luncheon upon the cliffs overlooking the white light-house tower upon the most seaward of the Mumbles.

"A shepherd was holloing and driving the sheep of the pasture furiously down a steep place into the sea, and a school of boys came running down the steep green slope, one of them playing 'Rosalie the Prairie Flower' on an accordian as he ran.

"A steam tug shot out of Swansea Harbour to meet a heavily laden schooner under a full press of canvass in the bay and towed her into port, *and the great fleet of oyster boats which had been dredging was coming in round the lighthouse point with every shade of white and amber sails gay in the afternoon sun* as they ran each into their moorings under the shelter of the great harbour cliff.

"As we went along the narrow cliff path among the gorse towards Langland and Caswell Bay, a flock of strange and beautiful black and white birds flew along the rock faces below us towards the lighthouse piping mournfully. They were I suppose a small kind of gull but they seemed to me like the spirits of the shipwrecked folk seeking and mourning for their bodies. Among the sighing of the gorse came upon the lift of the wind a faint and solemn tolling of a deep bell from seaward. It was the tolling of the buoy moored off the Mumbles, a solemn awful sound, for the bell seemed to be tolling for the souls of those who had gone down at sea and warning the living off their graves.

"When we came down from the cliff and were going through the town to our inn a furious whirlwind of dust arose and everything was hidden in a dense white cloud. People were obliged to grope for the walls of the houses and cry out to carriages which they could hear but not see not to drive over them!"

In 1883, Swansea Corporation's powers to control the fishery season were transferred to the Oystermouth Local Authority whereupon the regulations were made more stringent due to the forceful representations applied b y the Mumbles skiff owners. The close-time for the whole area was increased by one month, May, and dredging in Swansea Bay proper was confined to the months of December, January and February; while it was also laid down that no oysters should be taken which could be passed through a three inch ring. The advantage to the dredgers of the extension of the close-time for Swansea Bay was that it gave the beds a greater opportunity for improvement; and that part of the fishery, which was near home and more sheltered than the other, was reserved for those months which possessed the shortest days and usually experienced the worst weather. Another transfer of control powers took place in 1891 from Oystermouth to the Glamorgan Sea Fisheries Committee.

Among some of the well-known Mumbles skiff owners of the 1880's were (surnames in alphabetical order):
Captain Barrett, W., Sailors' Home, Swansea; Bennett, Susanna, Beaufort Arms; Bennett, W., Sheffield Place; Bevan, W., Park Street; Burt, W.; Davies, D.; Davies, J., Commercial Place; Davies, L.; Davies, Martha, Southend; Evans, D., Sheffield Place; Gammon, James, Clifton Terrace; Gammon, Richard, Clifton Terrace; Howells, D., Southend; Jenkins, James; Jenkins, Jenkin, Clifton Terrace; Jones, John, Sea View; Jones, Matthew, Westward Lane; Lloyd, D., Church Park; Lloyd, James, Overland; Matthews, J., Sheffield Place; Michael, D. E., Sheffield Place; Morgan, W., Clifton Terrace; Morris, W.; Powell, Stephen, Clifton Place; Powell, W., Oddfellows' Inn; Thomas, Hewitt, Gower Place; Thomas, John, Horsepool; and Webborn, J., Glass Row.

A number of the Mumbles-owned skiffs were built locally during the 1860's and 1870's at the Port of Swansea and on the Mumbles Beach. Numerous others came from the South-West Peninsula ports such as Bideford (Devon) and St. Ives (Cornwall). Messrs. R. and T. Bennett of Church Park, E. Prickett, "Marine House," were among the Mumbles boatbuilders and repairers of oyster skiffs. The oyster dealers possessed their own perches but these required rental payments made to the Duke of Beaufort.

The Mumbles skiffs did not only dredge Swansea Bay but worked as far east as the Nash, then all down the Gower coast as far as the Helwick. They also worked out of Tenby, where they dredged the Tenby and Caldy beds, the Stackpole beds, and other hauls in the vicinity.

Some of the old skiffs were used as floating workshops with sheds erected on their decks. One belonging to a Captain Davy Evans was well-known in its day, being nick-named the "Ark."

Along the beach sections near to Mumbles Head were once located a large number of "Perches" used b y the fishermen. Oyster perches were rough and ready divisions of the foreshore or small enclosures formed by lines of large pebbles, just above low water mark, with a floating log which marked the territory by each dredger. When an oysterman had completed his day's catch, he would steer his skiff to these perches in front of the village, made fast to his own particular log, tipped the oysters overboard and left them to feed until they were required for sale.

Outside the perches, so far out that they were uncovered except at spring tides, were similar enclosures known as "Plantations." In these the oyster merchant stored the main stocks of oysters during the close season, and here, any of these which were below the legal standard of size for sale were retained until they had grown to marketable bulk. The oysters on these plantations and perches needed constant care and attention. They had to be carefully spread over the ground, for if they were allowed to lie in heaps they soon died off.

Thousands of oysters were destroyed annually by their natural enemies among which could be numbered the starfish and whelk. The latter shell fish when cooked by part-boiling and then fried with bacon, made a palatable breakfast, and consequently were gathered in by the dredgers and others as an additional source of food to eat as well as sell. Whelks could also be pickled for winter consumption.

The five-rayed starfish, termed locally the "five-finger" were sometimes so plentiful that they formed a solid mass a foot thick on the bed and caused enormous damage to the oysters. Mussels too, sometimes, destroyed large quantities; at times they spread like a pall over an entire bed and killed everything that was under them. In addition, a hard frost at low tide, when the oysters were uncovered, would destroy them by the thousands in spite of preventive measures such as covering them with mats and old sails as soon as the tide went down. The severe Spring weather of 1895 killed off more than 150,000 oysters when the tides were at their lowest.

In their desire to seek out the mussels, limpets and periwinkles, some 19th century day trippers could disturb, damage or sometimes simply steal the oysters from the available perches. It was not uncommon for fights to break out between watchful dredgers and unmindful visitors.

The oyster skiffs, craft of about seven to nine tons, were usually manned by three men or dredgers. As a rule , one skiff towed two dredges; a single dredge weighed nearly eight stones.

When a skiff arrived at one of the hauls the two dredges were thrown overboard, and the boat sailed slowly along, or usually, if there was a light wind, drifted sideways, until the dredges were full. The dredge itself was was a bag-shaped net, of which the bottom or "belly" was constructed of iron rings, and the "back" of netted cord. The "foot," a wooden bar, kept the end of the dredge open and straight while the mouth was of iron, with a scraper called the "sword" which drew the oysters into the net. Iron "arms" connected the net with the ring to which the dredge rope was fastened. The dredge rope, about sixty fathoms long, was fastened to a winch on deck and the subsequent winding operation was operated by two of the dredgers.

It was laborious work; and in the early days of skiff dredging could prove to be an extremely dangerous occupation as referred to previously. Then the vessels did not possess a pawl (i.e. a short bar lying against a toothed wheel to prevent a windlass etc. from running back), or check, to ease the strain when the skiff jumped or the dredge caught the ground. When this happened men's arms were almost torn from their sockets and if the dredgers failed to hold the winch in such a situation, its handle would spin round rapidly and cause a severe accident or even death. The unexpected warping of a vessel's rope could also ensare a man's legs and drag him overboard to his death.

Eventually the dredge was hauled up on deck and the contents turned out. The oysters were separated from any "trash" and the latter was returned to the sea together with the very small oysters. Then the skiff was put about and the dredging continued again until the state of the tide compelled the fishermen to finish for the day. When they reached their particular moorings, the oysters were thrown on the perches where they were sorted, and the bulk put on the plantations until required for market or until they had grown to the required size.

During the period circa 1876-78, several local skiff owners made contracts with a number of London merchants to dredge oysters for them. The location was at Luce Bay in the Solway Firth and the London merchants had rented the oysters beds for a fixed period.

Consequently, for two seasons, a number of Mumbles skiffs sailed northwards and dredged for Scottish oysters. On these occasions they were away for a month or so and it was understandable that the relatives of the men concerned, in those days of large families, viewed these particular operations with some concern and anxiety.

On one of these voyages, the Mumbles skiffs experienced a particularly heavy gale and news of this event caused a great deal of worry to the relatives. Fortunately, as W. Ll. Jarvis recalls, there was a happy if somewhat amusing ending in store for those villagers awaiting confirmation that the menfolk were safe and sound. On the morning after the gale, one of the Mumbles owners of the skiffs received a a telegram from Tenby worded thus: "Arrived all safe in Caldee Roads; me, one more, and another". It took a little time afterwards for the skiff owner to find out exactly who "me, one more, and another" were precisely!

Successful dredging locally depended upon so many changing circumstances. A good season could never be guaranteed or even two consecutive days' work at times, and dredging was impossible during strong winds. Sometimes in winter, the skiffs remainded idle for days and weeks due to prolonged, stormy weather. Chance played a part too; one skiff could have located good "strings" of oysters one day while another equally skilled group would have dredged practically nothing but stones.

Some guide to 19th century prices may be judged from the following account selected from an oyster merchant's books. However, the catches quoted were rather below than above the average, for prices varied greatly from season to season.

In the season 1869-70, the "Pearl" caught 89,200 oysters which were sold at 32s. 6d. a thousand; in 1870-71 she caught 80,000. During 1871-72, the "Sally" caught 140,900 at 45s. per thousand; and in 1873-74, the "Wasp" caught 68,000, sold at 62s. 6d. At the end of 1874 prices rose to 75s. and 80s. per thousand. In 1877 the prices were 70s.; in 1878, 1879 and 1880, 77s. 6d.; in 1881, 79s.; 1882, 87s. 6d.; 1883, 80s.; 1883-1886, 75s.; 1887-1889, 67s. 6d.; 1890, 65s; and in 1895, between 55s. and 60s. By the mid-1890's, a skiff would catch, on a good day, around 800 oysters which would earn each man nine shillings; but the average catch represented only about 500. Consequently, some weeks a dredger-man would pick up £2 or more, while at other times he would be lucky to obtain a few shillings.

The oyster beds of the late 19th century and onwards were situated between Nash Point and the Helwick Lightship off Worms Head. Within this area scores of beds or "hauls" were scattered about over the bottom. The exact location of these hauls was accomplished by taking bearings from objects viewed on the shore or nearby land formations. A dredger had to take bearings immediately a new haul was discovered so that he was able to return to it. Here and there, some of the beds were only a few feet wide.

The local dredges were usually made at the Mumbles Smithy of John Henry Libby, the father of the late Cllr. Harry Libby. J. H. Libby, a ship and general smith, worked in his first forge at the Ship & Castle Quarry, i.e. behind the Conservative Club, and afterwards, on a site which is occupied today by the squash court of the Bristol Channel Yacht Club, Southend. In respect of these dredges, Dr. P. E. King and A. Osborn state in page 3:

> "The type was unique to the area. It was approximately 110 lbs. which is much larger than those used on the East coast at that time and had an iron drag curving down to the scraping blade, referred to as the 'sword.' In other parts this was called the 'scythe.' It was presumably given this name because of its scraping action on the bed but also perhaps because it had to be returned periodically to the smithy for resharpening. The blade was normally 4-6 inches wide, but some much-used ones became half this width and often had strips attached to them to widen the blade again. The opening to the bag was between 3 and 4 feet wide, which is large for a hand dredge but it was only 4-6 inches high. In most dredges the bar connecting the arms of the iron drag is some distance from the 'mouth' so leaving a wide opening but in the Mumbles pattern this bar is near the 'sword' so narrowing the mouth. It has been said that the dredges often contain more stones than oysters and although no record has been found, the narrowing of the mouth suggests that it was done to exclude larger stones. The beds

were, and still are, very stony and in places small rock projections must have presented problems. Boats under sail from Port Eynon would beat against the Westerly wind to Rhosili or Pitton then turn and put over their dredges and work in an Easterly direction but to avoid well known snags on the sea bed, navigation had to be accurate. The purse or bag was connected to a wooden bar by four 'eyes' at its posterior end and to the 'sword' at the other end by a series of 'S' links. The ventral part of the belly or purse and part of the postero-dorsal were made of iron links or 'O's' of two sizes, the larger ones called rings, had a diameter of approximately 2 inches and the smaller ones, called joiners were less than half this diameter, their role being to connect the rings. The diameter of the rings determined the size of oyster taken."

Oyster skiffs gliding off Southend, or already out at sea on a fine day, their reddish-brown sails glistening beneath a sun-lit sky, must have presented a picturesque sight to those visitors with an eye for colour and detail. It was formerly a common practice to dye or stain the ropes and sails of fishing craft a brown colour by the application of powdered bark obtained from oak trees.

Some unusual names were given to particular hauls and among these may be listed: the Fenian Hall, off Pwll Ddu Head, found at the time of the Fenian scare; Metz, discovered during the Franco-German War, 1870; Abyssinia, off the Scarweather Lightship in 1871; and the Bantam Haul which ran from Oxwich Bay to near the Helwick Lightship, but three or four miles from the land. In particular, the Metz was one of the best paying beds ever found, for at that time oysters were worth 70s. per thousand and the catches here were both extensive and rewarding.

Then there were the Hen and Chickens, Musselly Haul, Itchy Poll, Trashy Ground, Robin's Patch, Middle Drift and Duck Haul. California, Red Hole and East India were sited in Swansea Bay. The Zulu bed, found off Barry during the Zulu War posed problems at times for the dredgers. Although thick with oysters, it was a rather small bed which attracted too many skiffs on certain days from different harbours. Some craft fouled each other continuously and ended up hopelessly entangled. On several occasions, skiffs were forced to run ashore in order to avoid being run into and sunk. Quite a number of the hauls were also named after the men who had discovered them such as Jenkin's Haul, Llewellyn's Haul etc.

In the hey-day of the dredging industry, it was not unusual to see numbers of old skiffs, no longer sea-worthy, drawn up and placed as high and dry as the curve of the shore would allow. Inevitably, some of them were used as store-houses, carpenters' and sailmakers' sheds, places where longshore work was carried out without fear of interference from officialdom. Later, however, the seawall replaced much of what had been a nicely-shelved beach, against which these skiffs frequently dashed themselves to pieces throughout the stormy periods of winter. Time and tempest eventually disposed of them all.

As some form of compensation for the disappearance of their natural haven, the Mumbles Railway concern constructed a wooden groyne for the boat-owners. Unfortunately, Oystermouth U.D.C's refusal to preserve it and the subsequent severity of some gales throughout the Edwardian era hastened its extinction.

There were numerous occasions throughout her lifetime when the much admired "Emmeline," SA 14, displayed her true worth as a swift sailing craft. "Mermaid" in his particular contribution to "The Gowertonian" school magazine, volume 3, no. 3, dated July, 1913, refers to her highly successful partisipation in the Swansea Bay Regatta held at the Mumbles on the 18th June of that same year.

> ". . . The next race was for the fishing trawlers, five of whom started, but the wind was not strong enough and a poor race, or shall we say, a drifting match was won by the Hermes. Great interest was taken in this event because it was for the Prince of Wales' Cup, but the race was disappointing.
>
> "The smaller yachts did not arouse great interest, but their races were good, in fact better than most of the larger races. The local fishing skiffs were not seen to much advantage but the *Emmeline,* which won, was far and away, the fastest boat in the last three or four races."

One of her closest contenders in this regatta was the "Scorpion." The latter skiff was one of those vessels built at Bideford.

By the turn of the century, there was a marked decline in oyster dredging. Many boats which were family owned had to be sold and with the outbreak of the Great War in 1914 there were just under a dozen skiffs left in the Mumbles. The defence of coastal waters in wartime, 1914-18, and the fact that many men formerly engaged in oyster dredging now joined the Navy, caused a severe curtailment of activities in an already much reduced oyster industry. Nevertheless, some fishermen remained in the oyster fishery trade and more than one million oysters were brought ashore in 1920.

In that same year, however, a virulent, mysterious virus attacked the oyster beds of Europe. As a result, the fertile but equally frail oysters deposited along the European coastline were almost destroyed outright by the "Great Death." In common with some other United Kingdom oyster localities, the 1920-21 disaster signalled the end virtually of the Mumbles oyster trade. In addition, quite a number of local dredger-men who returned home after the first World War, looked for regular employment within the various industries of Swansea rather than contend with the irregular working periods, insufficient wages and diminishing returns then associated with oyster fishing.

Prior to the second World War, two smacks worked the grounds, the "Rising Sun" SA 22 and the "Secret" SA 74. Both were motor auxiliaries built in 1926 and 1928 respectively at Appledore. There were also two other motor craft which did a little oyster dredging, the "Morning Star" and the "Kathleen" but these were rather too small to be classified as "smacks."

The last of the Mumbles sailing skiffs, the "Emmeline," SA 14, was laid up during circa 1930-31. She was one of those working vessels which ended her days with dignity both as a working craft and yacht. Another companion and late stayer was the "Hawk," SA 24.

The "Emmeline" was built by William Paynter, of St. Ives, in 1865, for William Burt, a notable 19th C. owner of Mumbles skiffs. It was a type of skiff similar to the one used for oyster dredging at Colchester in Essex which was adopted for use in the Mumbles by approximately the middle of the last century. There is a handsome model exhibit of the "Emmeline" on display in the maritime section of the National Museum of Wales, Cardiff, donated by the "Friends of the National Museum of Wales."

There is also housed within the Royal Institution of South Wales, Victoria Road, Swansea, a large, striking model of a Mumbles oyster skiff, the "Beaufort," SA 22. Of ten tons burden, she was registered on the 3rd March, 1869, Master, Stephen Powell, and her original owner being Thomas Richards. Eight years afterwards, the SA 22 was sold to Cardigan, out of register.

By the 1930's, the oyster beds had ceased to be of any significant value commercially, except, perhaps, in a rather limited sense, when these could be sold and purchased for immediate local consumption. The very much reduced fishing activities for oysters throughout this decade came to a close with the commencement of World War Two.

Any strong hopes of even a minor post-War Two revival in the trade were soon curtailed by a realistic report written by H. A. Cole, D.Sc., (Principal Naturalist, Fisheries Department, Ministry of Agriculture & Fisheries), in 1949 for the South Wales Sea Fisheries District Committee. He also produced a paper on "The British Oyster Industry And Its Problems" in 1951. Among other factors, the former account entitled "Swansea Bay—Mumbles Area Oyster Fishery," established that the remaining inshore beds were extremely polluted, while the idea of restocking the offshore beds was considered not to be a viable economic proposition. The report reads as follows:

> "The area was *surveyed* during the period February 27th-March 5th. I was assisted by Mr. R. H. Baird, of Conway, and Lt.-Cmdr. T. A. Gibson,

Clerk and Chief Fishery Officer to the South Wales Sea Fisheries Committee.

"At my suggestion Lt.-Cmdr. Gibson had spent four days dredging on the outer grounds in the Bay during the week preceding our arrival, and we were, therefore, able to concentrate on the inner grounds and the shore in the vicinity of the Mumbles.

"Particulars of all the dredge hauls taken are summarized in Table I (attached).

"It will be seen that no commercial concentration of Oysters was found anywhere, and that the proportion of young Oysters (under 3 inches in diameter) was very small.

"The shores of Mumbles Bay were examined at low water on March 1st, when, owing to the prevalence of offshore winds during the preceding few days, there was a very good ebb. The remains of the 'Plantations,' formerly used for storing oysters prior to sale, were uncovered and were examined. Only one live oyster was found, in the vicinity of the Pier. There was abundant evidence of sewage pollution throughout the Bay in the shape of fragments of paper, tea, leaves, etc. A sample of Mussels was collected from the foot of the pier legs, and on bacteriological examination at Conway was found to be grossly polluted.

"The oyster beds in Swansea Bay were for practical purposes in the open sea. The young oysters produced by parent stock on these beds would be widely dispersed by tides and currents during the 10 to 14 days of their free swimming life. Even when the beds were actively worked, only certain areas of bottom offered suitable surfaces for the attachment of Oyster Spat, e.g., the Road Hauls, White Oyster Ledge, Green Grounds, etc.

"To obtain any appreciable settlement of spat on these widely scattered areas it would be necessary to produce a sufficient concentration of young oysters, in the pre-settlement stages, in the overlying water. Since young oysters take 10-14 days to complete their development, even under the most favourable conditions, it is impossible to prevent the wide dispersal and great dilution, in such open waters, of larval oysters produced by parent stock laid down close inshore. To produce a dense concentration of larval oysters over the formerly productive beds, at the end of the free-swimming period, it would be necessary to lay down very large amounts of breeding stock. Only in this way could the initially dense multitude of larvae needed be provided. This would require the laying not of thousands , or tens, or even hundreds of thousands, of oysters, but of millions. To realise the truth of this conclusion it is only necessary to recall that before the great oyster mortality of 1918-20, when the beds were thriving, *they produced annually a million or more saleable oysters.* This implies a stock of at least 5 and, more probably, 10 million oysters of all sizes on the grounds. To produce a similar concentration of oysters' larvae now it would be clearly necessary to lay down breeding oysters in similar numbers, i.e. by the million.

"Even if it were possible to find the money to purchase French oysters in this quantity, there is still another more serious difficulty to overcome. In order to provide surfaces on which the young oysters would settle it would be necessary either to cultivate the bottom over a wide area or to lay vast quantities of shell clutch. The purpose of the cultivation would be to uncover clean shell on the old grounds on which the spat would settle. Unless this work was done much of the value of the new breeding stock would be lost, since on uncultivated grounds surfaces suitable for attachment are few and widely scattered. On beds which are thickly populated with oysters the necessary clean surfaces are provided in the main by the shells of freshly dead oysters and the new fringe of growth on the edge of the shell of living oysters. These are supplemented on efficiently cultivated beds by the laying of clutch and extensive harrowing of the bottom. With few and widely scattered parent oysters such surfaces are very scarce, and consequently the quantity of spat settling is very small. The old cultch, overgrown and encrusted with worm tubes, barnacles, and corallines is useless.

"To undertake the necessary cultivation on the scale required, over a wide area, would mean the employment of numerous boats and men during the early summer months. It would be quite impossible to find or pay men on the scale required. The conclusion is reached, therefore, that revival of the Swansea Bay oyster beds as a self-supporting fishery by this means is out of the question.

"There remains the possibility of establishing a relaying, as distinct from a breeding, *fishery.* On such a relaying fishery, half grown oysters, usually three years old, are put down annually and taken up for sale when sufficiently well-grown, usually 18 months later. There are a number of such fisheries in the country which are profitable under favourable conditions. Often no particular attempt is made to obtain naturally set spat from the oysters laid down but, incidentally, a small amount is often obtained, particularly when the beds are established in shallow land-locked bays or river estuaries.

"It would be possible to lay down French oysters in the Plantations at low water springs, beside the Mumbles Pier, or in the Roads Haul, and to fish them for sale when sufficiently large and fat. If the Plantations were utilised the oysters could be collected and cultivated from the shore, but in the Roads Haul dredging would be necessary. These are the only two areas sufficiently sheltered for this type of fishery. Unfortunately there are several very serious objections to this form of oyster culture in this particular area. Firstly, it is very highly polluted by sewage, and it would not be possible to sell oysters for direct consumption without purification. In practice this would mean either the erection of a purification plant at a capital cost of at least £10,000, and possibly much more, or the selling of oysters for relaying on grounds elsewhere not affected by sewage pollution. The necessity for relaying oysters elsewhere since it is considered that the cost of purification would be prohibitive in this particular set of circumstances, would halve the returns from the oysters landed and would indeed make the whole proposition doubtfully economic. Secondly, the re-establishment of oyster beds close inshore, in dangerous proximity to the sewer outfall, would be unsound from a Public Health point of view. It would be practically impossible to ensure that oysters were not sold in small quantities, direct to the public at the Mumbles and in Swansea, without purification, or to prevent the public from poaching small quantities for their own use. The

> general prevention of poaching in such an easily accessible area would also require an almost continuous watch. The establishment of a relaying fishery in such unfavourable circumstances could only be justified if there was a substantial number of inshore fishermen, without an adequate livelihood, interested in the venture. There is no evidence that this is the case.
>
> "It is not practicable to undertake re-stocking and cultivation on the vast scale required to revive the offshore beds in Swansea Bay.
>
> "The establishment of an oyster fishery, based on the relaying of imported oysters, in the Plantations area at the Mumbles or on the Roads Haul, while possible, is not recommended, as the area is grossly polluted.
>
> "The long and well documented history of the Mumbles Oyster Fishery must now be regarded as closed. It is probable that the beds have now reached equilibrium, and the small natural population now present may be expected to maintain itself almost unchanged , until some new cataclysm, e.g. exceptional mortality due to disease, abnormally severe weather or poisonous industrial effluent, causes a further reduction or complete extinction."

Meanwhile, in addition to man-made pollution problems, the nation as a whole felt the effects of the very severe winters of 1947-48 and 1963-64, when even the sea waters round our coastline froze. A repetition of such circumstances together with the possibility of future flooding damage caused by exceptionally high tides are some of the situations committees have to bear in mind in relation to any proposed schemes to restore former oyster fisheries of the United Kingdom.

During the early 1960's, some 35,000 oysters were spread about the foreshores of West Wales in an effort to revive a once flourishing industry. The Welsh contribution to a resurgence of the oyster trade of the U.K. lies, perhaps, in the present work undertaken at the government research centre in Conway, North Wales. Here, the eggs from such species as the fast-growing Pacific Oyster are reared on treated sea water and food particles created on site. Protected within the hatchery's battery environment, the small oysters are then transferred to farms after approximately six to eight weeks. Under further scientifically controlled conditions, these ripen into seed for sale commercially or later develop into fully-grown oysters.

Mumbles Oyster Vessel, 1875. *Permission of Swansea City Council*

Mumbles Oyster Vessels. Circa 1875. *By permission, Roger David Studios*

Circa 1880's and prior to the loss of the skiffs' lay-up enclosed by the Mumbles Railway embankment of 1893.

By permission, Roger David Studios

Mumbles 1888. *By permission of Swansea City Council*

Era prior to the Mumbles embankment, 1893. Note the camera apparatus and tripod in the foreground and fairly crowded natural harbour in the background.

By permission, Roger David Studios

Mumbles Railway Embankment 1893.

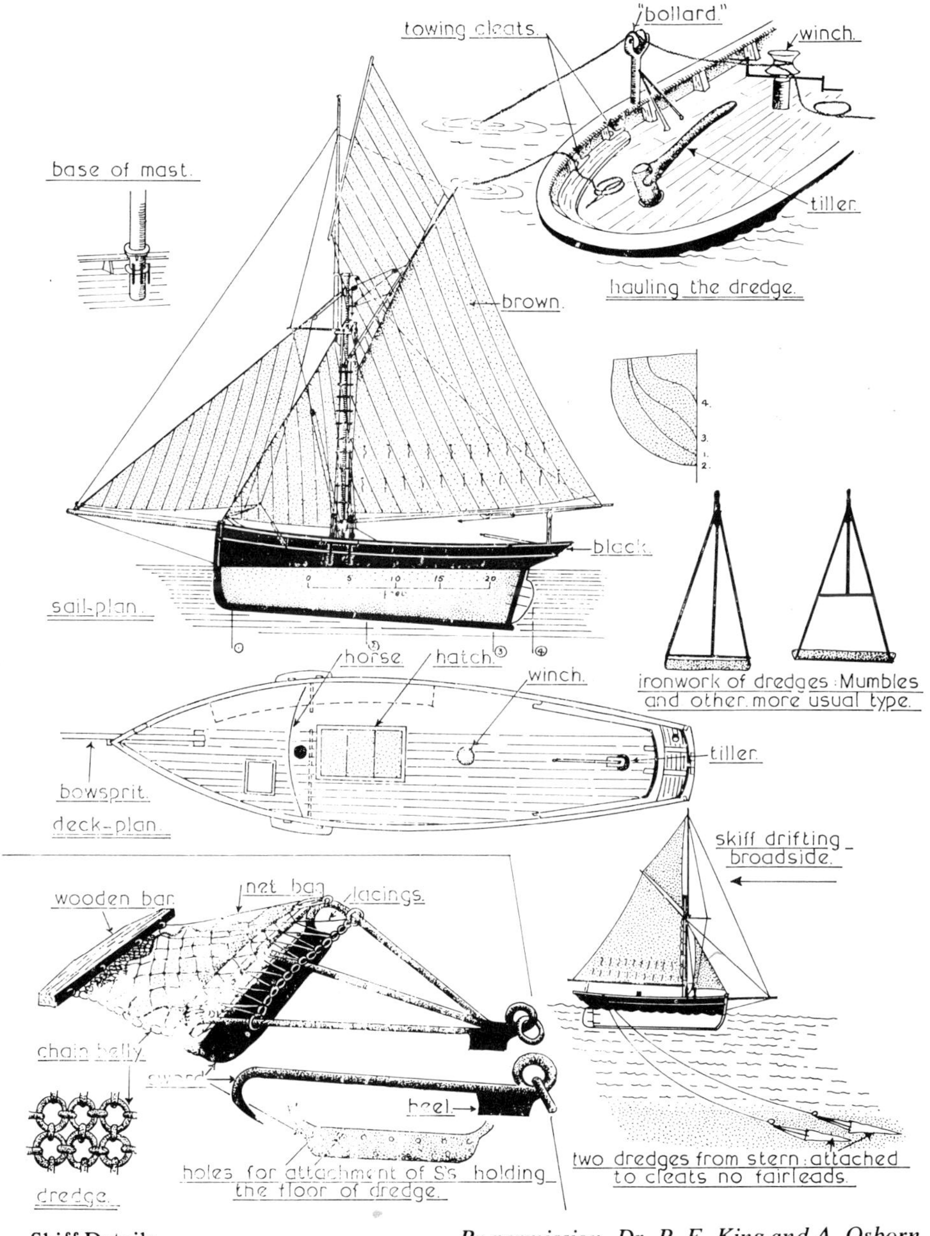

Skiff Details

By permission, Dr. P. E. King and A. Osborn

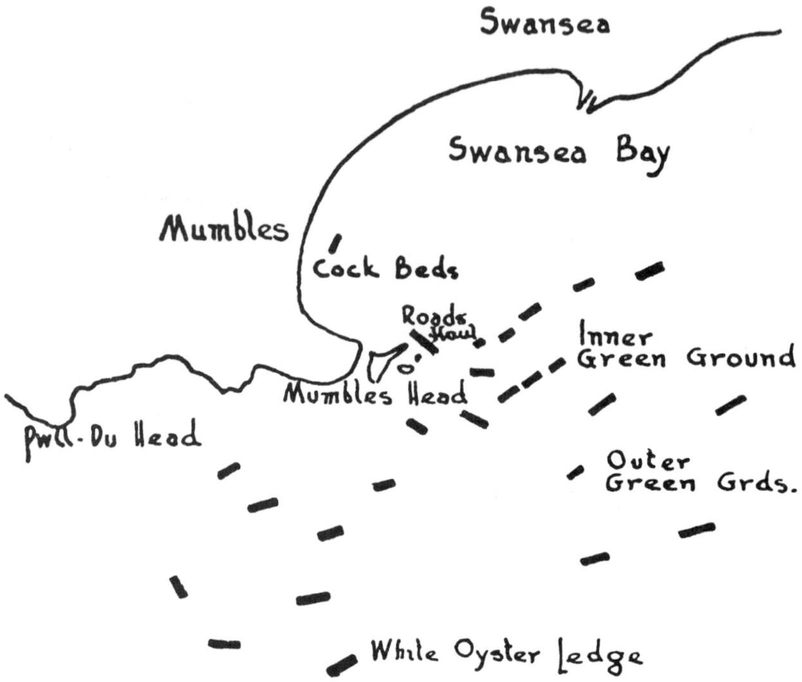

SWANSEA BAY & MUMBLES AREA OYSTER BEDS

▬ ~ Oyster Beds Examined Feb/March 1949

CHAPTER SIX

WATER SUPPLIES AND ASPECTS OF PUBLIC HEALTH

"The use of history is to give value to the present hour and its duty."
Emerson: Society & Solitude: Works & Days.

"The rocky plateau spreading east and west and facing the Atlantic, is being more and more recognised as the future residential quarter of this district. Its southern slades expand out into the sandy bays of Bracelet, Langland and Caswell, which from their shelter and picturesqueness constitute the attractive charm of this place to visitors. Bracelet Bay has been already opened out by road and railway, and when this sea drive is continued under the cliffs to Langland and thence to Caswell, we may be prepared for an important addition to our present responsibilities."
A. Lloyd Jones, M.O.H.: "The Annual Report For The Year 1901, On The Oystermouth Urban District."

"Again, do you know where the five ships are in the Mumbles that have never been out to sea? They will be found at Langland Corner, and are the work of stonemasons who built the wall around the house known as 'Gilberts Cliff.' Look carefully the next time you pass it. . .

"No one can really ever tire of the many views that Oystermouth and Mumbles have to offer residents and holiday-maker alike.

"Even at night-time, your interest is maintained, especially in the summer season. Stretching from the pier, through Southend into Oystermouth Square, are the overhead multicoloured light bulbs linked from tree to tree, while following the curve of the coastline towards Swansea, is a line of yellow beacons whose rays penetrate the sudden inrush of sea mists and fogs.

"Another night scene is provided by the yachts and small boats at anchor in the shadow of Southend: dark shapes silhouetted on a silver tide when the moon is out, or the white hulls of laid-up vessels caught in the glare of evening lights from nearby buildings or passing cars."
N. L. Thomas: "The Story Of Swansea's Districts And Villages." Enlarged Edition, 1965.

As mentioned in Chapter One, the need for adequate supplies of drinking water within the Mumbles area became increasingly apparent from the mid-1850's onwards. While the wells and shallow streams of the district proved sufficient for local needs throughout the 18th century, and early 19th century, the subsequent rise both in population and dwellings began to emphasise the lack of drainage facilities as well as limited sources of unpolluted water. Sewage matter permeated those sections of ground adjacent or near to buildings and a number of wells were contaminated as a result. At one time, it was not unusual, in such localities as Newton, to see notices erected which displayed the warning message that "The water of this well is not fit for cooking or drinking purposes."

In some respects, perhaps, an economic motive lay behind the proposals for a more effective improvement in the sanitary conditions of Oystermouth at this time. There were those prominent citizens of Swansea & District who visualised Oystermouth as a kind of 19th century "Brighton" of West Wales and any such development would have provided an outlet for a number of commercial projects. Although several reservoir schemes were investigated during the 'Fifties and 'Sixties, it was not until the late 1870's that a positive plan of action materialised. Hitherto, it was maintained, the absence of a satisfactory watershed had proved something of a stumbling block.

In circa 1879, a private undertaking produced a workable project and obtained a provisional order for the construction of a service reservoir at Kiln Green, Newton, which was to be linked to a system of mains from a spring located at Caswell Bay. The spring was tapped at the point known as the Freshwater Caves, at the western corner of Caswell Bay. Other water mains from the Kiln Green Reservoir were to be installed to supply various parts of the Mumbles. The original promoters of the scheme, as the Oystermouth Waterworks Company Ltd., were: Messrs. R. W. Bear, solicitors, Swansea; Mr. H. Ludlow, Neath; and Mr. W. Whittington, engineer of Neath.

The "great reproach," noted "The Cambrian" for the 5th May, 1882, "which has attached itself to the Mumbles for the last two generations has been wiped off. Oystermouth has now a water supply." The weekly newspaper also reminded its readers that, "Nature has done everything for Oystermouth; Art has as yet done nothing."

Of the opening ceremony it was stated:

> "Actual operations were commenced about six months ago (late 1881). Major Morgan of Caeforgan, having purchased the water rights under his land from His Grace the Duke of Beaufort, transferred them to the Company. The work was designed by W. Whittington and the contract for laying the pipes &c. was undertaken by Mr. W. Jones of Neath (late of the firm of Jones & Jepson), contractors.

"These works consisted of the blasting of the rock in Caswell Bay, so as to allow of the placing of a powerful steam-pump at the mouth of the spring, a 5 inch main pipe thence to the service reservoir at Kiln Green, a 4 inch main to Dunns and Church Park, Mumbles, and other supply pipes within the district, extending as far eastward as the West Cross Post Office. The Company has power to extend its supply as far eastward as the high level railway bridge at Blackpill.

"The district proposed to be supplied by the Company comprises the greater portion of the parish of Oystermouth, and a part of Bishopston. The number of *houses* already erected in the area is no less than 1,000, with a *population* of about *4,000* and a *rateable* value of *£14,000.* (The 1881 census recorded 3,915 inhabitants).

"It is estimated (dry season) that about 260,000 gallons per day can be obtained from this source which will be sufficient to supply 65 gallons per head of the present population or 20 gallons per head for a population of 13,000."

The pumping engines and boiler were built by Dyne Steel & Son, engineers of Swansea, who supervised operations on the opening day. The component parts consisted:

". . . of a pair of inverted steam cylinders, each 12 inches diameter which work two rams, each 7 inches diameter and are capable of pumping 7,500 gallons per hour. They are fixed, as well as the boiler, which is of the vertical type, 14 horse power, fed from the rising main, about 15 feet above the water well and the water is forced by them through 1,800 yards of pipes, 5 inches diameter, to the reservoir, which is situated at the top of the hill, 270 feet vertically above the pumping engines, giving a pressure of 125 lbs. per square inch of water due to this height and against which pressure the engines have to force water."

While its installation was a move in the right direction, the limitations of the small pumping station were publically acknowledged by the Urban District Authority towards the close of the 19th century. The availability of water supplies via the Newton Reservoir scheme was restricted to a period of several hours per day; as more houses were put up, this was further reduced to about two hours daily, a state of affairs which continued to exist throughout the early part of the 20th century until after the end of the First World War, at a time when Mumbles had been absorbed into the County Borough of Swansea during 1918. Moreover, particularly high tides at Caswell tended to penetrate the source of the fresh water spring within the limestone strata here and consequently produced a salty taste to the local water supply on such occasions.

Supplies were supplemented in the usual manner by collecting rain water in wooden barrels or galvanised containers as well as making use of existing wells. There was also a limited number of public pumps within the area: at Southend, for example, one was placed near the Antelope Inn and the other close to the George Hotel.

As a whole, however, the water supply proved insufficient to meet not only the increasing requirements of householders and market gardeners but also those demands of local farmers who needed water to wash out their dairies, cow-sheds and outbuildings. Prior to the turn of the century, councillors at their U.D.C. meetings had more or less agreed that a possible solution to the problem rested in their hands if they could purchase the Oystermouth Waterworks Co. Ltd. at a negotiable figure.

During 1893, the mains were extended to Dickslade and Tichbourne but Newton and Norton remained inadequately supplied. It was during periods of drought in particular that the reservoir failed to meet local needs. The summer drought of 1894 was but one example when water supplies became barely intermittent at best. Such occasions added to the burdens of the respective Medical Officers of Health who knew that the inhabitants would resort to the use of well water which was frequently subject to pollution of one kind or another. People were warned repeatedly to boil water obtained from streams, brooks and wells, before they drank it. Under the Public Health Act of 1875 and its subsequent amendments or additional statutory decrees conferred by Acts of Parliament, it was the M.O.H.'s arduous responsibility on behalf of the Urban District Council, as directed by the Local Government Board, to prevent or contain infectious diseases; maintain healthy surroundings and conditions; and inspect as well as supervise those important aspects in respect of sanitary arrangements such as sewerage, refuse disposal, roads, houses, workshops, dairies, cemetries and water supplies etc.

By 1901, the pumping-station, at the mouth of the Caswell Basin, had been equipped with two oil engines which pumped about 12,000 gallons hourly along the five inch pipe into the reservoir above Newton situated at an elevation of approximately 270-280 feet. The reservoir possessed no filter bed and supplies remained intermittent during the few hours each day it was in operation.

In contrast, the volume of water which emerged from the Caswell source was estimated at the time to average 50,000 gallons per hour. This constant supply was further augmented directly after rain, and yet was not seriously diminished during the drought periods. Unfortunately, the restricted storage capacity of the reservoir prevented a better and more adequate use being made of the seemingly abundant flow and overflow from the foot of Caswell Hill. The reservoir was shaped like an inverted short pyramid, the perpendicular of which was approximately 15 feet and its side twice that measurement. The inflow pipe entered at one angle of the surface while the outflow pipe emerged from the apex at the bottom. As a result of this somewhat obsolete pattern, the greater body of the water was practically stagnant at the other angles and sides, conditions which produced deposition and growth. Moreover, the small reservoir was also uncovered and provided a natural haven for the flourishing growth of insect and vegetable life in its still crevices; frequent scavenging hardly kept the water clear in these circumstances, especially during the summer season.

Irrespective of Rural Sanitary Districts, Oystermouth was one of 19 Urban Sanitary Districts which featured in "A Sanitary Survey Of Glamorganshire," 1895, by William Williams, M.A., M.D., the County Medical Officer. Its short account reveals a number of interesting aspects of public health and social conditions of the time. The district was recognised as a "well-known watering place" with a constant population of some 4,000 inhabitants, "which is considerably increased during the summer months," within a limited area of 2,615 acres.

The report noted the inadequacy of the water supply as a whole and advocated its extension to the villages of Norton and Newton as well as the closure of suspected, contaminated wells. Of the sewerage system, it was written:

> "There is one long sewer about a mile or more in length, laid under the main street. From this there are cross branches connected with the side streets and dwellings on the higher level. The main sewer has but a slight gradient, and extends from West Cross to South End. At West Cross there is a flushing tank, which is said to be emptied only once a fortnight. At South End the sewage is collected in a tank and emptied into the sea at every spring tide. The villages of Newton and Norton are not sewered. The slight gradients of the main sewer is a source of annoyance, and this renders flushing the more necessary.
>
> "Disposal of Excrement, Refuse, &c. There are about 280 water closets, 500 pails, and some 130 privies within the district. The contents of the water closets enter the Authority's sewers, but the pails are periodically emptied and their contents disposed of with the street and other refuse. The villages of Norton and Newton are entirely unconnected, and without the statutory distance. Slop and surface water is allowed to accumulate or to flow in open surface channels.
>
> "The pail closets are emptied twice weekly by the sanitary staff."

Housing accommodation was described as follows:

> "Many of the houses are of the better class, and occupied by business people. The smaller houses are in a fair condition, except some in the villages of Norton and Newton, and in Village Lane. There are no common lodging-houses within the district, no back-to-back, no cellar, and only a few back-to-earth dwellings. There are some houses without through ventilation . . .

"There are four slaughter-houses, and with one exception, they cannot be said to be fit for the purpose. They have been lately registered."

Those visitors on holidays, or even day-trippers, who sometimes explored the village background after experiencing the obvious delights of the district's marine walks and views during the mid-1890's, would not have failed to notice that the streets, lanes and numerous areas in and around dwelling-places presented a neglected appearance at the time. These were often unpaved and not drained sufficiently while many of the smaller abodes were damp simply from want of eavespouts.

It was also then one of the few districts within the county which had not implemented the regulations laid down by the "Dairies, Cowsheds, and Milkshops Order of 1885." Therefore, it was impossible to ensure efficiently that premises, cattle and milk were maintained in adequate hygienic conditions.

In 1902, "The Annual Report For The Year 1901, On The Oystermouth Urban District," compiled by the Medical Officer of Health, A. Lloyd Jones, D.P.H. Camb., was published. The author's detailed survey contains several far-seeing observations, reveals a practical administrator of imagination who was determined to bring about an effective improvement in the health and social welfare of the district. Some of his statistics, facts and comments are as follows:

"The incidence of the decennial Census with the year 1901 gives us a correct estimate of the population of the district. On the 31st of March last year there were 4,460 persons accounted for, including 33 on board vessels in the offing, and of these, there were 1,920 males and 2,540 females. The number of inhabited houses on the same date was 1,017, giving a dwelling rate of 4.38 per house, as compared with the 4.5 inhabitants for each house at the former census. The total number of houses in the district was 1,145; viz., the 1,017 inhabited, 38 uninhabited, 81 unlet, and 9 uncompleted houses. Our estimate for last year was 800 in excess of the actual population, owing to the inclusion of other rateable property than dwelling houses, to be a deficient allowance for unoccupied houses, and to the exaggerated dwelling-rate handed down from the preceding census . . .

"The area of the district is as of old 2,615 acres in extent, which gives a rate of 1.7 inhabitants to the acre. In this connection it may be pointed out how desirable it would be if the adjoining parishes of Bishopston and *Brynau* could be united with Oystermouth for sanitary purposes, and so make the three parishes co-terminous with the parochial Eastern District of the Gower Union. The other 16 parishes of the Gower Rural District would still cover an unwiedly area, whereas the delimitation of the above two would make with Oystermouth a compact square, that would obviate the overlapping of parish and public-health work as at present."

In many respects, the healthy climate of the district made up for the shortcomings of the sanitary arrangements which existed during the end of Victoria's reign. This was borne out by the low general death rate recorded for the years 1893-1901 but it was noted that, as in other neighbouring rural and town areas, whooping-cough among very young children was still the dreaded killer. Of 77 deaths listed in 1901, the M.O.H. wrote:

> "Eighteen died in infancy (12 under one and 6 under 5) of whooping-cough, diarrhoea and convulsions—death more or less preventable, and nearly always accelerated by chronic or acute food poisoning. The 9 from whooping cough equal the high death rate of 2.01."

However, in 1901, the whooping-cough rate for other County Urban District fell below Oystermouth's at 0.35; the five cases from diarrhoea also worked out at 1.12 as against the County Urban rate of 0.7. Eight died of heart disease, mainly in advanced age, the result of early rheumatic fever.

The M.O.H. recognised the fact that:

> "As the nature of the soil has an important bearing on residence we enjoy the advantage in this district of the larger area being on dry rock, covered over in parts by a light layer of glacial drift. To this natural circumstance, rather than to sanitation, we owe much of the salubrity of this seaside resort; for whatever contamination the surface may be subjected to from cesspits and refuse heaps, the next shower helps to wash it away into the innumerable fissures below."

Aspects of future housing developments were also correctly visualised thus:

> "The rocky plateau spreading east and west and facing the Atlantic, is being more and more recognised as the future residential quarter of this district. Its southern slades expand out into the sandy bays of Bracelet, Langland and Caswell, which from their shelter and picturesqueness constitute the attractive charm of this place to visitors. Bracelet Bay has been already opened out by road and railway, and when this sea drive is continued under the cliffs to Langland and thence to Caswell, we may be prepared for an important addition to our present responsibilities. As this sea slope is eminently fitted for bungalows, it is to be hoped that no rigid bye-law for nine-inch walls will debar intending residents establishing these tenants' fixtures if they choose; for so long as they conform to other sanitary requirements these detached residences must be healthier than jerry-built houses in a row."

(The subsequent housing expansion did materialise but beyond the scale perhaps ever envisaged by A. Lloyd Jones and others. Nearly eight decades have passed since the M.O.H.'s publication; yet sparse farmland still continues to decrease in acreage today as more houses emerge on the sky-line. The disappearance of Woollacott's Farm, Thistleboon, is another recent example while permanent holiday bungalows have mingled with Neo-Georgian private residences approaching Plunch Lane from the Limeslade Bay direction. Post-War Two pre-fabricated dwellings on either side of Fairwood Road, West Cross, have now been replaced by well set-out houses and flats, suitably landscaped, to form a particularly attractive municipal development of the late 1970's).

Topographical descriptions of the early 19th century frequently referred to the lack of winter sunshine at Southend due to the close proximity of the cliff formation which overlooked this section of the village. The continuance of such circumstances tended to create a health hazard:

> "The abrupt Thistleboon headland unfortunately so over-shadows the Southend and Hallbank extension of the Mumbles, that during the winter months this locality receives little or no sunshine and thus loses a vital factor towards cleanliness and healthiness. Upper Church Park shares part of the same drawback, and has on occasions shown an exclusive preference for diphtheritic troubles."

Council members were left in no doubt about the shortcomings of their sewerage arrangements or the inadequacies of the water supply system at the turn of the 20th century, although some improvements in other aspects of public health had been put into effect since the County M.O.H.'s 1895 report. (However, it was not until Mumbles had been oficially embraced within the Swansea County Borough extension of 1918 that its sanitation problems were eventually resolved by the town's network of sewers being laid down together with the installation of huge storage tanks under Mumbles Hill between the early 1920's and mid-1930's. New pipelines then linked up Mumbles with the Cray reservoir , built between 1892-1907, during the same period, and from the mid-1950's onwards, the Mumbles Ward was receiving the benefits of the huge Usk Reservoir operation as well as subsequent projects).

Edwardian Mumbles was to experience numerous emergencies in connection with its sewerage system which A. Lloyd Jones' report reveals:

> "Our sewer system consists of a main sewer along the sea front, from opposite West Cross Hotel to beyond the Oyster Perches and near the Pierhead, with five supply branches, viz., from Norton, Castleton, Upper and Lower Church Park, and Thistleboon. Its commencement is *provided with an inconstant flushing tank supplied by the Company's water,* and near its extremity at Southend is a valve opened and closed with the ebbing and flowing tide. The fall in this sewer curve of one mile and three quarters

is barely 15 feet, consequently, it has no scour, and necessitates several manholes en route for the clearing of its sediment and sludge. The diameter of this circular main sewer is only 18 inches, and it has to meet the supplies of tributary sewers of 15, 12, 9, 9 and 9 inches respectively which when full make nearly the double the volume of the main (or as 612 is to 324). The result of this insufficiency is that during storm-floods *fountains of sewage* issue out of the manholes, and that with the growth of the district an enlarged main will become an early necessity. Every facility is made for the separation of gutter water, but roof and yard water still enter the sewers.

"The sewerage of Newton is partially completed to include Nottage and Newwell Lane, the village proper being so far left as an open drain. This incomplete system discharges itself onto the Underhill fields, which during winter months present the spectacle of a lake several acres in extent. Originally this water-course emptied itself into a cavern alongside Glyncerrig, towards which it still makes its way, and it might be better to utilise again this ready outlet than to add to the already surcharged main.

"Excepting along the lines of sewers, other parts of the district are drained into their own cesspools, and where the bye-law for cementing sides and bottoms has not been enforced, such cesspools serve their purpose the better. In consideration of the connected houses being relieved of their sewage at the public expense, the Council have extended the same relief to the unconnected, and the night visitation of cesspools, periodically and as occasion demands, meets public requirements."

While nature had endowed the district's immediate hinterland with a number of picturesque localities, even these could not disguise the fact that there were several ugly sites which marred those parts of the rural environment. These were the places where the contents cleared from ashpits, middens and refuse heaps were dumped upon on appointed days. At one time, a tipping ground opposite St. Peter's Church served Caswell and Newton; and the top of Thistleboon Lane catered for the Langland area. The largest dumping ground of all was placed on the north side of Oystermouth Castle where a bank of hundreds of tons of rubbish built up to become once a nuisance and a menace, when disturbed, to the fields and gardens of the neighbourhood. A squalid mess became a regular occurrence on dry, windry days when soiled papers were scattered over a wide area. (Now built over or cleared in the course of time, these former sites fortunately present a very different picture today).

Another public nuisance of yesteryear, especially in the summer months, was the dust thrown up by traffic passing on the friable limestone roads. The restricted amount of water available daily then frustrated the efforts of the cleansing staff in their attempts to allay this menace so that the M.O.H. pointed out the need for "the erection of a number of tanks all over the district," as well as the possibility of "sinking shafts along the beach" in order to trap supplies of sea water for the task." However, he anticipated a great improvement in the metalling and rolling of the much used sea front roadway which had become the responsibility of the County Council.

By now, the district's three slaughter houses had been licensed and registered under the Public Health Act regulations while its four retail bakehouses had complied with the Factory & Workshops Acts. Under the "Dairies, Cowsheds and Milkshops Order," 28 were registered in the district in accordance with the Act, but the Sanitary Inspector's report indicated that approximately another 28 had yet to be registered. "Seeing the extensiveness of this trade," wrote the M.O.H., "and the possible connection between tubercular milk and infantile tuberculosis, something more must be done, such as the veterinary inspection of the cattle and the frequent analysis of the milk, if we are to do all in our power to keep down our increasing children's death rate."

Intense, mounting dissatisfaction was increasingly voiced about the water supply situation by ratepayers throughout the Edwardian era and at the beginning of George V's reign. Nevertheless, in 1911, members of Oystermouth's U.D.C. succeeded in presenting a bill for Parliament's perusal and ratification, whereby they could legally purchase the Oystermouth & District Waterworks Co. Ltd., maintain it and proceed with plans for future expansion projects. This was at a time when informed Mumbles residents were only too aware of Swansea's healthy position in terms of water storage and distribution. Under Borough Engineer R. Wyrill's management, some 864 million gallons of water were stored at Cray, while a million gallons per day were being supplied to the town's outlying districts from the Townhill Reservoir.

The necessary Act was passed by Parliament on the 18th August, 1911. A fortnight earlier, "The Cambrian" reported the outcome of a stormy private meeting of the Mumbles' ratepayers held at the Oddfellows' Hall. The very hot July weather for that year had revealed yet again the inadequacies of the water supply; many people were forced to rely entirely on the contents left remaining in their water butts for daily use. Mr. Viner Leeder chaired the ill-tempered meeting which some ratepayers asserted was not advertised or publicly announced. This was refuted by the chairman who stated that private circulars were sent out.

It was generally accepted that the Caswell source of water was ample enough for district needs, but its supply to consumers was marred by the Company's limited distribution network, neglected maintenance and lack of foresight. Leakage of water at source was quoted as one example of slackness and ineptitude. Ratepayers' grievances lay not with the officials concerned but rather "with the Company as a Company and the controlling spirit of that Company." Consequently, the public had suffered for years at the hands of an organisation which appeared to have failed to face the fact that "the place was increasing rapidly." Towards the end of the meeting Mr. V. Leeder made clear his desire to vacate the chair and he was succeeded by Mr. R. L. Sails. It was then resolved to convene a legal meeting of the ratepayers to consider the whole question again.

Meanwhile, the Oystermouth Urban District Council Water Act, (1 & 2 Geo. 5), of 1911, was passed in Parliament. As such, it was an Act "to transfer to and vest in the Council of the urban district of Oystermouth the undertaking of the Oystermouth and District Waterworks Company Limited to authorise the Council to maintain the existing waterworks and construct new works and to supply water within the urban district of Oystermouth and adjacent places and for other places. 18th August 1911." Some aspects of its proposals are recorded as follows.

The Act recognised that Oystermouth, in the county of Glamorgan, was, "an urban district within the meaning of the Local Government Act 1894 and is under the management and control of the Oystermouth Urban District Council (hereinafter called 'the Council')."

Finances permitting, the Act, Ch. LXI., reveals the aims and methods proposed by the Oystermouth U.D.C., some of which are contained in the following selected clauses:

> "And whereas by the Oystermouth Water Order 1879 . . . which was confirmed by the Gas and Water Orders Confirmation Act 1879 certain persons therein named . . . were authorised to make and maintain certain waterworks in the parishes of Oystermouth and Bishopston and to supply water within the parish of Oystermouth and that portion of the parish of Bishopston known as Herbert's Houses Herbert's Lodge Millstone Acres and Redlay all in the county of Glamorgan:
>
> "And whereas by section 6 of the Order the undertakers were authorised to raise share capital for the purposes of their undertaking not exceeding six thousand five hundred pounds and to borrow on mortgage of the undertaking any moneys not exceeding one thousand five hundred pounds:
>
> "And whereas the said undertaking is now vested in the Oystermouth and District Waterworks Company Limited (hereinafter called 'the company'):
>
> *Works and Lands*
>
> "16. From and after the transfer the Council may maintain and from time to time alter improve and renew or discontinue the existing works of the company.
>
> "17. Subject to the provisions of this Act the Council may wholly in the county of Glamorgan in the lines and situation and upon the lands delineated on the deposited plans and described in the deposited book of reference make and maintain the following works shown on the deposited plans and sections (that is to say):-
>
> "Work No. 1. A tank or service reservoir in the parish of Oystermouth on the west side of and adjoining the existing service reservoir of the company

situate partly on the lands of the company and partly on the enclosures numbered 437, 436 and 434 on the Ordnance map (scale $\frac{1}{2500}$) 2nd edition 1899 of the said parish commencing about twenty-five feet southward from the south of Summerland Lane and terminating at a distance of one hundred and fifty feet or thereabouts from the south side of the said lane:

"Work No. 2. A conduit or line of pipes commencing in the parish of Bishopston in the existing pumping stations of the company and passing into and terminating in Work No. 1:

"Work No. 3. A conduit or line of pipes in the parish of Bishopston commencing at or near the Redlay springs of the company situate on the western side of Caswell Bay and terminating in the existing pumping stations of the company.

"22. Subject to the provisions of this Act the Council may purchase and take and hold for the purposes of the water undertaking the lands waters rights and easements hereinafter mentioned and held by the company on lease from His Grace the Duke of Beaufort,"

which were in respect of those lands which formed the sites of the then existing pumping stations at Caswell Bay and for the easement of maintaining and repairing the line of pipes from Redlay Springs to the pumping stations within the Parish of Bishopston as well as for,

"The easements for maintaining and repairing the existing lines of pipes from the said pumping stations to the rising main in the public road leading from Caswell Bay to Oystermouth in through or under the lands delineated on the deposited plans and described in the deposited book of reference and numbered 1 and 5 in the parish of Bishopston and 7 and 8 in the parish of Oystermouth."

"38. The Council shall not be bound to supply with water otherwise than by measure any building used by an occupier as a dwelling-house whereof any part is used by the same occupier for any trade or manufacturing purpose for which water is required.

"39. The price to be charged for a supply of water by measure shall not exceed one shilling and sixpence per thousand gallons.

"40. The water supplied by the Council need not at any time be delivered at a greater height than can be reached by gravitation from the service reservoir or tank from which the supply is taken *nor need the water be constantly laid on under pressure* until the works by this Act authorised are constructed."

Item 46 (1). was a shrewd clause for it gave the Oystermouth U.D.C., the legal powers, if pursued, to obtain water in bulk from Swansea Corporation or other bodies in order to supplement or expand existing supplies. This reads:

"The Council may enter into and carry into effect agreements with the mayor aldermen and burgesses of the borough of Swansea and with any

> other local authority water board company or persons able and willing to supply water in bulk for the supply of water to the Council in bulk for the purposes of the water undertaking for such remuneration and on such terms and conditions and for such period as may be agreed upon.
>
> "46 (2). For the purposes of enabling the Council to take a supply of water under this section the Council shall have and may exercise any of the powers of the Public Health Acts in regard to the construction and maintenance of waterworks (including the Powers of a local authority for carrying water mains without their district) and the purposes of this section shall be deemed to be purposes of those Acts."

Any differences which were likely to arise with road authorities, railway companies, canal companies or other companies, in respect of the Council's powers to cross over their lands, were to be settled by an engineer or "other fit person" to be appointed by the Board of Trade at the request of either party. No works or installations were to be placed below high-water mark without the prior consent, in writing, of the Board of Trade. Clauses 72 and 73 covered these eventualities accordingly.

After several discussions with Lord Glantawe, namely, John Jones Jenkins of the Grange, West Cross, a leading businessman and tinplate manufacturer, during September, 1911, Oystermouth's Urban District Council Parliamentary Committee failed to reach an agreement in respect of the price to be paid for the Waterworks Company. Lord Glantawe was the main controller of the Company's shareholders. It now meant that the matter would be subjected to an arbitration procedure and the Committee also resolved "to hear in camera a more detailed report of what transpired at the meeting with Lord Glantawe." All too soon, however, the outbreak of the First World War over-shadowed any subsequent considerations and future plans until 1918 when the Mumbles became part of the enlarged Swansea County Borough. Moreover, Lord Glantawe died in 1915.

Between approximately 1922 and mid-1936, Swansea Corporation pushed ahead with its main drainage scheme in the face of early post-War I economic cutbacks. Among other districts, Mumbles residents shared in the resulting benefits of the completed programme although there were those who decried the construction of the Clydach to Mumbles main sewer ending here and its contents being discharged some 750 feet into the sea eastwards of the Mumbles Lighthouse. This latter main trunk, intercepting sewer, was not commenced until the last month of 1931, and its eventual completion in July, 1936, included the placing of large storage tanks under Mumbles Hill.

The sewer section from Brynmill to the Mumbles Head, the work of Messrs. Melville, Dundas & Whitson, Ltd., Glasgow & London, was constructed of brick. The massive scheme involved a cost in the region of one-

and-a-half million pounds but Swansea Corporation received some financial support from the Government of the day by way of an unemployment grant.

Swansea Corporation also honoured its obligation to the Mumbles Ward in respect of the question of an up-to-date public water system. They implemented a scheme whereby consumers were supplied initially with water from the Cray (Crai) Reservoir during the early post-War I years. Crai water was delivered to the Townhill Reservoir which served as primary storage.

A 12″ diameter main carried the water via Sketty Cross and Derwen Fawr to Blackpill from where a 10″ diameter main went to Oystermouth. By means of the mains in existence previously, the water was then distributed within the Mumbles area as far as it would go under the Townhill pressure head. It is not precisely clear how long the existing works, the Redlay springs and the tanks near Summerland Lane, continued in use.

Crai Reservoir was built between 1892 and 1907, on the River Crai, at a cost approaching £700,000. In spite of many difficulties encountered with the foundations for the dam, the Reservoir was successfully completed and brought into service on the 2nd October, 1907. The outlet from the Reservoir, a tunnel, 5 ft. high by 3½ ft. wide and 4,770 yards long, cuts through the hills dividing the Crai and Tawe Valleys and passes for a third of its length under the Reservoir.

The Crai reservoir is formed by a blue Staffordshire, brick faced Dam, giving a capacity of 1,007 million gallons at a water depth to its lowest draw-off point, at 81 feet below. The top water level is 1,001 feet above Ordnance Datum and the Reservoir supplies approximately eight million gallons per day to parts of the City of Swansea in addition to the villages in the Swansea Valley. During the period of construction, a cast iron main, 17″ diameter and 23 miles long, was laid to an open Service Reservoir of 3 million gallons capacity, constructed on Townhill. A second main was later laid, 24″ diameter and 20 miles long, part reinforced concrete and part steel, to supply the Service Reservoir at Morriston, into which the Lliw main was also diverted. The latter, completed in 1911, was the first covered reinforced concrete Reservoir in the Borough, and is formed by two similar circular tanks which together possesses a capacity of 4.5 million gallons. Water from this Reservoir is treated with ammonia and chlorine at Nantyrwydd.

By 1930, however, the Mumbles area was feeling the inconvenience of a long supply main. Consequently, the Newton Reservoir was built to iron out demand peaks, but was supplied by the same route. Twenty years later, mounting demands in the lower areas began depleting Newton

Reservoir's capacity and with the construction of the 1950 Clyne Reservoir the present basic pattern of water distribution was established. This also received its water from the Townhill Reservoir via Sketty Cross and a new 10″ diameter main link direct to Newton was laid. A County Borough of Swansea, Water Department's commemorative Clyne Reservoir plaque records a capacity of 750,000 gallons, with a top water level of 417 feet A.O.D. Messrs. Hussey Egan & Pickmere Ltd. were the contractors; Trevelyan Price, Borough Water Engineer & Manager; T. B. Bowen, Town Clerk; and Richard Henry, Chairman of Committee.

The only difference since 1955 is that Clyne Reservoir is supplied from the Cockett Reservoir (Usk Water) instead of Townhill. Currently, therefore, the water supply to Oystermouth and Mumbles derives from the Usk Reservoir.

The large impounding Usk Reservoir of 12 million cubic metres (m^3) or 2,700 million gallons was completed in 1955 and is the source for the whole of Western Swansea and East Gower. When full, the water area of some 290 acres, stretches for a distance of about 2¼ miles upstream from the dam and supplies upwards of 12 million gallons daily to Swansea & District. Swansea being outside the watershed of the Usk the supply cannot be drawn off in the normal way down the valley, and a supply tunnel, 2,370 yards long through the adjoïning mountainside is necessary. Steel pipes, lined and sheathed with bitumen, possessing flexible couplings have been used throughout the pipeline to the city. The thickness of the steel is varied to suit the changes of pressure occurring along the line, the maximum being 750 feet head at the Afan Sawdde, one of the Valley crossings. The flexible joints permit some movement of the pipes, if ground settlement should happen, without leakage.

In order to limit the static pressure which would develop in the pipes if the terminal valves at Swansea were closed, the line is divided into three roughly equal lengths, the pressures being limited to that due to the small reservoirs at the Supply Basin, Filtration Plant and a Break Pressure Tank. Furthermore, the diameters of the pipes are varied to suit the gradient available in each section. The first section is 28 inches diameter and about 10 miles long; the second, from the Filters to the Break Pressure Tank is 27 inches diameter, 9½ miles long; and the third is 26 inches diameter for the first seven miles to where it divides into two 20 inch pipes, each about 3½ miles long, which feed into the service reservoirs at Cockett in the west and Clase in the north of Swansea.

The water is treated at Bryngwyn, near Llandeilo, by sand filtration and chlorination before passing via the 27″ diameter steel pipeline, mentioned above, down to the 20″ pipeline size to the terminal Reservoir at Cockett. This feeds a subsidiary service Reservoir on Clyne Common, referred to earlier, which in turn feeds the Newton Reservoir. The latter is a traditional covered service reservoir in reinforced concrete with a capacity of 2250 m^3 or 500,000 gallons. It has a top water level of 89 metres above sea level (290 feet), affording adequate pressure to all parts of the area.

In addition, Oystermouth and Mumbles also share in the benefits of the River Towy scheme and the huge Llyn Brianne Reservoir & Dam of the 1970's. Mr. R. J. Lillicrap, C.Eng., F.I.C.E., F.I.W.E., was the Engineer and Manager of the West Glam. Water Board at that time. In times of drought the Usk Reservoir is used to reinforce the flow in the River Usk and the supplies to Cardiff. When this happens, water is pumped from the River Towy, near Llandeilo, and treated at Bryngwyn, and thereby replacing Usk-derived water in the local system.

As we approach the last two decades of the present century, the storage and consumption of the nation's water supplies for industrial and domestic purposes have become of paramount importance. Water officials bear a heavy responsibility in this matter, for they have to plan ahead constantly, seek major new water sources and anticipate long-term requirements. As a result, the vital programmes of expansion since the 1950's, have produced administrative changes. In 1966, the West Glamorgan Water Board was instituted by the amalgamation of the Swansea, Neath and Port Talbot Water Supply Authorities, together with six surrounding urban and rural districts. Messrs. Binnie & Partners, Consulting Engineers, have played an important role here in advising authorities concerned in the search for new sources to meet long-term needs. Later, the Welsh National Water Development Authority came into being, embracing among others, the Glamorgan Water Division. Early in 1978, this was superseded by the establishment of the Wales Water Authority.

The inhabitants of South-West Wales, therefore, are more than well provided for in the distribution and excellent maintenance of their public water system. The peak drought year of 1976 is one recent but most significant reminder of this fact; consumers of Swansea and Gower, among others, were extremely fortunate in that period of national emergency, when householders in some areas of the United Kingdom found themselves rationed to a few hours daily supply only, or, in other cases, had to depend entirely on water-containers being brought in by lorries.

CHAPTER SEVEN

OYSTERMOUTH CASTLE

"The perfect history of a town or village will be one that can be read with pleasure even by people who have never set foot in the place."
H. P. R. Finberg & V. H. T. Skipp.

"The Assize Roll for Wales (No 1150) for 34 Edward I gives us the record of evidence, from which we gather for the first time the nature of the injuries and oppressions imposed by De Breos upon his tenants. For instance, it is alleged against William de Breos, John Owayn, his seneschal or steward, John Lardner, and others, that they, with force and arms, took William de Langton, of Kilvrock, from his house, and carried him to De Breos's manor of Ostremuere, where he was detained against his will until, by his deed in writing, he had given De Breos a release of all actions pending between them. At the enquiry De Breos denied the injury, and claimed that the question should be tried by the law of the marches; but William de Langton pleaded that he could not be so tried, raised the old objection that Gower was a member of the corpus of Carmarthen, and that it was not held by barony but by knight's fee."
W. H. Jones: "History Of Swansea & Of The Lordship of Gower."

"In addition to its permanent role as a tourist attraction, the castle has become a focal point for some of the absorbing 'Ostreme' events held in the Mumbles during the late summer season . . . Afternoon performances of church and historical plays are held within the castle grounds watched by hundreds of spectators. The evening musical presentation here of 'Son Et Lumiere—The Bells Of Santiago,' an Extravaganza in Music and Light, is a particularly spectacular production . . . On such nightly occasions, suitably bedecked and floodlit, the castle's surroundings become admirably enhanced, a fitting spectacle and tribute to its newly-found role as a scenic stage for man's more positive and creative endeavours."
N. L. Thomas: "Mumbles: Past And Present."

The strategic position of Oystermouth Castle, placed on an eminence, upwards of 120 feet above sea level, continues to serve as a tangible reminder of our past heritage. As such, it is also a picturesque site which commands sweeping views of Swansea Bay, Oystermouth, together with the Mumbles Lighthouse, Lifeboat Station, Pier and adjacent coastline.

Limestone cliffs on its western side afforded a certain amount of additional protection. Remains of the original stone stronghold are in evidence today and have been dated to about circa 1280. As in the previous century, the present-day castle functions as a definite tourist attraction as well as an historical locality visited by historians and students engaged in environmental studies.

The emergence of Oystermouth's first stronghold and subsequent fortresses is due to the Norman conquest and colonisation of Swansea with the Gower Peninsula. Swansea's first castle, circa 1099-1101, erected by Henry de Newburgh and his knight-adventurers, was most likely a mound, the habitable area on top being protected by a surrounding of wooden palisades, an early type of motte and bailey construction. This was followed by similar strongholds put up in Gower at Oystermouth, Penard, Penrice and Weobley etc. Later, these were replaced by more durable stone-work fortifications which guarded the eastern entrance to the Lordship of Gower.

There were those occasions throughout its history when Oystermouth Castle sustained numerous attacks and sieges, some of which the defenders repulsed successfully. On the other hand, it was sometimes heavily damaged or razed to the gound by Welshmen in revolt against their feudal overlords. However, the Normans clung tenaciously to their immediate possessions; recaptured or rebuilt lost castles and generally managed to dominate the Lordship of Gower, an area which extended from Gowerland northwards to the Amman Valley.

There is not sufficient evidence available, in respect of early records, to determine who was actually responsible for building the first castle at Oystermouth . It may have been constructed by order of Henry de Newburgh or Beaumont, as the first Norman Lord of Swansea and Gower, circa 1106, in connection with his early subjugation of the peninsula. (The name of De Newburgh or "Novoburgo" was taken from the castle or town of Neuborg, near Beaumont-le-Roger, in Normandy, where he was born. De Newburgh was also created the first Earl of Warwick).

It has been suggested that the builder was William de Londres, Lord of Ogmore Castle, who had taken part in the conquest of Glamorgan. Whatever the case, Sir William de Londres was given the manor of Oystermouth at this time as a fief from Henry de Newburgh, and, as such, De Londres must be seen as the earliest holder of Oystermouth.

At a much later date in the 12th century, the De Londres family and their connections with the manor of Oystermouth are referred to in the charter of Earl William of Warwick granted to the burgesses of Swansea, circa 1158-1184. W. H. Jones writes: "But the charter was, most probably, dated at Swansea, since the witness whose name is copied was a neighbour of Warwick's, 'Willelmum London,' Lord of Kidwelly, who also probably had the mesne manor of Oystermouth. He was grandson of the William de Londres, a knight of Fitzhamon's, who had Ogmore for his share of Glamorgan. The witness to our charter was second in succession from this William, and inherited Ogmore and Kidwelly, holding the latter by the service of guiding the king's army, when necessary, from Neath across Gower to Laugharne. It is unfortunate that we have no precise date connected with de Londres which will assist us in establishing the date of our charter." In addition, the holding of the manor of Oystermouth by the De Londres family is verified by an entry in the "Historia Monasterii St. Petri Gloucestriae," which reads "De Ewenny—Anno Domini 1141, Mauricius de Londonia, filius Willelmi de Londonie, dedit ecclesiae Sancti Petri Gloucestriae . . . Insuper et ecclesiam de Ostrenuwe in Goer." Towards the close of the 12th century, a William de Londres was custodian of Swansea Castle in 1188 and 1192.

Even if Henry de Newburgh was not involved directly in the building of the first limited type of motte and bailey castle at Oystermouth, he saw to it, as the chief Lord of Gower, that his useful stronghold came under his jurisdiction very soon after the initial domination of the peninsula. Furthermore, Oystermouth Castle and its subsequent rebuilt versions, was considered important enough to come under the immediate command of successive Lords of Gower in conjunction with their main Swansea fortress.

At one stage in its history, but for a brief period only, it superseded Swansea as the Lordship of Gower's principal centre of defence. However, Oystermouth was generally recognised as being second in over-all military importance to Swansea, although it must have been a popular stronghold, situated as it once was, within a heavily forested area suitable for those hunting pursuits associated with the Mediaeval period.

The close proximity of Oystermouth Castle to Swansea's, approximately five miles distant, meant inevitably that both strongholds were liable to be attacked within a short time of each other, or almost simultaneously, when Welsh uprisings embraced the peninsula. As a rule, the Welsh insurgents, in victory, would burn down or destroy, as far as possible, the Norman castles of Gower, rather than hold on to them. These castles, such as at Oystermouth and Swansea, would afterwards be rebuilt and often further strengthened, in the wake of successful Norman counter attacks.

Although the dates quoted in the Chronicles of the Princes, such as the "Brut y Tywysogion," sometimes conflict with other historical accounts, their descriptions provide some guide to past conflicts in Gower as elsewhere. The Chronicles note in 1116 the destruction of a Gower castle which was most likely the one based at Oystermouth. This was the work of the forces under Gruffydd ap Rhys ap Tewdwr, a Prince of South Wales, who led a campaign from circa 1113 onwards to win back ancestral territories. Reference to the account of "Brut y Tywysogion" about this attack upon a castle of Henry de Beaumont near Swansea is also mentioned in a deed of Gower land presented to St. Taurin's Abbey, Evereux, in Normandy, by Henry, Earl of Warwick.

It is recorded:

> "Afterwards he sent his companions to attack and to alarm a castle which was near Abertawy (Swansea), and which belonged to an Earl named Henry Beaumont (De Newburgh), and after burning the outworks and attacking the garrison defending the tower, and killing a few of them, he retreated again . . . He committed great depredations round about him . . . for there was a castle in Gower (Oystermouth) which he burnt entirely, killing many men therein."

However brief, reference must be made to subsequent 12th and 13th century attacks upon nearby Swansea Castle and invasions of Gowerland, in view of Oystermouth Castle's particular geographical location in relation to such happenings. Absence of information about Oystermouth Castle's involvement in *some* of these battles or incursions does not preclude, however, the obvious premise that the stronghold and its defenders were bound to be affected, directly or indirectly, at times, by the course of events which then prevailed.

Henry de Newburgh who died 1119 was succeeded as Earl of Warwick by the eldest of his three sons, Roger de Newburgh. The latter's forces suffered a notable defeat in 1136, on Garngoch Common, at the hands of the Welsh led by Hywel ap Meredudd. Roger de Newburgh was apparently more interested in his other inherited possessions rather than the Gower Lordship which appears to have been taken over by one of the younger sons, Henry.

In addition, the South Wales coastline with that of the peninsula's was open to periodic attacks of Danish and Irish marauders. In the "Orkneyingers Saga," circa 1139-48, some exploits of the former are recorded; among the localities they landed at was Jarlsness, or Nash Point, eastwards of the Swansea coastline. When repaired, the Normans in their Oystermouth Keep were in a position of some strength to face up to invasions by sea or land. Alternatively, from the close of the 12th century onwards, other inhabitants would seek refuge, no doubt within the strong, embattled tower of Oystermouth Church, as was the case in respect of similar other Gower churches. This strong tower of the parish church served obviously as a kind of alternative keep when needed throughout different periods of the late 12th and 13th centuries.

Among other areas, Swansea and Gower were overrun by the followers of Meredudd and Rhys, sons of Gruffydd ap Rhys, in circa 1150-51. Their raids were initially of a retaliatory nature in order to avenge a treacherous attack made upon their brother, Cadell, at Tenby, by the English of Gower. A succession of victories saw them drive the Normans out of their numerous settlements in western South Wales, as far afield as Pembroke; eastwards to Swansea; and beyond that point to Aberafan Castle which they took from one, Caradoc ab Iestyn, Lord of Rhwng Nedd ac Afan.

Roger de Newburgh died in circa 1153 and was succeeded by his mother, countess of Henry de Newburgh, most likely by the provisions of her husband's will and the fact that Roger de Newburgh's son was not yet of age at the time. The Welsh, meanwhile, were in firm control of Gower between 1150 and 1157, but in the latter year Rhys was persuaded to do homage to King Henry and left Gower. As Henry de Newburgh died apparently without issue, the Lordship of Gower was consequently inherited by his nephew, William, Earl of Warwick, in 1158.

Well within the early part of the last decade of the 12th century, Gower was despoiled yet again by the Lord Rhys ap Gruffydd who had renounced his previous allegiance to King Richard I. However, this same Rhys, supported by his quarrelsome sons, Gruffydd and Maelgyn, failed to take Swansea Castle, defended by William de Londres in 1192, after a near starvation siege for the garrison of some ten weeks.

In 1203, the whole of the lands of Gower were granted to William de Breos (Braose) by King John who, at this time, was seeking as much military support as possible in his war with the barons. De Braose received ten marks in the following year "for the use of Leision, son of Morgan, who was bringing 200 Welshmen to join the King's Forces."

Part of the charter of King John to William de Braose reads:

> "John, by the grace of God, King of England, Lord of Ireland, Duke of Acquitain, and Earl of Anjou, . . Know ye that we have given and granted, and by our present charter confirmed to our beloved and trusty William de Breos, all the land of Guher with all the appurtenances, in Wales, to have and to hold to him and his heirs of us and our heirs, *by the service of one knight* for all service."

The service due for a single knight's fee was that of one fully-armed horseman who had to serve in the king's army for forty days in the year during time of war. In addition to military service, the holder could be subjected to other burdens such as aids, fines on alienation, relief, wardship, scutage (i.e. a tax levied instead of service) and escheats (i.e. properties which fall to the state or king for want of an heir, or by forfeiture).

After the death of William de Braose in 1211, the De Braose's concerns were looked after by his two surviving sons for a time, Giles and Reginald.

On numerous occasions throughout the greater part of the 13th century, the Welsh maintained their intermissive raids upon the Lordship of Gower and attacked with unfailing regularity the principal Norman strongholds entrenched therein. Swansea suffered again in 1212 when Rhys Gryg, "Rhys the Hoarse," otherwise known as Rhys Fechan, son of Lord Rhys, set fire to the town. Two years previously, King John had visited Swansea briefly on his expedition to Ireland.

As well as others, the castles of *Oystermouth* and Swansea bore the brunt of another determined invasion in 1215, the year when King John granted his charter to Swansea. The town was burnt by young Rhys ap Gruffydd, the grandson of the lord Rhys, and a nephew of Rhys Gryg. The Welsh chronicles describe the events thus:

> "Young Rhys collected also an army of vast magnitude and obtained possession of Cydweli and Carnwyllion (the district between Kidwelly and Gower, and in the present day known as the Hundred of Carnwallon) and burned the castle. From thence he drew to Gower, and he first reduced the castle of Llwchwr, and afterwards he fought against the castle of Hugh (Castell Du in Llandeilo Talybont), and the garrison essayed to keep the castle against him, but Rhys obtained the castle by force, passing the garrison and castle through fire and sword. The following day he marched against the castle of Ystum Llwynairth in Sein Henyd (Seinhenydd, i.e. Swansea) and from fear of him the garrison burned the town. And they, without being diverted from their purpose, proceeded to the castle of Ystumllwynarth (i.e. *Oystermouth),* and he encamped about it that night, and the following day he obtained the castle which with the town he burned, and by the end of three days he reduced all the castles of Gower and thus happy and victorious he returned home."

Oystermouth Castle's subsequent reconstruction after this devastation would have continued most likely on the lines of a modified motte and bailey design. The motte, of course, consisted of a raised bank or mound of earth and stones upon which a castle was placed for defence. The bailey or uncovered courtyard together with the castle would be protected by a surrounding of high walls. In respect of *Oystermouth,* at this time, as was the case with other Gower strongholds, the mound would support a wooden hall-residence of the lord and, perhaps, a large timber gate-tower entrance. High, earthen banks of packed earth mixed with rough stones then encircled and protected any wooden dwelling places together with the open courtyard. A strong, wooden fence-work or stockade could also be erected on and around this raised wall of earth and stone to form an additional means of defence. As a rule, outside and at the bottom of the fortress, stood a deep, well-dug ditch around the mound which increased the effectiveness of the rampart's steep sides and presented attackers with a difficult obstacle to overcome in the initial stages of any assault.

The stone castles of Gower did not begin to emerge until around the middle of the 13th century, and it was only towards the close of that century when the stronger more durable, high stone walls, conspicuous towers and keeps came into prominence. Oystermouth Castle's middle section of buildings which made up the present keep is of late mid-13th century construction.

The Lordship of Gower continued to feel the impact of further Welsh invasions in 1216, 1217 and 1257. The occupation of Gower by Rhys Gryg in 1217 and his successful attacks upon Swansea Castle and neighbouring strongholds, which must have inevitably involved Oystermouth, is referred to once again by the Brut y Tywysogion as well as other chronicles.

In particular, the years 1216 to 1230 witnessed the dominant power and notable victories of Prince Llywelyn ab Iorwerth and his allies, like Rhys Gryg, within the peninsula and beyond. By circa 1217, Reginald de Braose had personally acknowledged Llywelyn's military supremacy, whereupon the Prince rewarded De Braose's pragmatism by presenting him with the custody of Swansea Castle in place of Rhys Gryg. Later, in 1219, Llywelyn consented to the marriage of his daugher, Margaret, to Reginald's nephew, John, the eldest son of the young William de Braose, who had been starved at Windsor, and who, with more title to them than his uncle had, now looked for an opportunity to acquire the family estates.

Due to Reginald's desertion of Llywelyn, John de Braose as the Prince's son-in-law, became the Lord of Gower and repaired Swansea Castle in circa 1221 by the consent and advice of Llywelyn, his father-in-law. Consequently, the De Braoses of the day held Gower, not only under the 1203 grant from King John, but also as a gift from the powerful Llywelyn.

After Reginald's death in 1228, his son, William de Braose succeeded to the family inheritance but in the following year he was hanged by Llywelyn ab Iorwerth at Aber, North Wales. This action was prompted principally because of an ancient feud Llywelyn had maintained with the elder William de Braose and his wife, Matilda de St. Valéry. Consequently, John de Braose, as Lord of Gower, then took possession of all the family estates.

A riding accident in 1232 caused the death of John de Braose. As his son, William, was a minor, the Lordship of Gower, once again came under the custody of the crown for the next nine years.

During 1256-57, Llywelyn ap Gruffydd, the last of the princes of South Wales and grandson of Llywelyn ab Iorwerth, swept through South Wales and overran Gower. At this time, King Henry III warned William de Braose, son of John de Braose, to take defensive precautions for the safety of his marcher lordship but these proved to be of no avail. With Swansea, *Oystermouth's* fortifications were overcome in 1257, and of the English in

Gower 200 were slain; 194 men and six women. The Annales Cambriae states:

> "He burned all that belonged to the English in the aforesaid land (Gower), as also in Abertawy, and having freed all the Welshmen thereof, he joyfully returned home."

Some time after these fierce engagements, William de Braose erected the first stone stronghold or keep, parts of which at least form the core of the present Oystermouth Castle's fabric. As such, the castle's construction as an Edwardian type fortification may be traced to circa 1280. In the Barons' War, De Braose was amongst those barons who successfully supported the king at the Battle of Evesham, 1265, and by such action, he strengthened his independent power over the Lordship of Gower.

For two decades after 1257, Llewelyn ap Gruffydd's influence and power remained virtually absolute although Gowerland was not permanently occupied by his forces.

Llywelyn ap Gruffydd as the last of the Welsh princes, was killed in a skirmish at Cilmeri, near Builth Wells, in December, 1282. His death meant the end of any substantive, united Welsh opposition to the English until the commencement of the 15th century. Soon afterwards, within two years, Llywelyn the Last's principality was divided into three counties by the Declaration of Rhuddlan; each county now came under a justice of the crown.

A noteworthy but peaceful occurrence in Oystermouth Castle's history took place during the last month of 1284, when William de Braose entertained the mighty Edward 1st and his wife here for two days. Edward was determined to pacify as well as subjugate Wales, and a royal tour gave him some opportunity to "show the flag" as it were, and to make judgements about military or provincial matters which then prevailed in those places he stayed at throughout the journey. The king arrived at Oystermouth from West Wales via Kidwelly and remained at the castle for two days, on the 10th and 11th December.

A royal writ dated at "Oystremuth" for the 10th December, 1284, confirms Edward's visit. It would appear that, on this occasion, Swansea Castle was not befitting enough to receive the king and his queen, Eleanor.

There is, incidentally, a tradition which maintains that Oystermouth Castle was being specially prepared for the reception of Queen Eleanor who was pregnant at this time. The anticipated birth did not materialise then, however, so the queen journeyed on to Caernarfon, where the first Prince of Wales, the future Edward II, was born.

In 1287, the peace between Edward I and the Welsh princes was broken due to an uprising headed by Rhys ap Meredudd of Dryslwyn and Dinefwr, the Lord of Ystrad Tywi, a former ally of Edward I who had fought against Llywelyn. Among other grievances, Meredudd, as one of the South Wales Marcher lords, had not taken kindly to the suppression of Welsh laws and customs; in addition he had openly quarrelled with the King's chief-justice at Carmarthen about pillages and atrocities committed by the English in his Ystrad Tywi domains. The Annales Cambriae describes his initial victories as follows:

> "Rhys ap Meredudd, Lord of Ystrad Tywi, having quarrelled with Lord Robert Tibotot, then the King's Justicar at Carmarthen, on the Sunday before the feast of the blessed apostle Barnabas took the castles of Llanymddyfri, Dinefwr, and Carreg Cennen, and afterwards burnt the town of Swansea and the Manor of Ysterlwyf *(i.e. Oystermouth),* and the greater part of the district, and the town of Llanbadarnfawr, and the town of Carmarthen to the very gates."

On this occasion, the two stone castles at Swansea and Oystermouth provided stubborn opposition in the face of Rhys' forces. While the town of Swansea was burnt on the 10th June, 1287, its castle appears to have sustained ineffectual damage. Rhys proceeded in some haste to Oystermouth Castle but failed to achieve a swift, successful outcome here. The Oystermouth defenders held out until the 26th June which involved a siege of 17 days.

Rhys ap Meredudd's revolt was prompted perhaps by more personal feelings; the grievances of a marcher-lord, rather than by patriotic motives. De Braose's writ of trespass against Rhys was upheld by the King's Court at Carmarthen; and eventually, after four years of pursuit, his lands confiscated, Rhys was captured and put to death. The failure of this rebellion, within five years of Llywelyn the Last's death, practically completed the triumph of Edward I's forces in Wales, although there were other revolts prior to the King's death in 1307.

William de Braose, the elder and the second of his name, as Lord of Swansea and Gower, died in 1290. He was succeeded by his eldest son, another William, who had already distinguished himself in the eyes of Edward I by his military prowess on behalf of his sovereign. This William de Braose, the last of the Gower de Braoses, remained as Lord of Gower as the result of a mutual agreement with his father's widow in respect of her dowry. (The elder De Braose had married Isabel, daughter of Earl Gilbert de Clare; he also married Agnes de Moels, and Mary de Roos, who died in 1326). The widow relinquished her Gower possessions but retained her Sussex estates.

Irrespective of his skill and undoubted bravery at home or overseas, in the service of Edward I, he nevertheless, locally, became a despot, fraudulent and deceitful in the extreme, hated even by members of his own family. De Braose's excesses finally forced him to grant his Charter to "Sweynes" of 1305-6, at a period in time which marked approximately two centuries of Norman occupation of Gower.

De Braose granted one charter to the Swansea burgesses while the other was presented to the English and Welsh within Gower. It was a singular triumph for both the burgesses and tenants; their liberties and traditional privileges were now clarified and legally endorsed. Contravention of the charters by the lord or his heirs incurred a fine, payable to the king, of five hundred pounds in silver and "to him, them, or the burgesses aforesaid and their heirs, to whom wrong shall have been done, contrary to the tenor of this present charter, in five hundred marks of silver, by way of pure debt, to be paid within half a year from the time of the wrong committed, as often soever as we shall have done or attempt to do anything contrary to the premises or any of them."

On the other hand, De Braose succeeded in maintaining his marcher-lord rank independent of the county court at Carmarthen. In recognition of William de Braose's unstinted support of the crown in military matters, Edward I had, in 1304, reconfirmed the conditions laid down by King John to De Braose's ancestor whereby the family held Gower on par with the other prominent marcher-lords in Glamorgan (Morgannwg) under the sovereign of England.

Oystermouth manor featured in the course of events which led to the charters of 1305-06. Sir William de Langton, knight of Kilvrough, was involved in an incident whereby he had been forcibly removed from his home by armed men led by De Braose's steward and taken to the Lord's manor of "Ostremuere." De Langton had been a thorn in the flesh as far as De Braose was concerned, for this knight had brought several charges of misconduct against him to the notice of Edward I at the very commencement of the 14th century. At Oystermouth Castle De Langton was kept a prisoner until he had signed a release of all grievances and accusations made against De Braose.

During a previous visit to the castle, it appeared that De Langton had originally withdrawn his complaints voluntarily and not under duress. However, the very surroundings must have proved somewhat intimidating under the circumstances and in view of De Braose's reputation. De Langton afterwards, changed his mind apparently, returned to the castle next day and requested to see the document he had signed. He then damaged the parchment paper and left in some haste. It was this act which subsequently led to de Langton's abduction by the Lord's steward and his retention in Oystermouth Castle.

The policies and intrigues of the De Braoses throughout the 13th century and early part of the 14th century reveal, therefore, that the position of a marcher-lord of Swansea and Gower was at times one of unique power. There were those occasions when the De Braoses openly defied their sovereign over-lord or his legal representatives. The authority, privileges and dues bound up with such a lordship tempted them, perhaps, to feel and act as a separate entity. It was left to the odd royal visit of a monarch to remind lords and barons of their status as liege-lords under the feudal tenure of ownership.

Consequently, Edward I, during his visit to Oystermouth Castle, mentioned previously, in 1284, must have viewed with some obvious apprehension the noticeable degree of influence exercised by the elder William de Braose. In this connection, W. H. Jones, in his "History of Swansea," writes:

> "King Edward must have seen much in De Breos's surroundings to confirm his determination that the power of these marcher lords must be broken. For example, the king moved of necessity with all the machinery of state at his command, and the impedimenta of his chancery accompanied him, his writs being sealed with the seal of the royal chancery at *Oystermouth;* whilst here, too, was De Breos, maintaining his own chancery of his lordship, using the royal 'We' in the wording of his writs, and sealing them with the seal of a district chancery as lord paramount of Gower, a lordship marcher in which the king's writ would not be recognised."

The De Braoses were, by now, well-established at their Oystermouth manor and castle. The settlement was suitable enough to receive royal guests in preference to Swansea Castle at this particular time in history. Although William de Braose had been a staunch ally of the crown, Edward must have meditated somewhat upon the fact that this marcher-lord had organised his court on par with a county court. Those who came here, from time to time, were the lord's vassals, skilled in the arts of war and the owners themselves of useful strongholds.

As a manor, Oystermouth was one of twelve such divisions of land held by the English within the peninsula. It will be recalled that under the feudal system, after a sovereign over-lord had ganted his vassal or liege-lord a number of manors, the latter would often give small sections of his "fief" (i.e. land obtained as a fee), or a separate manor itself, as a "Knight's Fee" to his own selected followers. They in turn swore to obey as well as follow their lord, the king's vassal, and pay all relevant dues to him. The system sometimes reacted against a monarch when his liege-lords supported enemies of the crown in times of strife.

When a lord died, the king could grant his fiefs to someone else; so too, could the lord or baron when one of his knights died. However, if the liege-lord's eldest son, as in the case of William de Braose, the eldest son of William de Braose the elder (died 1290), was of age and ready to take the customary oath of allegiance, the monarch then granted the estate to him as a rule.

Eventually, the malpractices of the last of the De Braose lords, William, reacted severely against him; not only did he alienate his own relatives but also the burgesses of Swansea as well as the English tenants of Gower. As a result, the men and tenants of Gower issued a petition against William de Braose and his followers, such men as, for example, John Owayn or Sir John Iweyn, De Braose's principal steward of Gower together with his assistants. In 1305, Edward I appointed a commission to conduct an inquisition at Swansea to investigate the long list of grievances levelled at the Lord of Gower. Five years earlier, De Braose's oppressive tactics within his own lordship had been brought to the attention of Parliament.

In the end, the petitioners won their case which resulted in the bestowing of two charters by William de Braose during 1305-06. Among the numerous concessions listed, a particular significant one reads:

> ". . . Nor will we henceforth carry off our burgesses, nor any of their domestics in time of peace or war, or compel them to go beyond the limits of Goher' into an army or into any expedition or military force; but within the limits of Goher' they shall go forth with us in manner as is contained in their original charter."

Defiant to the end, William de Braose managed briefly to repossess the Lordship of Gower in circa 1324 by way of an assize of novel disseisin but then surrendered his estates to the Elder Dispenser. This devious manoeuvre hastened somewhat the outbreak of the Barons' War, which, in turn, caused the capture and death of John de Mowbray. In a marriage of convenience, and at the age of eleven, De Mowbray had been wedded to De Braose's daughter of approximately seven years of age, in order to bring about the unification of two substantial estates. Childless by his second marriage, and his only son having died, De Braose's links with Gower were finally cut with his passing in circa 1326.

De Mowbray's widow, Alina de Braose, was fortunate enough to recover the Lordship of Gower in 1327, married a Richard de Penshall in the following year, and held her newly won estates up to her death in mid 1331. She is credited with the responsibility for having certain modifications carried out to Oystermouth Castle in order to change it into something more of a residential fortress.

The next Marcher Lord of Gower during the period 1331-54 was John Lord Mowbray whose inheritance as a young man embraced huge estates in the north and south of England. As far as Gower was concerned, he was a typical absentee owner, a baron concerned chiefly with the maintenance of his English possessions. However, Baron Mowbray undertook a few visits to Gower, rebuilt Swansea Castle, and repaired Oystermouth Castle, as acknowledged by Leland, ". . . to be likelihood *Ostermuth,* also for the defence of the haven."

Mismanagement of fiscal dues collected from tenants and others by local officials as well as a general feeling of dissatisfaction with the shortcomings of absentee ownership in the lordship alienated considerable sections of the local populace throughout the 14th and early 15th centuries. It was not surprising, therefore, that their anger erupted into open rebellion when the opportunity presented itself. Owain Glyndwr's uprising, 1400-12, which became a national struggle, found ready support in South Wales and Gowerland. Oystermouth was one of a number of castles successfully attacked and damaged at a time when, it is believed, many historic documents may have been destroyed within its confines in the resulting pillage and destruction.

As Glyndwr's successful attacks gathered momentum during the opening years of the 15th century, the English began to appreciate the true significance of this widespread revolt which posed a real threat to their suppression of Wales as a whole. In 1403 and 1406, for example, the Bristol Merchants were commissioned to supply the garrisons at Newport, Cardiff, Kenfig, Swansea, Gower and Cardigan with provisions and stores. A Parliament of 1407 drew attention to the obligations and duties encumbent upon the Marcher Lords to defend their own castles and lands. In many respects, it was fortunate, as far as the English defenders were concerned, that the Welsh did not possess an abundance, if any, of heavy siege appliances, which consequently hampered their efforts to raze some castles to the ground or complete withering attacks to a final victorious conclusion.

Nevertheless, widespread damage and ruin engulfed Glamorgan; castles, buildings, hamlets, cultivated lands were despoiled and orchards and hedges laid waste by fire. Gower had been retaken by the English in 1406, according to the Welsh Annals, its castles at Swansea, Oystermouth and elsewhere within the peninsula having received reinforcements brought across the channel from Bristol and Devon. The Lordship of Gower had also sustained a great deal of devastation at the hands of Glyndwr's insurgents, so much so, that officials estimated in 1409-10 that two-thirds of the Lordship already in the King's possession, were not worth, in monetary terms, more than £100. Much of Glamorgan remained neglected and desolated until the reign of Henry VII, when Jasper Tudor, Duke of Bedford, the last Lord of Glamorgan, undertook to improve the County's husbandry.

When another John de Mowbray died in circa 1432, one of his former possessions was listed as Oystermouth Castle which encompassed an area of ground worth £12 per annum. In 1436, the third Duke of Norfolk succeeded to the Lordship of Gower. One of the Duke's leading officers in Gower was Sir Hugh Johnys who became the Constable or Warden of Oystermouth Castle in 1451 as well as the Reeve (Steward) of the Manor of Oystermouth.

A valiant warrior, Sir Hugh Johnys had a distinguished military record. It was at Jerusalem that he was knighted, in 1441, having fought against the Turks and Saracens under John, Emperor of Constantinople, for five years. He was honoured as a knight marshal of France for five years, and then a knight marshal of England.

At one time, Sir John was a suitor for the hand of Elizabeth Woodville, who afterwards, became the queen of Edward IV. Eventually, he married Mawde, a cousin of Sir Matthew Cradock of Place House, Swansea, first high sheriff of Glamorgan, and went to reside at Landimore Castle (Bovehill Castle). Norfolk favoured him with several annuities and also made him a surveyor of the Lordship of Gower.

From the late 15th century onwards, the inhabitants of Gower witnessed several changes of ownership. In circa 1470, Swansea Castle and the Lordship of Gower, together with other castles and lands, passed, by charter, to William Herbert, Earl of Pembroke. Estates in Swansea, Kilvey, the Lordship of Gower with Oystermouth, were owned by a Sir John Herbert throughout the early part of the 17th century. Among other appointments, Sir John was King James I's Principal Secretary.

Researchers can neither confirm nor deny whether Oystermouth Castle took an active part in the English Civil Wars of the 17th century. Originally, twin round towers flanked the gateway entrance but the external halves of these two towers were, in a period as yet unknown, taken down. With their firm control of the seas, Cromwellian forces in the west must have been aware of the castle's possibilities as a defensive site. Therefore, historians are, perhaps, at liberty to suggest that some sort of demolition here may have been undertaken by Cromwell's soldiers after their swift, successful entry into Swansea.

An entry in the minute book of the Corporation dated the 19th May, 1648, records that there "came into this Towne the truly Honorable Oliver Cromwell, Esq., Lifftenant Gennerall of all the Forces of this Kingdome of England, under the command of the Parliament, Lord of this Towne, the Seigniory of Gower, and Mannor of Killvay with the members thereof," and his gift of £10 to the poor is also noted. Oliver Cromwell was awarded the confiscated estates of the Marquis of Worcester in Gloucestershire and Monmouthshire by Parliament in May, 1647, and subsequently the estates in Glamorgan were included in the settlement, which explains his title as being "Lord of this Towne, the Seigniory of

Gower, and Mannor of Killvay." (Afterwards, as Lord Protector, he granted two generous charters to the burgesses of Swansea," a Town Corporate," in 1655 and 1658. The latter charter gave Swansea, for the first time, a representative in Parliament, as distinct from the Cardiff group of boroughs).

Consequently, Oystermouth Castle became a possession of the Lord Protector, although, as such, the building was worth very little. It is mentioned in the Survey of the Seigniory of Gower, 1650, undertaken by Bussey Mansel and others, under a Commission issued by Oliver Cromwell, as "an old decayed castle, called the castle of Oystermouth," within the manor of Oystermouth.

With the restoration of the Stuarts, these confiscated estates were released, and over a period of time reverted eventually to the Marquis of Worcester's descendants, the Ducal House of Beaufort. The Seigniory of Gower formed but one part of a large group of county estates owned by the Beaufort family throughout the centuries.

For very nearly two centuries, the castle remained virtually neglected and left in a dilapidated condition, a process of deterioration hastened by the effects of inclement weather and the passing of time. Yet, this is not the complete story, for on the west side of the building some marks of repair work, or modifications, reveal themselves as dating from the Middle Ages up to the 18th century. The castle must have been seen as a picturesque, ivy-clad and ancient ruin to those 18th century travellers hardy enough to negotiate a return journey, along the very few narrow, winding trackways leading in and out of Oystermouth. Samuel and Nathaniel Buck, of Garden Court, Middle Temple, London, selected it as one of their admirable, separate castle views of Gower. The brothers have again included Oystermouth Castle as part of the distant background within their detailed 1748 print, "East View of Swansea," but have rather incautiously listed Oystermouth itself as a "Town."

Throughout the later decades of the 19th century, the castle became one of the principal tourist attractions for visitors who travelled to the Mumbles in ever increasing numbers as road and rail transport facilities improved as never before. The horse-drawn coaches of the Oystermouth Railway or Tram Road together with the subsequent opening of the 1826 turnpike road made a noticeable improvement in the early decades. In the 1830's, permission to view the castle was obtained by way of its Warden, W. Collier, who was also a schoolmaster and a postman to the Mumbles. Then the reopening of the Mumbles Railway horse-drawn service in 1860 followed by the 1877 introduction of steam-hauled carriages on the line catered for the interests of the travelling public of the late Victorian era.

In 1840, the then Duke of Beaufort appointed Colonel George Grant Francis to supervise essential repair and restoration work at the castle, a task which must have been a labour of love as far as this noted, local antiquarian was concerned. Any further or anticipated decay within the structure was thereby curtailed for a considerable time afterwards as a result of this enlightened project.

As the art of photography developed throughout the later stages of the 19th century, the castle's elevated site was often used as a natural vantage point. Local History owes a debt to former amateur and professional photographers whose engaging views of late 19th and early 20th century Mumbles recapture the past in much detail.

In 1927, the Duke of Beaufort, as Lord Seigneur of Gower, agreed to the purchase of the castle and its surrounding ground from him by the County Borough of Swansea. Since that date, the area has remained an attractive and popular open-air public amenity; thousands of people, residents and visitors alike, explore the castle within annually which is open to sightseers normally during the summer months.

The ancient structure has been well maintained by Swansea Corporation who fully appreciate the castle's potential as a permanent tourist attraction. They also have to cater for the safety of the visiting public and, consequently, between 1956 and 1968, the castle was closed to visitors in order to permit the carrying out of urgent repairs to the stonework. Among others, several skilled stonemasons were engaged in a process which involved the application of patient renovation techniques. At a cost of several thousand pounds, particular care was taken to retain the original character of the limestone building and to preserve as much of the stonework as possible. Any new materials used have been carefully blended in with the old.

At the time, the Corporation's Maintenance Department worked in conjunction with the then Ministry of Works' officials. In addition to its historical importance and as a tangible reminder of one's heritage, Oystermouth Castle is most worthy of such necessary attention for it is, after all, one of the Borough's outstanding landmarks. Its architectural features with a short historical summary are contained in W. H. Jones' "A Brief Description And History Of The Castle Of Oystermouth" in which three original sketches of the main entrance, courtyard and prison by Harold Morgan are reproduced. This free booklet is generally available to those who visit the castle during the summer season and the admittance fee is a modest one.

Within the castle walls there is much to interest a discerning visitor. The gateway was originally protected by a ditch and drawbridge. A modern reproduction of the stronghold's portcullis is placed at the entrance and immediately in front of this, in the roof, remain two square holes through which defenders could pour down boiling oil etc. upon the enemy beneath. The grooves for the wheels which took the chains of the bridge are still visible above.

On the highest section of the rising terrain stands the main Edwardian block; subsequent additions represent a feudal layout more in keeping with that of a residential arrangement rather than a defensive network. Inside are the preserved remains of a guard-room, barracks, kitchens, prisons, store-rooms as well as the fine chapel annexe attributed to Lady de Mowbray.

The oldest section in evidence today, the keep, approximately twenty metres by eighteen metres, formerly housed the principal apartments of a three-storeyed building. At first floor level, in line with the porch, the square-shaped keep consists of two separate quarters: the first area complete with spacious fireplace was either a hall or Assize room; the second room above served most likely as a dining compartment in which one of its doors gave access to the chapel located on the south-east corner of the structure. Another room may have been placed above the dining area and if so appears to have lacked a stairway to it.

Additional rooms, above the basement area, are found in the northern half of the keep. The ground floor or drawing room possesses an ornamental fireplace with three striking lancet windows, The room overhead was originally a banqueting hall while the windows here are of the Early English period.

The chapel area is the higher of two upper apartments approached by a well-preserved circular stairway. As an integral part of the castle, the chapel is the largest one of its kind among the remaining castles left standing in Glamorgan. The splendid tracery of the large east window and the two windows on each side belong to the early 14th century, the three having been restored during the mid 1840's. Two further items of particular interest in this section are the finely-carved piscina and an ambry.

Therefore, throughout its history, Oystermouth Castle did possess most of those architectural features normally associated with a Mediaeval stronghold, even down to the inclusion of a pigeon house. Pigeon flesh provided an alternative source of food for the garrison, especially in the winter months, when it relieved a little the monotonous diet of salted beef.

Archaeologist and local historian, Bernard Morris, draws attention to this important aspect in an article of his published in "The South Wales Evening Post," dated the 28th February, 1968. He writes:

> "Many castles had these pigeon houses, but until recently it was assumed that Oystermouth Castle did not have one. A combination of careful research and good fortune has, however, now produced evidence that one did exist there, and we can even say exactly where it stood.

"Among the fine collection of nineteenth century drawings of local antiquities kept at the Royal Institution of South Wales (Swansea Museum) there is a drawing by William Butler, a talented local drawing-master, dated 1849, and showing 'the pigeon house at Oystermouth Castle.'

"The drawing shows a circular stone building similar to the pigeon house at Penrice and Oxwich, and another drawing by the same artist shows the interior, with the characteristic rows of square pigeon holes. The roof appears to have been covered with stone tiles not corbelled as in the other local examples.

". . . An examination of the first large-scale Ordnance Survey Map of Oystermouth , prepared in 1877, gave no immediate clue to the whereabouts of this distinctive structure . . . The answer to this tantilising puzzle came when I happened to see some old photographs of Oystermouth belonging to Mr. Stanley Williams, of West Cross.

"These were taken about 1870, and one of them showed the castle dominating the middle distance. On the seaward side of the castle was a clump of tall trees and below the trees—very small on the photograph, but quite unmistakable, was the elusive pigeon house.

"The 1877 Ordnance Map was quickly consulted again, and there, beneath the feathery drawings of the trees and largely concealed by them, was a neat circle, the site of Oystermouth Castle pigeon house.

"It had stood within what are now the castle grounds, 70 yards north-east of the castle, at the corner of the stone wall bounding the present allotments. Not a stone of the old structure is visible today, but a barely visible raised circular area marks where the foundations lie beneath the turf. Perhaps sometime in the future they can be carefully exposed and preserved."

In addition to its permanent role as a tourist attraction, the castle has become a focal point for some of the absorbing "Ostreme" events held in Mumbles during the late summer season. Since the early 1970's, the Ostreme programme of activities has been a special feature of Mumbles life witnessed by thousands of people, visitors and residents alike. Many local organisations and their members, supported by the City of Swansea Council and the various services under the Ministry of Defence and other national organisations, are involved in the excellent presentation of such events as the Swansea Bay Associations' Regatta, Mumbles Council of Churches Pageant, sports, exhibitions, competitions, plays, lectures, musical items, entertainments, contests and various displays which last for nearly two weeks.

Afternoon performances of church and historical plays are held within the castle grounds watched by hundreds of spectators. The evening musical presentation here of "Son Et Lumiere—The Bells Of Santiago," an Extravaganza in Music and Light, is a particularly spectacular production. (Based on the story of a tragedy in Chile, in 1863, the first production was written and recorded for Ostreme' 73 at All Saints Church, and engaged the combined choirs of the Mumbles Women's Institutes, the Brian Morris Singers and the Aelian Singers, the narrator being Timothy Perkins). On such nightly occasions, suitably bedecked and floodlit, the castle's surroundings become admirably enhanced, a fitting spectacle and tribute to its newly-found role as a scenic stage for man's more positive and creative endeavours.

Oystermouth Castle *By permission Roger David Studios*

Oystermouth Castle circa 1910 *Photo by D. G. Bowden*

All Saints, Oystermouth Parish Church circa 1850's *By permission Roger David Studios*

CHAPTER EIGHT

TOPOGRAPHICAL DESCRIPTIONS OF YESTERYEAR

"In a certain sense all men are historians."
Carlyle: Essays On History.

"It was in 1850 that his (Rev. John Pugh of Killay) activities centred on Mumbles, and after many visits to the vicinity of Norton and Blackpill, he secured the lease of a plot of land at Longfields, Mumbles. It was here, in the middle of a field that he had built, Bethany Baptist Church, to serve the needs of the rural community of Bishopston and Murton, as well as the little village of Mumbles. It should be remembered that Mumbles itself at that time was a very small place, and with the exception of a few fishermen's cottages on the front, there were very few people living in the area we know as Mumbles today. The two villages of Newton and Norton were the centres of population. Lady Barham had sponsored the building of a chapel at Newton, known as Paraclete, which was founded in 1818, John Pugh was now to provide for the needs of the village of Norton and its surrounding district by having Bethany built."
Robert Barnes: "The Church In The Lane." Bethany Baptist Church Building Centenary, 1867-1967.

"All Southenders lived 'outalong'; those at Oystermouth were 'inalong'; those at the top of Newton Road, Castleton District, were 'upalong'; and those at Langland were 'down backside.' The last expression needs some explanation. It arose from the dredgermen who, when they went dredging and rounded the Mumbles Head to go westward, always talked about going 'down backside,' and to some of us the names have stuck."
H. Libby: "The Mixture: Mumbles And Harry Libby." 1964.

1802.

"The village of Oystermouth is singular for losing all sight of the sun for upwards of three months in the year. There are several small houses for the accommodation of travellers, particularly the Old and New Mermaid, kept by Mrs. Stephens and Mrs. Phillips. On the higher part of the village stands 'Thistleboon House,' the residence of Mrs. Shewen, occasionally let as a lodging-house during the season to families of distinction."

("The Swansea Guide"—containing Such Info. as was deemed useful to the Traveller, through the counties of Glamorgan and Monmouth. Swansea: Printed by Z. B. Morris; and sold at Oakley's and Evans' Libraries, 1802).

1803.

An interesting and revealing description of Swansea in Nelson's days was written by the Rev. J. Evans. On visiting Gower, he described Caswell Bay as an "epitome of Lulworth Cove", a statement reiterated afterwards by some other writers of local guide books. The village of Oystermouth also impressed him and he noted that the "sea here abounds with soles, plaice, brill, turbot, sewen, crabs, lobsters, prawns, limpets, shrimps and other shell fish; and the rocks with a *small delicious oyster in high season,* during the summer months, when all others are out."

("Letters Written During A Tour Through South Wales, In The Year 1803." Rev. J. Evans, B.A.).

1813.

"We next reach Oystermouth Village, situate near the shore, under a vast rock of limestone, which from the beauty of its veins has been converted into chimney slabs, and other purposes for which marble is commonly used, and is not inferior in appearance to foreign marble.

"This village is singularly situated, not having the benefit of the sun for several months in the year.

"The sea here abounds with fish of all descriptions, and during the summer months, when all others are out of season, with a small delicious oyster, in the highest perfection.

"There is a house of good accommodation kept by Mrs. Stevens, where everything is good and reasonable, with great civility.

"Not far distant from the village, is the Castle. . . . Passing the village of Newton about two miles you reach Caswell Bay, famed for the number and beauty of the shells which the sea frequently throws upon the sands.

"This place is said to resemble Lulworth Cove. . . . To those fond of the marvellous, this secluded spot will furnish abundant food for the imagination. The violence of the sea has produced wonderful excavations of various shapes and dimensions, some assuming the appearance of temples, with mighty Gothic arches; and others of subterraneous passages, with a circular canopy.

"A little further is Langland Bay, famed also for its shells, and beauty of its situation."

("A Description Of Swansea And Its Environs". 1813. Printed and sold by David Jenkin, Castle Street).

1819

"OYSTERMOUTH, a sea-port and parish in the cwmwd of Gwyr, cantref of Eginoy (now called the hundred of Swansea), and County of Glamorgan, South Wales, is situated on a small promontory, which forms the western boundary of Swansea Bay, in the Bristol Channel. The eastern extremity of the parish is called 'The Mumbles Point,' opposite to which, at a short distance from the shore, a light-house has been lately erected. *This place might be made an excellent station for shipping at a very trifling expense,* either by walling in the sounds between the Mumbles Head and the shore, or by running a pier out under the east point of Mumbles Hill. Vessels bound for Falmouth with coals from Swansea generally lie here when waiting for wind and convoy; frequently to the number of one hundred and fifty sail at one time. Along the shore hence to Swansea, a railway has been constructed, by which *coals and manure* are brought down, and *lime* returned from the limestone quarries, which are situated close to the village of the Mumbles, and where *several lime-kilns* are established.

"In digging the stone of these quarries many human bones of large dimensions have been discovered; and tradition says, this spot was formerly the site of a chapel, but no vestiges of it now remain. The existence of such a building, however, is not improbable, *as the sea has made great encroachments on this part of the bay.* A large wood, called *'Crow's Wood,'* frequently mentioned in ancient records, has been submerged, and traces of it are still evident in the sand at low water. Vast quantities of shell-fish, but particularly *oysters,* are caught or dragged on the coast here: hence the origin of the term Oystermouth as the designation of the parish, which, according to the Parliamentary returns of 1811, contains 200 houses and 761 inhabitants.

"On a knoll or eminence east from the church stand the ruins of Oystermouth Castle, supposed to have been erected by the Norman Beaumonts, who conquered Gowerland. It has suffered less from the ravages of time than any ruin in this part of the country, the principal walls being as yet in good condition, and most of the apartments entire. The general figure is polygonal, and the ramparts are conspicuously lofty, but there are no flanking towers except on each side of the entrance gateway. Here, according to tradition, the chancery court for the seigniory of Gower was anciently held. This edifice is now the property of the Duke of Beaufort, as lord of the seigniory, *and is much resorted to by parties of pleasure* from Swansea and the neighbourhood. In one of the dungeons of the castle is a circular stone pillar, into which almost every visitor sticks a pin, conformably to an old custom, practised from time immemorial. The whole ruin is covered with a profusion of ivy."

("The Cyclopaedia; or, Universal Dictionary of Arts, Sciences, and Literature." Abraham Rees, D.D., F.R.S., F.L.S., S. Amer. Soc. London, 1819. Vol. XXV).

1823

"Near Oystermouth is the marble manufactory of Messrs. H. Griffiths and Co. equal in beauty and durability to any in the kingdom; near which is Norton, a hamlet belonging to Oystermouth; Norton-lodge; West Cross, the residence of Captain Andrews; and other neat, small cottages. Here the majestic ruins of Oystermouth castle presents itself, on the brow of an eminence surrounded by broken cliffs of limestone, said to be built by Henry Beaumont, Earl of Warwick. The principal walls of this ruin are not much injured by time, and most of the apartments may be readily distinguished; the general figure is polygonal, and the ramparts are conspicuously lofty; but unflanked by towers, except at the entrance: a profusion of ivy overspreading the ruin, rather conceals than adorns it. The entrance is at the south-west end, which forms a projection and breaks the square; it seems to have been protected by a portcullis and double gates. On a level with the wall on the east side is thc keep, whence the prospect is extremely fine. The whole building is a good specimen of the Gothic; the upper rooms were large, and communicated with each other by small doors. It is said there is a subterraneous passage to Swansea, and even to Neath, but for the truth of this we have no good authority; there are many private arched vaults and staircases, and it must have been originally a place of great strength. This castle, with much of the land adjoining, formerly belonged to the lords of Gower; and are now a part of the possessions of his Grace the Duke of Beaufort.

"A little further on is Oystermouth church, an object from many situations very picturesque. The Rev. Mr. Davies, Vicar. The village lies along the bottom of a high limestone rock, the headland of which boldly terminates one of the peninsulas of Gower, and by its stretching far into the bay affords a safe anchorage to vessels harassed by foul winds in the channel. On the head of the peninsula a light-house was erected by the trustees for the improvement of Swansea harbour.* (*All the shipping that pass the Nash point, in the county of Glamorgan, and Horestone—otherwise Horsedown point, Somersetshire, and Leadstep point, near Manorbeer, Pembrokeshire, and Hartland point, in the county of Devon, contribute towards the support of it). This building is much admired and frequently visited; the light consists of a large iron lanthorn (lantern), cast at the foundery of Neath Abbey, with eleven grand lamps and reflectors, which is seen very brilliant across the channel."

("The New Swansea Guide", 1823. Printed And Sold by H. Griffith, 17

Wind Street; Sold Also By D. Jenkin, Castle Street: In London, By Longman And Co. And Baldwin And Co.).

1830

"The Mumbles having of late become a place of fashionable resort by the Visitors of Swansea, from the variety and beauty of its scenery, and the excellent road thereto (than which a finer piece is not to be found in the Principality, for which the Commissioners deserve the public thanks). It has now several good Lodging Houses, and bids fair to be a still greater attraction, if some enterprising persons were to provide further accommodation in the establishment of an Hotel. New roads are intended to be made and others improved, so as to form a delightful drive round the romantic shores of the Peninsula of Gower. The Castle of Oystermouth, has, with the Lordship thereto belonging, been almost constantly the property of the Lords of Gower. The first of which, were the Beaumonts, Earls of Warwick, and by them it was conveyed to the Crown. King John, afterwards gave it to the Breoses, Lords of Brecon; from them it came by marriage, to the family of the Mowbrays; from thence to the Herberts: and by marriage of an heiress, to the family of the Somersets, in which it is now vested in the person of His Grace the Duke of Beaufort. It has been a place of great strength, but little is known of its local history; it has been fenced around, but the ruins may be viewed by applying to the Warden, W. Collier."

"Rev. Samuel Davies, Minister of Oystermouth.

Churchwardens:

Mr. Samuel Gammon

Mr. John Jenkins.

Schoolmaster, Warden of Oystermouth Castle and Postman to the Mumbles—W. Collier.

RESIDENTS

Andrews—Esq., Norton.
Jefferies Richard, Esq., Norton.
Thomas T., Esq., Norton.
Thomas Lieutenant T., R.N. Ditto.
Griffiths Mrs. Susannah
Hammerton Rev. William
Lloyd Mr. David, Tide Surveyor.
Nicholls Mr. John
Powis John, Esq.
Summerfield T. B. Esq.

LODGING HOUSES

Bennett Mrs.
Harncorne Mrs.
Hill Mrs.
Knight Mrs.
Morgan Mrs. E.
Masters Mr.
Morgan Mr. Lilliput
Thomas Mrs. Sophia

VICTUALLERS

Evans Jenkins, George Inn.
Jenkins John, Butchers Arms.
Phillips George, Ship and Castle.
Rees Morgan, Ship Inn.
Stephens Mrs. Jane, Mermaid Inn.
Taylor Daniel, Nag's Head.

AT NEWTON
John Davies, Ship.
Matthews Wright, Dove, Norton.
Mary Jenkins, Three Salmon.

BRINNEY
John Harris, Brinney Inn."

(Matthew Mathews': "Swansea Directory For The Year 1830." Printed And Sold By The Editor, M. Mathews, 71, High Street; And By The Booksellers).

1851

"The Mumbles, from its proximity to Swansea, and from the variety and beauty of its scenery, has become a place of fashionable resort, more especially during the Summer season. Following closely all the way the line of Swansea Bay, and being overlooked throughout the distance by graceful woodland eminences and gentlemen's country seats, the road from Swansea to the Mumbles affords a most pleasing drive and very delightful prospects. By the most competent authorities, it is considered there are few places of shelter for shipping on the British coast comparable to the Mumbles roadstead. In a channel destitute of a harbour of refuge, it is invaluable; and occasionally as many as 500 or 600 sail of vessels are anchored in this small roadstead, which is well sheltered from all except north-easterly winds. The length of the rock is about a mile. At the eastern end are two islands, which, in effect, form part of the promontory, as the tide usually leaves a dry passage between, at low water. On the farthest is a well-known lighthouse, which is much admired and frequently visited. The light consists of a large iron lanthorn, cast at the Neath Abbey Foundry, with eleven grand lamps and reflectors, which is seen with brilliant effect across the Channel. Below the Lighthouse, to the south, is a vast cave, locally called 'Bob's Cove,' accessible when the tide is out, and much frequented by the curious.

"The Mumbles headland consists chiefly of excellent limestone, which is quarried and exported at from 1s. 3d. to 1s. 6d. per ton. This limestone, from the beauty of its veins, has been converted into chimney slabs, and is not inferior in appearance to foreign marble. A valuable vein of iron ore was discovered in 1845, which has been worked, much to the disfigurement of this romantic spot, which commands scenes of great beauty, and a view of the Channel, from Nash Point to Lundy Island on one side, and Swansea Bay, backed by graceful hills, and studded with many sails, from the three-master to the pilot-boat, on the other. On the south of the headland, just in the track of ships, is a shoal, called 'The Mixen,' distinguished at its western extremity by a buoy. In strong weather, at early flood, the sea runs 'mountains' over this sandbank. A short time ago, *one of the Cuba ships,* loaded with a *valuable cargo of copper-ore, struck here, and almost immediately became a total wreck.*

"In an old 'Cambrian,' dated April 7th, 1810, the following singular occurrence is related:

'The labourers employed by Mr. Yalden in the limestone quarries at the Mumbles lately cut through a complete cemetery, in which were found immense quantities of human bones, of a very large size: from the position and confused state they were discovered in, it is highly probable that this spot was the burial-place of a vast multitude who perished nearly at the same time, either by pestilence or the sword, at some very remote period.' These bones (says Mr. Dillwyn, in his 'Contributions, &c.'), 'were found on the eastern back of shallow declivity in the rocks, nearly halfway from the village to the Mumbles point, where there was a deposit of earth or some detritus, about three or four feet deep, and one of those which I saw was remarkably large, nor could they by possibility lie in greater confusion than the bones in the ancient cemetery of Margam Abbey, which I assisted the late Rev. Dr. Hunt to examine shortly afterwards. From some of the oldest inhabitants of Oystermouth I heard a tradition, that there was once a chapel near the edge of the cliff above where these bones were found, though its foundations had long since been quarried away, and they were aware that the spot had been a burial-ground belonging to it.'

"The village of Oystermouth is a genuine fishing village, the oyster fishery giving employment to upwards of 400 men in the height of the season. The oysters are caught in the bay and near the village, and are exported in great quantities to Liverpool, London, Bristol, Gloucester, and other parts of England. The village is singularly situated under a vast rock of limestone, and from this circumstance, it is said that the sun does not shine on it for three months in the year. To those fond of 'breezy downs scented with thyme and other wild plants, sloping to an iron-bound coast broken by bluff and vast headlands,' of delicious little bays, where one can dream away the day in gazing, . . . this neighbourhood will be found full of charms, particularly the Mumbles Hill, from which is to be seen one of the most magnificent marine prospects in the kingdom. There are inns and good lodging houses in the village, and in the neighbourhood of Norton. Some good accommodation will be had at the Mermaid, the George, and the Ship and Castle, all of which are famed for the quality of 'the cup that cheers,' and other refreshments, which they provide at a moderate rate. The omnibuses run from Swansea to the Mumbles throughout the day: from Rees's, the Horse and Groom, College Street, twice a-day; from Barter's, the Rutland Arms, and from the Bush Inn, High Street, each three times a-day; and from the Railway Booking Office, Wind Street, several times a-day.

"Not far from the village is the Castle, considered one of the most majestic Norman fortresses in the Principality, although but little appreciated until very recently. The structure, which stands upon a picturesque eminence, was so much hidden by ivy, that its outlines were hardly distinguishable. In 1843, Mr. G. G. Francis, of Swansea, induced the Duke of Beaufort to expend a small sum in repairs and restoration, which arrested the work of dilapidation, and a very fine example of Mediaeval military architecture has been disclosed. The foundation of Oystermouth Castle has been ascribed both to Henry Beaumont, Earl of Warwick, the Conqueror of Gower, and to Richard de Granville, one of Fitzhamon's Knights, and the founder of the Castle and Abbey of Neath. It now forms part of the extensive possessions of the Duke of Beaufort. It is said that Oliver Cromwell marched part of his army from Oystermouth across the isthmus, in a line to Penclawdd, where he forded the river, on his way to Kidwelly Castle. A guide is generally in attendance to conduct visitors over the commanding ruin of Oystermouth."

(John Lewis, Reporter To "The Cambrian" Newspaper: "The Swansea Guide" 1851. Published By William Matthias Brewster).

1870

"A little beyond is the village and watering-place of Mumbles (Inns: Mermaid, George), which has considerably increased since the formation of the docks spoilt the bathing at Swansea. It is snugly situated underneath the high escarpment of mountain-limestone cliffs which terminate seawards in two rocky islets, on the furthest of which stands the Mumbles Lighthouse. Much stone is obtained from the quarries and sent to Swansea.

"The Bay, which is thought by many to bear a strong resemblance to that of Naples in its outline, is seen to advantage from here, and is singularly graceful. Since the time of man, however, ancient records point to a considerable extent of wood which has been submerged by the sea, a fact borne out by geological appearances, such as the discovery of trunks of trees, hazel-nuts, &c., at low water.

"The sea has made great encroachments here within living memory, and not so many centuries back the high road to Bristol ran along a tract now constantly covered by the waves. The Mumbles roadstead, as affording a perfectly secure shelter to shipping in all winds, except those from the N.E., is very important as a harbour of refuge, and many hundred sail are occasionally detained here whilst waiting for more favourable weather. The oyster fishery is valuable, and affords employment to a number of vessels and many men.

"At Lilliput, close to the village of Norton, Sir. W. Logan found a seam of coal cropping out on the sea-shore with only a thin covering of sand.

"2 m. W. of the Mumbles is Caswell Bay (where is a tolerable hotel and boarding-house), an extremely pretty bit of marine landscape. Here are some copious springs of delicious water, covered by the tide at high water. The pedestrian should walk along the cliffs from the Mumbles by Langland's Bay and Whiteshell Point, where the coast is fine and rugged. At the former bay is the marine residence of R. Crawshay, Esq."

(Murray's "Hand-Book—South Wales." 2nd Edition, 1870).

1875

"Oystermouth, or Mumbles. This pleasant suburb of Swansea is situated five miles S.W. of the borough; and since the rapid increase of factories, &c., in the latter, has become the chief sea-side resort and bathing-place of Swansea folks. From its peculiar position under a high limestone rock, which deprives it of sun during several months in the winter, it is but a dreary residence during that period of the year. The higher grounds command noble views of Swansea and Carmarthen bays, the peninsula of Gower, and the Bristol Channel. As implied by the name, the oyster fishery is carried on extensively during the season, chiefly for the Bristol market, and large quantities of salmon are caught in the weirs in Swansea Bay.

"The general character of the coast is sandy burrows the whole of the way round, especially at the mouths of the rivers, Tawe, Neath, and Afon, which discharge into the bay. Outside these flats come the Green Grounds, which extend 2¼ miles in an easterly direction from the Mumbles Head . . . Mumbles Lighthouse is situated at the extremity of the point bearing that name, but at low water the rocks are uncovered 280 yards further out to the Cherrystone. The lighthouse is octagonal in shape, shows a white fixed light, 114 feet above high water, and visible 15 miles off in clear weather. From the Mumbles Head the coast trends inwards to the N.W. for a mile, and then curves eastward for 4 miles to the harbour. Mixon Shoal is a fine sandbank, lying just outside of the Mumbles Head to the S.W., and a black bell buoy marks the outside or southern edge of this danger. It is high water at the Mumbles, full and change, at 6 hr. 1 min. local time, and 6 hr. 17 min. Greenwich time. Equinoctial spring rise, 31 ft.; ordinary springs, 27 ft. 5 in.; and neaps 20 ft. 5 in.; the latter ranging 13 ft. 5 in. At low water the mud flats all round the bay are laid bare on an average of half a mile from the shore, and on the western side are intersected by numerous fishing weirs, and the bar at the entrance of river channel up to the Swansea docks and harbour is also quite dry at low tide.

"All Saints' Church is a neat and appropriate edifice, containing a monument to Thomas Bowdler, the editor of the 'Family Shakespeare' and Gibbon's 'Decline and Fall of the Roman Empire.' On the summit of a knoll, surrounded by broken cliffs, a little to the N.W. of the church and commanding a fine sea view are the remains of the ancient castle. It has been partly restored by the Duke of Beaufort, under the antiquarian superintendence of G. G. Francis, Esq., of Swansea. The plan of the castle is irregular, its general figure being an isosceles triangle. The gateway has been flanked by two towers, which have been removed at some early period, so that the inner and concave segment forms now the outer wall, and thus throws forward the gateway. What may be called the keep is certainly the oldest part of the building. This, placed at the N.E. angle, is quadrangular, of three stages, heavily buttressed, with recessed chambers in the buttresses. The upper storey is the chapel. It is all of the same date, English Declension, and the additions are not much later. It was probably built by Henry de Beaumont, to serve as a link in the border chain of castles. There is frequent communication with Swansea by the railway skirting the bay; and the rateable value of the parish is £11,111.

"Caswell Bay is situated a couple of miles W. of the Mumbles, between White Shell Point and Pwll du Head. The aspect being almost due S.W., added to the fact of a fine sandy shore, on the beautiful bay, which renders the sea-bathing unsurpassable, it is peculiarly adapted to the requirements of delicate people, and a more agreeable marine resort in South Wales could scarcely be found. Some copious springs of delicious water are situated here. There are two postal deliveries daily . . .

"London and North-Western Railway Station, Blackpill,—Station Master, Richard Alfred Davies. Oystermouth Railway Station,—Station Master, William Pressdee. Police Station,—Supt. John Baker. Coastguard Station, Mumbles,—Supt. Capt. Thomas Dickenson, R.N.; Chief Boatman, James Salter. Assembly room, Dunns,—Proprietor, Daniel Clement.

("Butcher & Company's Directory of Swansea . . . 1875-6.")

1880

"Oystermouth, anciently Ostremuere, but now for the most part styled The Mumbles, is the most considerable centre of population in Gowerland, and only 4½ miles from Swansea. A higgledy-piggledy collection of poor cottages, respectable terraces, commodious villas, hotels, public houses, and shops, occupies the inner side of the excellent roadway that follows the curve of the bay; and, behind this varied line of frontage, extending backwards to the sheltering hill, and even scaling its steep slopes, the visitor will find a labyrinth of small streets that intersect each other, and double round upon those who attempt to follow them, and at last lead nowhere. The explanation is, that when the village of Oystermouth was built, there was no superintending Urban Sanitary Authority such as now exercises a jealous and beneficial influence over the place. The village has outgrown the designation 'Rural,' repudiates the intermediate epithet 'Suburban,' and assumes the fully-fledged dignity of an 'Urban' Government, though some things still remain to be done before the place can be seriously called a 'town.'

"The chief industry of Oystermouth is oyster-dredging, but the owners of a large number of the better-class houses depend upon the rents they receive from lodgers, who visit the watering-place in the summer months. The accommodation is fairly good, and the charges compare well with those of most English sea-side resorts. Among the chief hotels are 'The Mermaid,' a quaint old place, with rough-cast flower-veiled front, and cosy little tea rooms, and arboured garden, reaching down to the shingle at the water's edge; the 'Ship and Castle,' commodious and well-furnished; 'The George,' which is the headquarters of the Bristol Yacht Club, &c. There is much promenading all day, but especially in the cool of evening, along the broad smooth street, which, at its southern end, leads away along the shingle and under high limestone cliffs to the Mumbles Head, the Lighthouse and the Battery. On the way, just where it should be in case of need, is the Lifeboat House, containing the fine boat 'Wolverhampton,' which, following in the wake of its predecessor on this coast, has been instrumental in the hands of brave men in saving a great many lives. The path gets rougher as the explorer nears the Inner Sound, or narrow, rocky, sea-weedy channel, which divides the first round Islet from the mainland. At low water this may be crossed dry shod, and in the crevices of the rocks naturalists will find many things to delight them. The first island is a rounded outlying heap of limestone, on whose rugged surface there is nothing save a solitary telegraph post, that bears the strain of two wide spans of wire. The Outer Sound, or second channel, is wider and deeper, and more hazardous to cross.

". . . The Mumbles Head is a larger outlying mound of limestone, the high summit of which is taken up by a fine lighthouse, a battery, and some habitations and offices . . . The ancient brazier and the coal fire have long since disappeared, the tower has been raised, and the present light, which is maintained free of cost to the shipping, consists of a large dioptric lantern, . . . exhibiting a fixed white light, visible in clear weather from 15 to 20 miles across and down the stormy channel's mouth. The gallery outside the lantern is well worth a visit for the excellence of the view it yields.

"Within the last twelve months the advantages of the national and international telegraph system have been brought down to the water's edge at this spot, so that captains have only to signal with flags, or step ashore and write a message, and their arrival is known in a few minutes to the owners and shippers, however far away. This is the only convenience of its kind in the Channel."

(S. G. Gamwell: "The Official Guide & Handbook To Swansea & District.")

1901

"From Swansea to the Mumbles, $5\frac{1}{2}$ M., Steam Tramway, starting opposite the Victoria Station hourly during the day (fares 1st cl. $7\frac{1}{2}$d., 2nd., $5\frac{1}{2}$d.), The road skirts the sands of Swansea Bay, the natural beauty of which triumphs over many disadvantages. At St. Helen's Junction, the steam-tramway is met by the electric tramway from Gower St. We pass (on the right) the Victoria Park, Swansea Cricket Ground, Swansea Bay Recreation Ground and Singleton, the residence of Lord Swansea. On the left is a fine promenade (benches) overlooking the sea. At $1\frac{1}{2}$ M. St. Gabriels and 3 M. Mumbles Road are stations of the L.N.W. Railway. To the left are the remains of a submerged forest, and to the right, at $3\frac{1}{2}$ M.

Blackpill, are Clyne woods. 5 M. Oystermouth; $5\frac{1}{4}$ M. Southend; 2 min. from the hotels. Pony-chaise to Langland Bay or Caswell Bay, 1s. 6d. . . . 2s. 6d. $5\frac{1}{2}$ M. Mumbles Pier.

"The Mumbles. (Ship & Castle; Mermaid; George; lodgings) is a rising watering-place which has developed out of the fishing village of Oystermouth and has assumed the name that in strict parlance belongs to the detached rocks off the S. horn of Swansea Bay. The name is supposed to be derived from the resemblance of these rocks to projecting breasts (mammae). The oyster-beds here have recently recovered some of their former prosperity. From the Pier (adm. 1d.; restaurant), opened in 1899, steamers ply in summer to Bristol, Cardiff, Swansea, Tenby, Ilfracombe, Lynmouth, etc. The bathing is tolerable and the boating is good. A fine marine drive has been carried round the coast from Southend to Bracelet Bay, passing near the Lighthouse on Mumbles Head.

(K. Baedeker: "Great Britain—Handbook For Travellers" 1901).

1911

"But at the Mumbles you have left the copper-smoke far behind. The time to climb the Mumbles Hill is late on a summer evening, when the tide is full and the sun westering. But by broad moonlight on a clear night the bay looks just as fair: if the sea-surroundings are not so distinct, the furnace-glow on the left is mysterious to see. Seen by day, the view ranges along the Glamorgan coast, beginning with the superb curve of Swansea Bay, and traversing the mouths of the rivers Tawe and Neath, and scanning the smoke-cloud of Swansea Town and the dolorous valley of Landore . . .

"Outside Norton, we overtook a big herd-lad driving the proverbial three cows. They were three sisters; the first eight, the second seven, the third six years old: sleek, brown and dun animals, Alderney and Shorthorn crossed. The lad was fond of the creatures, and proud of their cross-bred qualities. 'They were good milkers, or fairly good,' he said, 'much better than your pure Alderneys.' 'An Alderney is not worth her salt' was a common saying among the Gower farmers."

(Ernest Rhys: "The South Wales Coast." 1911).

1919

"Our chapel faces due East, and stands back a little from the main road, above the level of which the main entrance is elevated a few feet, as the ground rises rapidly to the rear.

"Until a few years ago the sea rolled right up to the road whenever the tide was in; and when the easterly gales were on, the waves raced across the shelving beach and broke madly over the low sea wall in clouds of spray, which rendered the road impassable and the chapel itself unapproachable from the front. Then the front door of the chapel had to be kept closed, and those who lived on the main road used to go out at their back doors, and, with others who had arrived by devious courses, creep round to the back of the chapel, and get in by means of the little side door through which the preacher and the singers usually entered." (Page 1).

"Midway between the Glen and the Bay, and on rising ground which commands a view of both, stands the Castle from which the farm takes its name. For hundreds of years it was one of a chain of fortresses. . . Then it was dismantled. The hill where Oliver Cromwell did not place his cannon is still shown. Then it came into use as a debtor's prison, and finally degenerated into a mere shelter for cattle. Sixty or seventy years ago it was cleared and restored, and now it is properly cared for. Castles are now assets. On its hoary walls *are found some fifteen varieties of ivy,* amid the thick growth of which almost as many kinds of birds congregate.

"In courtyard and banqueting hall, where Dane and Norman, bailiffs and debtors, 'gloried and drank deep,' now echo only to the laugh of the holiday maker or the chatter of the *country people who come from afar to gather the medicinal 'pellitory of the wall'* which has chosen this, of all places, for its local habitation.

"From the look-out over the entrance where the thrushes build, you can see straight pass the village, and the headland with its light, across twenty-five miles of salt water, to where, on the other side of the channel, great hills slope down, verdant even to the water's edge. When you can make out the different colours of the fields, or if there is a bloom on those distant hills almost like that on a blue plum, then you may be sure it is going to rain—and whatever the outlook from the Castle window may be, you can never be sure it is not going to rain." (pages 10-11).

C. W. Slater: "The Corner Pew." 1919).

"There were quite a number of shops at the Dunns where visitors could purchase most items, especially presents. Among the ever popular gifts bought by the dozen were the small china plates, mugs, jugs, bowls and so on, suitably inscribed, 'A Present From Mumbles.' For cheapness and appeal the miniature ware was much in demand, the Stoke-on-Trent firms catering specifically for this trade, as in other holiday resorts. 'Wilton' china, to quote but one of several examples, would contain views of the Pier, Swansea Bay, Mumbles Head and Lighthouse. Many of these small ornaments, including pink German ware, are being sold in antique shops today."

(N. L. Thomas: "The Story Of Swansea's Districts And Villages." Enlarged 1965.)

Mumbles Lighthouse Battery Naval Gun, circa 1860's at Swansea Marina, 1978.

By permission, South Wales Evening Post

Caswell Bay, early 19th C. print.

New three-storey houses in Newton Road, 1872. Taken from Overland Road; original restored by Mr. Cyril Reed.

By permission, South Wales Evening Post & Roger David Studios

Edwardian Days. *By permission, Roger David Studios*

Pier—Edwardian Days. *By permission, Roger David Studios*

Pier—Edwardian Days. *By permission Roger David Studios*

The Parade, circa 1906 (Postcard)

Oystermouth Square 1920's. *By permission, Roger David Studios*

The Dunns, 1920's. *By permission, Roger David Studios*

Opening of Wales Tourist Office, Oystermouth, May, 1977, by Mayor & Mayoress of Swansea, Cllr. & Mrs. Werner Siversten.

By permission, South Wales Evening Post

The Gower Pony with Newton W.I. Members, 1977 *By permission, South Wales Evening Post*

Mumbles View 1962 by B. V. Parkyn. *Kindly loaned by Mr. & Mrs. L. A. Haines*

CHAPTER NINE

RESCUE AT SEA AND PROTECTION OF THE COASTLINE

"To be ignorant of what happened before you were born is to be ever a child. For what is man's lifetime unless the memory of past events is woven with those of earlier times."
Cirero: Orator. Sec. 34.

"At the end of April, 1947, a Memorial Service was held in the School Hall for the victims of the terrible lifeboat disaster, in which all eight members of the crew lost their lives. The school was closed in the afternoon on the occasion of the funeral, and Oystermouth School sent £61 to the Mayor's Life-boat Distress Fund."
Oystermouth School Centenary 1878-1978 Publication.

"The latest Look-Out Communications Centre situated on the Tutt, alongside the old 1921 structure, was built by Messrs. R. M. Douglas Construction Ltd. and opened on the 26th June, 1973, by Mr. Michael Heseltine, M.P., as the then Minister for Aero-Space & Shipping . . .

"Of special interest is the weighty but movable 'Dopples' binoculars which can be directed into any desired position and commands a particularly long range of vision. It was obtained from a former heavy gun emplacement installed as part of the German 'Atlantic Wall' defence system of World War Two. Another interesting feature concerns the Mumbles Lighthouse, half a mile distant; if thick fog breaks its beam, the fog horn is automatically set off by the Coastguard Centre."
Mumbles: Past And Present.

At national or local level, rescue at sea involves primarily the services of Her Majesty's Coastguard and the Royal National Life-Boat Institution. The protection of the coastline is the other principal responsibility of the former organisation and, in this connection, or when it forms part of a life-saving operation at sea or on land, H.M. Coastguard can call on the professional help of numerous different establishments and deploy them to the best advantage. Some of these relate to the "declared facilities" of the R.N.L.I.'s life-boats, Ministry of Defence helicopters, Nimrod aircraft and Royal Navy vessels. Help is also sought and given freely by Trinity

House, life-guards, police, ambulance personnel, medical staff, vessels at sea both commercial and pleasure, harbour pilot boats and members of the public. All involved, collectively or individually, give their time and effort to the saving of life and it is the basic task of H.M. Coastguard to co-ordinate these to the best advantage. Such an aim is best summed up in the words of Coastguard Officer D. Fairfield, M.R.C.C., Mumbles, Swansea, thus: "To get the right equipment to the right place at the right time."

Within a more restricted area, protection of the coastline is also the essential function of the South Wales Fisheries' District which stretches from Cardiff to the entrance of Cardigan Bay, a length of some 270 miles. This agency covers three main fishery industries and their activities: trawling, crab and lobster fishing, and the gathering of cockles.

The Coastguard Service has long been associated with the Swansea and Mumbles scene. Their first Look-Out Station or "Watch-House" was positioned on Mumbles Hill circa 1850; in those days it was reached by climbing the cliff pathway situated behind the George Hotel. The "building" was rather a make-shift arrangement: it consisted of half a boat turned on its end, the only immediate semblance of official status being represented by the adjacent flag-staff used in making appropriate signals to vessels out at sea. Although some improvements were made to this structure later, and its replacement, the Look-Out on this particular site was eventually dismantled in 1910. The natural vantage-ground and location of the Tutt was afterwards considered a suitable alternative.

Among others, Coastguard personnel are periodically referred to by "The Cambrian" for acts of bravery or devotion to duty and such was the case in respect of one fierce storm which hit the Swansea area from a south-easterly direction on the 27th September, 1856. Twenty-two vessels at the Mumbles sustained various degrees of damage, while eight sank and nine were driven ashore by the violence of the winds. Led by Chief Officer Dillon, the Coastguard boat was launched by the men under his command who "exerted themselves most energetically in rendering aid to the distressed vessels." They succeeded in rescuing the crews of the schooner, "Monkey" of Drogheda, Owens, Master, and those aboard the "Western Star" of New Ross. This occurred before the permanent establishment of a lifeboat service at the Mumbles by the R.N.L.I. in 1866.

As a nationwide organisation responsible for the co-ordination of search and rescue operations around some 2,500 miles of coastline of Great Britain and Northern Ireland, H.M. Coastguard celebrated its 150th anniversary on the 15th January, 1972. The force was brought into being originally to combat the once relentless activities of 19th century smugglers; it came under the control of the Board of Customs but the personnel were appointed by the Admiralty whose officers commanded 3,000 men at the commencement of 1822.

Men worked an all-night watch when they came on duty at dusk and went off at dawn, a grim existence on poor pay. Nevertheless, their counter-measures gradually won the day and by the mid-1850's smuggling was no longer widespread or such a profitable activity. By the Coastguard Act of 1856, the force was placed under the control of the Admiralty as a Naval Reserve which could contribute to the defence of the coastline; serve on board Royal Navy ships; and assist in the protection of the Revenue. It continued in this role until the end of the First World War. This particular Act made no reference to life-saving responsibilities which, under the provisions of the Merchant Shipping Act, 1854, was entrusted to the Board of Trade. The latter took over life-saving companies and issued them with equipment.

While Admiralty instructions to the Coastguard in 1911 again emphasised they were not responsible for life-saving systems or their inadequacies around the United Kingdom's coastline, coastguardsmen could "render every possible assistance to the life-saving services, as far as is compatible with their proper duties," which they did year in and year out. Most of the coastguards were mobilised into the Royal Navy at the outbreak of the 1914-18 War; many of them were tragically lost in the sinking of the three old battleships "Aboukir," "Crecy" and "Hogue" as well as other vessels.

In 1925 the Board of Trade (now the Department of Trade) took over the management of the Coastguard from the Admiralty and gave it the responsibility for search and rescue operations around the coast, the first occasion in the nation's history that a professional force had been created for this important function. The Board of Trade also retained the title of "H.M. Coastguard" for its members by Royal sanction.

The Treasury's 1922 Inter-Departmental Committee whose findings led afterwards to the passing of the Coastguard Act of 1925 made three basic recommendations for the peace time work of the Coastguard Service. These provided for a Naval Signalling Force to man selected stations as were considered necessary under Naval requirements; the Coast-Watching Force to perform duties in connection with the saving of life; the salvage of wreck; the administration of foreshores and certain other miscellaneous duties to be administered by the Board of Trade; and a Coast Prevention Force to be managed by the Customs for Revenue protection purposes. The Committee also further suggested that in the event of any future hostilities the Naval Signalling and Coast-Watching Forces should come under the authority of the Admiralty.

Between the 28th May, 1940 and 1st October, 1945, the Admiralty again took over the control of H.M. Coastguard in time of war as laid down in the 1925 Coastguard Act. As an Armed Force, its regular and auxiliary personnel were subject to the Naval Discipline Act. The importance of their unique contribution to the defence of the realm throughout those anxious years cannot be overestimated. Some indication of this can be gleaned by the short extract quoted from page 7 of "A Brief History Of H.M. Coastguard," which reads:

> "The greater possibility of invasion which arose in the early part of 1940 required that the watch on the coast had to be considerably intensified. It was accordingly decided , in consultation with the Naval Authorities, to increase the number of Auxiliary Stations and also to establish a large number of Coast Watching Posts, all of which were manned by Auxiliary Coastguardsmen. The main function of the Posts was to watch the beaches against landings by the enemy, the dropping of mines from aircraft, drifting mines at sea and other activities not observable from the Coastguard Station. At the outset, watch was kept by men working in pairs and generally was restricted to the hours of darkness and during thick weather . . .
>
> "Early in 1942 it became necessary that the Coastguard should undertake coastal patrols for security reasons. This involved a daily search of those portions of the coastline where enemy agents or saboteurs might be likely to land. To enable this to be done and also to meet additional operational requirements, the number of Auxiliary Coastguardsmen was further increased to something over 5,000."

On the 28th September, 1945, an Order in Council revoked the Defence (Auxiliary Coastguard) Regulations of 1941; and on the 1st October of the same year, the Admiralty annulled the Order of the 28th May, 1940. Once the Coastguard Service ceased to be under Admiralty control, it resumed its peace time duties of coast watching and life-saving with the support of the Auxiliary Force as the Coast Life-Saving Corps.

From the middle of the 19th century onwards, therefore, members of the Coastguard Service who have served at the Mumbles have played a significant part in the over-all history of the force as outlined briefly in the preceding paragraphs. The dismantled 1910 Look-out structure was afterwards replaced by a more traditional, timbered building erected on the Tutt in 1921. It has remained in existence for more than half a century but is used mainly today as an office quarters. On a raised, cemented base, its old naval signal loft is clearly evident and a reminder, perhaps , of more spartan days when it once housed the simple necessities such as a telescope, signalling apparatus, paraffin heater, small desk, table and bed.

A more permanent relationship between the Coastguard Service and the Mumbles began to emerge during the 1850's, if not earlier, at a time when the Lower Church and Upper Church Fields sloped downwards in the direction of the Parish Church and Methodist Chapel. Among other sources, these two fields are specified in a "Conveyance In Fee," Mrs. Mary Jones to Mr. John Burt, dated the 9th October, 1851, kindly loaned by Mrs. Gladys Barton of 8, Upper Church Pks. Selected extracts indicate the presence of Coastguard personnel here and the setting up of their first Station.

> "This Indenture made the 9th day of October 1851 between Mary Jones . . . Widow of the first part John Burt of the Mumbles . . . Merchant of the second part Thomas Roberts Davies of Castle Street in the town of Swansea . . . Stationer of the third part and William Jenkins late Chief Officer in the Coast Guard Service at the Mumbles aforesaid of the fourth part . . . She the said Mary Jones . . . grant bargain sell release and convey unto the said John Burt and his heirs ALL THAT field or close of Meadow Land called UPPER CHURCH FIELD containing by estimation three acres two roods and thirteen perches . . . AND ALSO ALL THAT Field or Close of Meadow Land called LOWER CHURCH FIELD containing by estimation two acres . . . which said fields or closes of land were formerly in the tenure or occupation of Henry Bath Esquire and now or late of the said Louis Marie Joseph Butel and Mary Griffiths his wife or their undertenants . . ."

The original Coastguard premises occupied a square containing approximately an acre of land: the men's quarters were located along the top and one side of the square; and at one of the bottom corners the rocket apparatus was housed under cover. The interior of the square was used as a garden. More precisely, the Coastguard Station and quarters became bounded on the north side by Westbourne Place, on the south by Overland Road, on the west by Upper Church Parks and on the east, in part, by the premises known as 13 Church Parks, and, in the other part, by No. 8 Overland Road. The Coastguard cottages were those dwellings built on that parcel of ground

> "formerly part of two fields called the Church Fields or Church Park Fields containing by estimation 3 acres 2 roods and 16 perches (less the area of road made through and out of the same) situated near the Church in the Parish of Oystermouth in the County of Glamorgan"

which was by an Indenture of Lease dated the 25th March, 1856, demised by John Burt to William Clement for 99 years from the 25th March, 1856, at the yearly rent of £40.

From the "Abstract Of The Title of Lynette Lowry" to the freehold property known as the Coastguard Station in Westbourne Place, it is revealed that the parcel or piece of land which formed a part of the

Church Park Fields referred to in the preceding paragraph comprised approximately 3 roods, 4½ poles and this section was outlined on a Lease dated the 28th April, 1859, made between William Clement and the Commissioners for executing "the office of Lord High Admiral of the United Kingdom of Great Britain and Ireland for and on behalf of Her Majesty her heirs and successors of the other part whereby the same were demised to the said Commissioners from 29th September 1858 for 96 years at the yearly rent of £20 payable as therein mentioned and subject to the covenants and conditions therein contained Together with the messuages and buildings erected thereon and then collectively known as The Coast Guard Station." This, of course, expired in 1954, the year in which the present, modern Coastguard Station H.Q. was erected in Overland Road at the junction with Western Lane. Additional Coastguard houses were built adjacent to it and on the opposite side of the road. The former terraced Coastguard cottages are well-maintained today as private residences complete with the original garden area and from this natural vantage point some pleasant views of the bay remain.

During the latter half of 1978, a major reorganisation of the U.K.'s Coastguard Service was undertaken and, as a result, the Mumbles Coastguard Rescue Headquarters has been scheduled for a programme of further expansion in recognition of its importance as an accessible location, by land or sea, within the revised scheme. Since the 1st September, 1978, as the Western Region's M.R.C.C., Marine Rescue Co-ordination Centre, Swansea, the Mumbles Headquarters' site at Overland Road and its modern Look-Out Communications Station on the Tutt, cater for an area stretching from the Bristol Channel to the Solway Firth. Nationally, six new regions have been formed to replace eleven previous ones; the Southern, Dover Strait, Eastern, East and West Scotland represent the other five regions. Mumbles is now responsible as a M.R.C.C. for six districts within its region instead of three formerly; Inspector R. Richards is the Regional Controller and the District Staff Officer and District Controller are respectively Messrs. R. Kirby (formerly Mr. R. Clayton) and P. W. Cross.

The principal aim behind this recent reorganisation is to increase the operational efficiency of the Coastguard Service and improve its capability to coordinate action on all marine emergencies including those involving pollution from vessels and other incidents requiring international cooperation. Consequently, the Mumbles, Swansea, functions both as an inter-governmental and international rescue centre in line with the recommendations brought out by the International Maritime Consultative Organisation.

An earlier operational and boundary change had taken place on the 6th April, 1973, when various divisions and districts were affected. Then the old Cambrian Division boundary was adjusted and renamed the Western Division. A former inspector of the Cambrian Division was the late Commander R. G. Hurst, who was stationed at the Mumbles between 1921 and 1946. In October, 1977, his grand-daughter, Mrs. N. Whitehead and family made a special presentation of her late grandfather's plotting instruments to the Mumbles Rescue H.Q. These were received on behalf of the Station by Inspector R. Richards and among those who attended this pleasant ceremony were Mr. W. Gwyther, a previous Station Officer under Commander R. G. Hurst, and Inspector R. Richards' predecessor, now retired, Mr. E. Williams, M.B.E., who served at this Station between 1961 and 1973 as District Officer and Inspector.

Previously, the Western Division comprised: St. George's Channel, Bristol Channel and Cardigan Bay, north of a line from Trebetherick Point to Stepper Point, thence to the coast of the Irish Republic and south of a line westwards from Borthwen Point to the coast of the Republic of Ireland. Hartland (North Devon), Mumbles and Milford Haven (St. Anne's) were embraced by this division which represented broadly an area from Aberdovey (Gwynedd) to Padstow (Cornwall). In 1977, coastguards went to the aid of nearly 150 small craft in the Western Division; carried out 67 cliff rescues; retrieved 48 people cut off by incoming tides; and undertook 31 shore searches. Twenty-two lives were lost in incidents around its coastline.

While, as before, Swansea's present Marine Rescue Co-ordination Centre based at the Mumbles embraces an area which takes in Hartland, Milford Haven, Holyhead, Mersey (Formby) and Ramsey (Isle of Man), today it covers in effect an extensive sea zone which stretches broadly from the River Camel (East Cornwall) out towards the mid-Atlantic and sweeps back and upwards to the Scottish border on its western side. These last five are classified as M.R.S.C.'s, Marine Rescue Sub Centres, with Swansea's Search & Rescue Region sited at the Mumbles' M.R.C.C.

In more precise terms, Swansea, as a S.R.R., relates to a line bounded from the north bank of the River Camel, near Trevose Head, 281° to the south-east corner of the Shannon S.R.R., thence northwards along the I.C.A.O. boundary to a point at 53° 55″ N 05° 30′ W on the Shannon S.R.R. boundary, thence north of the Isle of Man through the points 54° 34′ N 04° 24′ W and 54° 38′ N 03° 52′ W to the Scottish border. Regional responsibilities concern using the Bristol Channel and approaches, the Irish Sea and approaches to the Mersey. Offshore exploration operations and liaison with the Irish Republic are two other important aspects.

The Swansea S.R.R. can deploy a staff of 15 regular Coastguard personnel. Under the command of the Regional Controller and his Deputy, the present force consists of C.G.O. 1's: Messrs. D. Fairfield, D. Powell, R. Sellars, N. Thomas and R. Taylor; and C.G.O.'s V. Crosthwaite, J.

Livitt, I. MacDonald, T. Moore and M. J. Taylor. They are supported by a large panel of Auxiliary Coastguards, seven of whom are women members.

The latest Look-Out Communications Centre situated on the Tutt, alongside the old 1921 structure, was built by Messrs. R. M. Douglas Construction Ltd. and opened on the 26th June, 1973, by Mr. Michael Heseltine, M.P., as the then Minister for Aero-Space & Shipping. Welsh stone forms part of its construction in line with environmental requirements, for the Mumbles cliff section here falls just within the defined boundary line of Britain's first selected area of outstanding natural beauty, a title awarded to the Gower Peninsula. Its erection is principally due to the determined efforts of the Western Division's previous Inspector, Mr. Edward Williams, M.B.E., who had stressed the urgency for such a building to be placed here to cope with future demands.

Of special interest is the weighty but movable "Dopples" binoculars which can be directed into any desired position and commands a particularly long range of vision. It was obtained from a former heavy gun emplacement installed as part of the German "Atlantic Wall" defence system of World War Two. Another interesting feature concerns the Mumbles Lighthouse, half a mile distant; if thick fog breaks its beam, the fog horn is automatically set off by the Coastguard Centre. Encompassed by angled, anti-glare windows, the latter's interior presents a picture somewhat similar in many respects to that of a captain's ship's bridge. Here, as at other Coastguard Look-Out Stations, a constant watch is maintained day and night and additional support is rendered by intermediate stations.

The Swansea's District's immediate area for search and rescue measures would take in Ferryside up to Gloucester and down to the River Parrett (Somerset). As along other part of the U.K.'s coastline, regular Coastguard Stations within this sphere are also to hand and these include: Rhosili, Porthcawl, Llantwit Major, Barry and Weston-super-Mare. Then again, there is the valuable work of the Auxiliary Stations based at Pembrey, Oxwich, Port Talbot, Penarth, Chepstow, Clevedon and Burnham-on-Sea. Nowadays, under the Swansea District, Rhosili, Mumbles, Porthcawl, Llantwit Major, Barry, Newport and the Upper Severn are classified as "Sectors."

It was in 1966 that the Coast Life-Saving Corps was renamed the Coastguard Auxiliary Service; all volunteers, they help the regular Coastguards in various aspects of their everyday work. The Auxiliaries keep visual watch, man Auxiliary Station Look-Outs and their Rescue Companies go to the assistance of crews whose vessels have been driven ashore or to those individuals involved in cliff accidents etc. Nowadays, there are approximately 7,000 Auxiliaries available to support the regular force of some 550 men. Before its recent change-over to Regional status, the Western Division consisted of 70 regular officers and around 500 Auxiliaries who manned 18 permanent Stations and many Auxiliary ones at strategic points along the coast.

Much in evidence these days at the Mumbles is the Coastguard's blue-coloured Rescue Land Rover, which is driven speedily to an inshore incident or as near to a cliff saving operation as the terrain will permit. All Coastguard Stations are supplied with these mobile units, the flat, horizontal surfaces of which are painted bright yellow so that the vehicles are easily observed from the air by helicopters. A winch is fixed to the front part of the Land Rover and inside the vehicle essential items of rescue apparatus are carried, such as cliff equipment, rockets and lines, first aid, stretchers, VHF portable radio, box of pyrotechnics, lighting and megaphones.

While the now renamed Swansea M.R.C.C.'s main responsibility is the coordination of maritime search and rescue operations, it may, perhaps, be overlooked that its other duties are many and varied, demanding and exacting. As is required of other Rescue Headquarters, such work involves "patrolling the coastline in the vicinity of their stations for the purpose of finding and safe-guarding wrecked property, general supervision of the foreshore to prevent encroachment on land below the high water mark or illegal removal of sand or shingle." The Coastguard Service is now playing a greater role in anti-pollution measures directed against oil slicks which threaten the nation's shores from time to time. It serves as a part of the weather reporting organisation of the Meteorological Office and at the Mumbles Look-Out hourly records are kept of the wind's direction and speed, amount and types of cloud formation, dry temperature reading in the shade, wet temperature in the wet, temperature of the grass, concrete and glass, visibility over land and sea, rainfall and barometric pressure readings.

Another invaluable service is rendered by the owners of small, well-equipped pleasure boats, those volunteer members of the force, who are "Auxiliaries Afloat." The marked increase in the use of pleasure craft and yachts locally has added to the work of the Coastguards who anticipate annually that even more sailing enthusiasts, experienced or otherwise, will be numbered among the summer influx of visitors to the Mumbles and Gower as they arrive here in their thousands via the M4 and the Severn Bridge.

An information service is also provided for people who seek advice about such factors as the local coastline, sailing hazards, state of the tides and the weather situation. Additional radio apparatus, telexes, weather monitoring and control equipment are to be installed at the Mumbles to enable the Headquarters to fulfil its new role as a Regional Centre. By the close of the current decade, a new Look-Out and Operations Centre will have been established on the Tutt Head.

There is a fine esprit de corps between all Coastguards whose work is characterised by a high standard of self-discipline so necessary in a crisis. Whether the latest co-ordinate rescue techniques are used, or person to person rescues, they are committed, at any time of the day or night, to the saving of life in the quickest time possible. We are indeed fortunate in such men and women as these.

A tangible reminder of man's endeavours to provide protection at sea is supplied by the permanent presence of the Mumbles Lighthouse. By the Harbour Act of 1791, the Swansea Harbour Trustees were empowered to provide a harbour light on the Mumbles Head. Such a light had to be maintained constantly from one hour after sunset to one hour before sunrise. The Act stated:

> "That it shall and may be lawful to and from the said Trustees, with the consent of the Duke of Beaufort, his heirs or assigns, and of the owners of property whereon such Light House shall be built, but not otherwise, and making him or them full and adequate compensation for the same by rent or otherwise, to erect a Pier at The Mumbles , and sufficient building for the keeping of coal or any other Light at or near The Mumbles aforesaid, and to cause such light to be kept constantly burning in the night from one hour after sunset to one hour before sun rising throughout the year, for the benefit and security of the ships and vessels passing the said place called The Mumbles Head."

After some delays, the first lighthouse at the Mumbles was eventually constructed under the supervision of Mr. William Jernegan, a noted Swansea architect and surveyor. It consisted of two perpendicular coal lights at a distance of 18 feet from each other. Towards the close of 1795, a house and shed were built for the person responsible for the care of the lights.

By April, 1799, further progress and changes had been effected when oil burners were installed to replace the use of coal-fired beacons which involved Wm. Jernegan in adding a lantern and gallery within the scheme of alterations. His original fee of twenty guineas was doubled by a grateful Trustees Committee. The tide-table for that same year notes the conversion as being "altered to one large lanthorn of Argand lamps with reflectors." The large iron lantern was cast at the Neath Abbey foundry in 1798 and this housed eleven Argand lamps and reflectors, facts much beloved by the writers of early 19th century guide publications about Swansea and Gower. The title of "Argand" refers to a lamp and gas-burner invented by Aimé Argand (1755-1803).

The management of the lighthouse passed from the Harbour Trustees to the Corporation of Trinity House by Act of Parliament in 1834. By 1860, the lighthouse had been fitted with a dioptric light, a method whereby the illuminative power of the light was enlarged by refracting lenses. At a height of 114 feet, the light was visible up to 18 or 20 miles on a clear night. The diptric lamp remained in operation until 1905. Of that year, W. H. Jones in his "History Of The Port Of Swansea," Chap. 18, p. 258, recounts:

> "The occultation of the light was introduced for the first time on the evening of New Year's Day, 1905. Simple as is the present method of lighting, a much more simple device secures the periodical obscuring of the light which is necessary to distinguish it from neighbouring light signals. An opaque extinguisher or cap, of little greater dimension than the incandescent mantle, is operated by clock-work, so that the extinguisher descends, surrounds the mantle as to exclude the light, and after the proper interval rises again to reveal the light once more."

W. H. Jones also refers to the service of the lighthouse keepers:

> "Of the keepers of the Mumbles Lighthouse there have been but few. Two of them have already been named. (David Bydder and John Walker, but a Benjamin Llewellyn is mentioned too). Three Abraham Aces, grandfather, father and son, accounted for nearly three quarters of a century. The eldest died in the fifties, having already relinquished his duties to his son, long known as Abraham Ace, junior, and the latter carried on for over 50 years, dying on the 27th August, 1885. He was followed by his son, who continued to look after the light until 1902, when he was succeeded by his assistant, Jasper Williams, who gave place in 1914 to his own colleague, John Thomas, who is in charge of the lighthouse at the present day (1922)."

While others have had periodic connections with lighthouse service, such as the Cottles, it is generally considered that John J. D. Thomas was the last permanent keeper. Abraham Ace's two daughters, Jessie and her sister, Mrs. M. Wright, are remembered historically for their brave efforts, with others, in rescuing a survivor from the "Admiral Prinz Adalbert" disaster of 1883.

As an unmanned lighthouse of the present century its operation became later an automatic process dependent on the "light valve" principle i.e. automatic cameras governed by photo electric cells. In 1970, the present power beam beacon was fitted and the old lamp support presented to the Royal Institution of South Wales.

The lighthouse and its surrounds were taken over from the British Transport Dock Board by Trinity House Lighthouse Service in 1975 and the old fort leased from Swansea City Council on a 99 years' lease. During

1977-78, Trinity House carried out essential repairs and maintenance work on the structure: the rusted unsafe gallery railings cast originally at Neath Abbey Foundry in the last decade of the 18th century were replaced; some minor repairs made to the tower section; a small derelict building on the fort roof repaired for visiting mechanics in the future; and the whole premises cleaned down and repainted in line with the high, normal standards associated with the Lighthouse Service.

After taking away the existing lantern's (circa 1860) outer casing, its engineers have decided, as yet, not to recover it with a glass frame available from a redundant light vessel's lantern. Therefore, the existing 1970 optic is to be left uncovered for an experimental period of one year. With the exception of the lighthouse's altered appearance currently at its apex, Trinity House has succeeded in preserving the identity of the existing structure as much as possible and at the same time housed within the latest navigational aids "in an ancient but well-preserved and cared for Lighthouse."

Station Data for 1977 contains the following information:

"*Site:* Approx. 457 metres, E.S.E. of the mainland of Mumbles, Swansea. Admiralty Chart Nos. 1161 & 1165; Admiralty List of Lights No. 5358. Latitude, 51 34.0 N/W; Longitude, 3 58.2 N/W.

District: West Coast, Swansea Depot.

Status: Unwatched.

Established: 1793, Property of Swansea Harbour Board. 1975, Taken over from British Transport Dock Board by Trinity House. Fort leased from Swansea Corporation on 99 year lease.

Approach & Access: On foot across tidal beach at low water. By local boat at high water.

Premises: Tower, Fuel Oil Store, Engine Room, Mess Room and Battery Room, sited within the compound of the old fort. Fog signal is sited on the lower gallery of the tower.

Tower: Central octagonal stone structure, 17 metres in height, with an outer octagonal stone structure to a height approx. 10 metres from ground level. This is roofed and forms a lower gallery. 3 No. Bulkhead state of the Station Indicator Lights, mounted on lower gallery. Visible from Coastguard Station.

Attendant: Mr. Alan Jones, Lifeboat Cottage, Mumbles.

Water Supply: None.

Water Heating: None.

Space Heating: Calor Gas Fire.

Cooking Facilities: 2 Ring calor gas burner in mess-room. Gas cylinder under burner.

Electricity Supply: None. Calor gas lighting. Lanterns. Calor gas cylinders supplied under contract. (Calor gas supply is a temporary measure).

Battery Room: 1 No. Station Battery, 24 volt nickel cadmium 20 dual cells in hardwood containers. 'N.I.F.E.' type SV 42 E 840 A.H. 1 No. Control Cubicle, Austinlite Ltd. Navigation Light, Fog Signal and Battery Charging.

Engine Room: 2 No. Battery charging generator sets. Stone chance. Engines, Ruston 2YBA air cooled, electric starter motor; Generator, BKB 7.5 KW 26/34 Volts D.C. 220A.

Engine Starter Battery: Type Nickel Cadmium 18 cells XL3 capacity 37 A.H. In hardwood containers.

Fuel Oil Storage: 2 No. 300 gallons capacity each, Fuel Oil Tanks. Installed at rear end of fort, outside Engine Room.

Optic: Stone chance power beam BEACON MK3, 3RPM rotation. Half panel arrangement axis at 30 degrees.

Pedestal: Fixed.

Illuminant: Electric.

Lamps: Type EC 145 Volt 150 W. Quartz Iodine.

Lampchanger: Stone platt type L.C. 6, 6 position.

Character: White group flashing 4 every 10 seconds.

Intensity: 30,000 Cd.

Nominal Range: 17 Sea miles.

Focal Plane Height: 35 metres.

Geographical Range: 16 Sea miles.

F. 0.18 seconds
E. 1.48 seconds
F. 0.18 seconds
E. 1.48 seconds
F. 0.18 seconds
E. 1.48 seconds
F. 0.18 seconds
E. 4.84 seconds
10.00 seconds (Total)

Arc of Visibility: All angles from seaward.

Navigation Light Battery: (See Station Battery).

Navigation Light Battery Charger: (See Battery Room).

Lantern: 1st Order Walker Pattern, gun metal framing, with vertical astragals, flat glazing panes. Copper conical roof, murette panels marine plywood.

Type: Powerstone. Two stone-chance/Tannoy 500 Watt directional electric sound emitters, comprised of two vertical banks of five units. Mounted on lower gallery of tower.

Character: 3 Blasts every 60 seconds.

B. 1.3 seconds
S. 2.0 seconds
B. 1.3 seconds
S. 2.0 seconds
B. 1.4 seconds
S.52.0 seconds
60.0 seconds (Total)

Fog Signal Coders: Stone platt omniflashers, built within Austinlite Control Cubicle.

Transmissometer/Fog Detector: Receiver Unit sited on Mumbles Coastguard compound. Manufacturer, Lancashire Dynamo Electronic Ltd., Rugeley, Staffs. (Thorn Automation). Note, Equipment sales now leased under licence to Sacol Control Ltd., Commercial Road, Tolton, Southampton.

An exciting discovery was made during mid-1978 by Mr. Brian Price of Killay, when he came across a five ton, twelve feet long naval gun of the 1860's, embedded in the rocks and sand beneath the Mumbles Lighthouse Fort. With the assistance of the British Sub-Aqua Club, Swansea Branch diving members, the cannon was carefully extracted and prepared for a six miles' tow from the lighthouse to the Swansea Marina.

Despite the use of flotation bags, the gun was temporarily lost in relatively shallow water on the 5th August, 1978, 1¼ miles from its destination. Four days later, however, more flotation bags, wire hawsers, were attached to it together with lorry tyres' inner tubes to correct any imbalance. One of the divers monitored the condition of the lifting gear throughout the final tow accomplished by the Swansea fishing boat "Morning Star," Captain David Lawrence. Prior to being put on public display, the heavy gun was soaked in a sodium and water solution to remove salt and carbons, after which it was subjected to a thorough cleansing process.

The battery at the base of the lighthouse was erected in 1860, under the Palmerston administration, at a cost of £10,000. By the 1880's, it contained five 68-pounder guns which were maintained by a sergeant and two privates of the Royal Artillery. As a fixed gun then, it was most likely one of a pair run on a semi-circular track when used. Like numerous and even larger establishments sited along the British southern coastline in their day, these were never needed as defence points against supposed French invasion intentions and were dubbed subsequently as Lord Palmerston's follies.

The lighthouse continues to dominate the immediate skyline and overlooks a crowded Mumbles boating scene. On a capricious midsummer evening in 1978, for example, there were, from the smallest craft upwards, approximately 210 at their moorings, while nearly another 350 were laid up in the Southend and Village Lane boating parks.

Rescue at sea locally and out in the channel immediately recalls to mind the splendid service rendered to mariners of all countries and their vessels by the crews of the Mumbles Life-boats during the last century and up to the present time. It is a proud story of triumph and disaster, of fortitude, courage and devotion to duty, carried out in the finest traditions of the Royal National Life-boat Institution which celebrated its 150th Anniversary in 1974. As referred to earlier, a well-illustrated, detailed history of the Mumbles Life-boat from 1832 onwards, has been written by Carl Smith, a present serving crew member, entitled "The Men Of The Mumbles Head" and published by Gomer Press in 1977.

The R.N.L.I. is, of course, a highly efficient, voluntary body which is dependent consequently upon freely-given contributions and support. The sole reason for its existence is for the expressed purpose of saving lives at sea but there have been those occasions too when livestock have been rescued from the water or from vessels in distress. All lifeboatmen, when called out, can expect to undertake, if necessary, search and rescue work up to thirty miles out from their own coastline. Since 1824, life-boat crews of the R.N.L.I. have saved nearly 100,000 people.

The Mumbles Life-boat is one of approximately 134 boats positioned around the coastline of the United Kingdom and the Irish Republic at selected, strategic points. Like others, the Mumbles Life-boat Station possesses considerable autonomy and therein lies its strength and character, for such a system permits flexibility, promotes goodwill and strong community support, aids efficiency and creates that special brand of loyalty which life-boat crews display to their coxswain.

First of all, volunteers have to serve for a probationary year after which time the coxswain has to decide whether they have an aptitude for the job; if successful, they are put on the regular crew list. It generally takes about five years' service in order to become proficient in life-boat work and at the end of this period men are taken on as full-time members of crew. The age limit for serving crew is 60 in conventional life-boats and 45 in the inshore rescue service.

Usually, the only full-time member of the crew is the mechanic who is an employee of the R.N.L.I. However, at the Mumbles Station, both the coxswain and the mechanic are full-time members. The coxswain endeavours to retain a squad of twenty lifeboatmen in all although only seven men go to sea to form a crew at any one time. Among his numerous responsibilities, he ensures that the life-boat is put out to sea every six weeks from the last time it went into the water as an exercise or a service launch.

"Availability," stresses Coxswain L. Derek Scott, B.E.M., "is of prime importance when applying to join a crew. If a man is a yachtsman or generally 'mucks about in boats,' he will usually fit in. Professional men are hard to come by, the main problem being that they are, as a rule, away at sea when the life-boat is required."

The construction of the present Life-Boat Station was commenced in the fateful year of 1914 but further work ceased after the completion of the platform and slipway in 1916. The life-boat was kept on it under a canvas sheet for protection when not in use. Work recommenced in 1918; a second-hand house was shipped from Cornwall by ketch and erected on site. It has been in use since 1922 and contains a wealth of information about sea rescues undertaken from the Mumbles. By prior arrangement, organised groups of schoolchildren and students visit the Station frequently in connection with local studies.

Whether in peace or wartime, the dramatic rescues of the past, the successes and failures, joys and tradegies, usual and unusual happenings, and the names of the gallant life-boat crews involved, are all painstakingly recorded by Carl Smith. Among the life-boats based at the Mumbles since 1863, the year the R.N.L.I. put one into service from here, have been: the "Martha & Anne," "Wolverhampton," "James Stevens," "Charlie Medland," "Edward, Prince of Wales" (the first motor life-boat), "William Gammon" and the "Pentland." Relief life-boats are also stationed here from time to time and there also is the contribution of the inshore life-boat crews since 1965.

The Boat-House displays within a number of large notice boards which record in a very condensed form some facts about lifeboat activities in previous years. One such entry for 1964 states simply: "October 18th; Two horses, landed a dead horse." Behind these bare lines lies a story of true compassion and concern for animals.

The horses concerned had been frightened on Swansea Beach by some heedless youths who had chased them into the sea. Soon they were swimming out towards Swansea Bay as if attempting to cross a wide river. Fortunately, their plight was spotted by a passer-by who immediately reported the incident officially. The life-boat answered the call and went to the rescue of the struggling animals. By making use of the appropriate gear but under great difficulties, the lifeboatmen managed eventually to haul the exhausted beasts aboard. The sad condition of the horses greatly distressed the men at the time and the experience proved too much for one of the animals in the end. This one incident speaks volumes.

Each life-boat station is administered by an Honorary Secretary who is supported by his local committee made up of a Chairman, Honorary Treasurer, Honorary Medical Adviser, Fund-raising Secretary and a member of the Ladies' Life-boat Guild. Representatives of the Police, H.M. Customs, Lloyds and the Receiver of Wrecks may also be members of the committee. The Honorary Secretary's appointment is a very important one; once he is selected, the District Inspector of Life-Boats must be consulted by the Branch Committee which includes normally the Inspector of Coastguard, a Local Officer of Coastguard, Harbour Master, Customs Officer, Lloyd's Agent or Sub-Agent, a Minister of Religion and a Senior Police Officer. Their joint recommendation must then be confirmed and the appointment sanctioned finally by the R.N.L.I. Headquarters.

At the Mumbles there have been eight Honorary Secretaries since 1863: Mr. Alfred Sterry held the post for the first 11 years; Mr. Thomas W. Islay Young served for 26 years; Francis le Boulanger, 37 years; Mr. Thomas E. Kluge, 6 years; his brother, Mr. H. J. Kluge, 12 years; Captain E. H. Slater, 5 years; Captain C. E. Mock, 12 years, having served 18 years previously as Assistant Secretary; and the present holder of the position, Mr. Edward Beynon, who was appointed in 1973. Previously, Mr. Edward Beynon had been an Assistant Secretary, since 1967, under Captain C. E. Mock. Messrs. A. D. Morgan and L. Howell are Chairman and Honorary Treasurer respectively.

The Honorary Secretary's primary duty is the management of the Life-Boat Station. In this he acts as local representative of the R.N.L.I. and conducts all the general correspondence on behalf of the Branch. It is also his responsibility to give the orders for assembling a crew and launching the life-boat upon receiving intimation of a wreck or vessel in distress.

The role of the Honorary Secretary as a launching authority is a demanding one, in that he may be, in common with all crew members, on call throughout 24 hours of the day. At the Mumbles, two deputy launching authorities assist Mr. E. Beynon in this connection: Captain K. Carstens, Superintendent of Trinity House Depot, Swansea; and Mr. J. Whitford, a former life-boat crew member and business man. Mr. E. Beynon speaks for all Life-Boat Station Branch Honorary Secretaries when he writes thus:

> "When the launching authority is advised that there are casualties, usually by the Coastguard, whom the R.N.L.I. work with very closely and amicably, he has to make an immediate decision. Very many of the calls occur in the early hours of the morning, so that one moment he is in deep slumber and the next responsible for sending to sea a life-boat crew, all of whom he will know very well. The situation may be a very dangerous one and it is essential that he keeps calm and listens very carefully to the information given to him. There are, of course, occasions when he may discuss the situation with the Coxswain, always a man of very sound, practical experience, who, when the life-boat is at sea, is totally in charge; but the decision whether to launch must be made by the Honorary Secretary, or one of his deputies, and they have to stand by it, come what may, for a delay, even of minutes, can mean the loss of life. Their thoughts dwell equally on the lives of the life-boat crew and those of the casualties which makes their task both honourable and onerous."

In all kinds of weather, at any time of the day or night, lifeboatmen go out to sea in answer to all distress calls and face up to a variety of situations which will test their personal resources of skill, strength and courage. As volunteers, crews only receive small payments for services and exercises which are classed as expenses. Lifeboatmen are paid at the rate of 50p. per hour at sea after the first two hours, for which they receive £2.00! However, they would not want it any other way, for it is the spirit of voluntary service to and within a community which really matters to those who belong to the R.N.L.I.

A much loved boat, the "William Gammon—Manchester & District XXX," saw service at the Mumbles between late 1947 and the 27th August, 1974. She was, of course, named after the late Mr. William Gammon, gold medallist, R.N.L.I., Coxswain of the previous Mumbles Lifeboat, "Edward, Prince of Wales," which was lost with all eight members of the crew after two gallant attempts to save 39 men of the striken "Samtampa" off notorious Sker Point on the 23rd April, 1947.

It was as Coxswain of the "William Gammon" that Mr. L. Derek Scott was awarded the R.N.L.I.'s silver medal for his action in dealing with the fire-swept M.V. "Kilo" episode on the 18th November, 1963. Eight other members of his crew received the official thanks of the R.N.L.I. inscribed on vellum for their part in this event.

The "Petland" (Civil Service No. 31) replaced the "William Gammon" on the 27th August, 1974. She was brought from Littlehampton, Sussex, by Coxswain Derek Scott and Mechanic Alan Jones. A Watson 47′ 0″ cablin class life-boat, built by Messrs. J. S. White, Cowes, I.O.W., in 1957, she was converted to self-righting in 1972 by extensions to her casing. Her refit involved watertight subdivision and modifications to drainage and ventilation sections. With a displacement of 24 tons, the "Pentland" was formerly stationed at Thurso, Scotland, before being specially adapted for work in the Bristol Channel. Additional data reveal: register tonnage, 9.84; propelling machinery, twin Gardner 5 LW diesels, 1300 rpm, 70 bhp; speed, 8.56 knots; and equipped with MF/VHF radio, Echo Sounder and E.M.I. Radar. Forty-eight feet long, she can support 100 survivors.

When required the Mumbles Station can be allocated any one of ten suitable 46′/47′ relief boats from the R.N.L.I.'s reserve fleet at present. Inevitably, the cost of new life-boats has risen noticeably since 1974. The "Arun" type class then cost approximately £140,000; currently, it is nearer £250,000. At the opposite end of the scale, the 1974 inflatable inshore life-boat obtainable at £1,250 now demands a figure of approximately £3,000 excluding the trolley. This is ample proof why the fund-raising activities of local branches are so important to the upkeep of a vital service.

In "The Men Of The Mumbles Head," Chap. 4, p. 68, Carl Smith quotes a closing passage from a speech made by Coxswain L. Derek Scott, B.E.M., guest speaker at the R.N.L.I.'s annual meeting held at the Festival Hall, London, during the 150th Anniversary, which explains succintly but vividly what the Life-Boat Service is all about:

I have always believed that a coxswain is only as good as his crew. When you set off in the blackness of night into gales force 9, into God knows what, the feeling of unity between a life-boat crew is inexplicable, and no matter how frightened you feel you know that the crew of the ship who are waiting for you are a great deal more frightened. Then, maybe after hours of battling through heavy seas you arrive at the scene wet, cold and thinking 'What on earth am I doing here?' and then you see the casualty who may be in a terrible situation where life hangs by a thread, but this is the moment we have all been prepared for. From the time that lady sold her flag or arranged her coffee morning to raise funds—that was when this rescue started, not when the maroons were fired. Everyone who works for, or supports this Institution in some way is responsible for the preservation of life at sea. If you could share with me the look on a survivor's face at the moment of rescue, and the marvellous feeling with the crew when they are coming home in the boat and the job has been done, then you know that this last 150 years has been more than worthwhile."

Stained glass window, All Saints, Oystermouth, commemorating the loss of the crew of the Mumbles Lifeboat, "Edward Prince of Wales," in the 1947 disaster. Unveiled and dedicated, 6th May, 1977.

By permission, South Wales Evening Post

Presentation of gear by the Mumbles Round Table—to crew of the Mumbles Lifeboat, 1977.

By permission, South Wales Evening Post

SELECTED SOURCES AND ADDITIONAL READING

K. Baedeker: Great Britain (5th Edition), 1901.
R. Barnes: The Church In The Lane: Bethany Baptist Centenary 1867-1967.
D. G. Bowden & N. L. Thomas: Swansea Old & New 1974.
G. P. Butcher: Swansea District Directory 1875-76.
The Cambrian Weekly Editions.
Dr. H. A. Cole: Swansea Bay—Mumbles Area Oyster Fishery Survey Report 1949.
N. Cutmore: Trinity House Lighthouse Service; Mumbles Lighthouse Data 1977.
Walter Davies: General View Of The Agriculture And Domestic Economy Of South Wales: Vol I, 1814; Vol. 2, 1815.
C. J. O. Evans: Glamorgan Its History & Topography 1938.
Rev. J. Evans: Letters Written During A Tour Through South Wales 1803.
S. G. Gamwell: The Official Guide & Handbook To Swansea & District, (British Association), 1880.
The Gowertonian: Vol. 3, No. 3, July, 1913.
H. Grenfell & B. Morris: The Castles Of Gower 1970.
H. Griffith: The New Swansea Guide 1823.
A. Hall: History Of Oystermouth 1899.
E. Harris: Swansea Its Port And Trade & Their Development 1935.
D. Helme: A Little England Beyond Wales 1911.
D. Jenkin: A Description Of Swansea & Its Environs 1813.
A. Lloyd Jones, M.O.H.: The Annual Report For The Year 1901 On The Oystermouth Urban District 1902.
W. H. Jones: History Of Swansea & Of The Lordship Of Gower 1920.
W. H. Jones: History Of The Port Of Swansea 1922.
W. H. Jones: A Brief Description And History Of The Castle Of Oystermouth.
R. Jones: Gower Fact & Fable 1970's.
Dr. P. E. King & A. Osborn: Oyster Dredging 1969.
R. Lawson: A New Role For The Mumbles Railway 1976.
C. E. Lee: The Swansea & Mumbles Railway 1942, 1954 & 1977.
J. Lewis: The Swansea Guide 1851.
H. Libby: The Mixture: Mumbles & Harry Libby 1964.
M. Mathews: Swansea Directory 1830.
W. H. Michael, M.O.H.: The Medical Report On The Sickness And Mortality Of The Borough Of Swansea 1854.
D. Morgan: Ballad Of The Old Mumbles Railway.
Z. B. Morris: The Swansea Guide 1802.
The Mumbles & Gower News Monthly Editions.
Mumbles & Gower Holidaymakers' Guide (Mumbles Chamber Of Trade) Annual Editions.
Murray: Hand-Book—South Wales 1870.
Ostreme Mumbles Festival Booklet 1973 etc.
Oystermouth School Centenary Booklet 1878-1978.

Oystermouth U.D.C. Water Act 1911.
E. I. E. Phillips: Guide To All Saints, The Parish Church Of Oystermouth 1961.
E. I. E. Phillips: Golden Jubilee: 50 Years At All Saints.
K. Pryer & B. Radford: Luftwaffe Over Swansea 1939-45.
A. Rees: The Cyclopaedia; Or Universal Dictionary 1819.
E. Rhys: The South Wales Coast 1911.
S. W. Rider & A. E. Trueman: South Wales 1929.
M. & R. O. Roberts: Two Centuries Of Mumbles Methodism 1977.
E. E. Rowse: In & Around Swansea 1896.
J. G. Rutter: Prehistoric Gower 1948.
C. W. Slater: The Corner Pew: A Series Of Sketches Of Mumbles Methodism. 1919.
C. Smith: The Men Of The Mumbles Head: The Story Of The Mumbles Lifeboat From 1832. 1977.
The South Wales Transport Co. Ltd.: Souvenir Booklet 1928.
The South Wales Transport Co. Ltd.: The Oldest Passenger Railway In The World 1954.
The South Wales Transport Co. Ltd.: The Chain Of Progress 1960.
Survey Of The Lorship Of Gower 1650.
N. L. Thomas: The Story Of Swansea's Districts & Villages; Vol. 1, Enlarged 1965.
N. L. Thomas: The Story Of Swansea's Districts & Villages; Vol. 2 & Vol. 1 Combined 1969.
W. V. Thomas: Portrait of Gower 1976.
D. Williams & A. C. Wright: The Swansea Directory & Almanack 1883.
Capt. J. Williams: The History Of The Mumbles Lifeboat.
W. Williams, Cty. M.O.: A Sanitary Survey Of Glamorganshire 1895.

INDEX